IMPROVING
SPEED & ACCURACY
in KEYBOARDING

The McGraw·Hill Companies

Ober ISAK/1e
Online Software Registration Card

Log On & Get Started!

(See reverse side for instructions.)

10

Log On & Get Started!

1. Your instructor will provide you with a URL for accessing Ober/ISAK.

2. Open your browser to the specified site to create your student account.

3. Use the following registration code when creating your Ober/ISAK student account.

Scratch off to reveal access code:

B2PRNTYX3J78265C67

nwaters1
Florette56

ISBN 978-0-07-765740-6
MHID 0-07-765740-3

EAN

90000

9 780077 657406

www.mhhe.com

IMPROVING
SPEED & ACCURACY
in KEYBOARDING

Scot Ober

www.mhhe.com/isak

Connect
Learn
Succeed™

The McGraw-Hill Companies

Connect
Learn
Succeed™

IMPROVING SPEED AND ACCURACY IN KEYBOARDING

1 2 3 4 5 6 7 8 9 0 RMN/RMN 1 0 9 8 7 6 5 4 3

ISBN   978-0-07-339701-6
MHID   0-07-339701-6

Senior Vice President, Products & Markets: *Kurt L. Strand*
Vice President, General Manager, Products & Markets: *Brent Gordon*
Vice President, Content Production & Technology Services: *Kimberly Meriwether David*
Director: *Scott Davidson*
Executive Director of Development: *Ann Torbert*
Development Editor: *Allison McCabe*
Digital Development Editor: *Kevin White*
Executive Marketing Manager: *Keari Green*
Project Manager: *Kathryn D. Wright*
Senior Buyer: *Michael R. McCormick*
Designer: *Trevor Goodman*
Cover/Interior Designer:
Cover Image:
Media Project Manager: *Cathy L. Tepper*
Typeface: *10.5/12.5 Adobe Garamond Pro*
Compositor: *Laserwords Private Limited*
Printer: *R. R. Donnelley*

About the Author

Scot Ober has taught business education for more than 20 years, most recently as a professor of business at Ball State University in Muncie, Indiana. He received his Ph.D. from the Ohio State University in 1974. In addition to his high school and university teaching experience, he has served as director of research for the Gregg Division of McGraw-Hill Book Company in New York City and as a military secretary in Vietnam, where he was awarded the Bronze Star. He received the 1993 Distinguished Alumnus award from East Carolina University.

Scot is a past national president of Delta Pi Epsilon and a past national chair of the Policies Commission for Business and Economic Education. He also served a three-year term as editor of the *Business Communication Quarterly* and was named a Distinguished Member of the Association for Business Communication in 1997. He has chaired or served as a member of more than 100 accreditation teams of the Accrediting Council for Independent Colleges and Schools, and won the organization's Distinguished Public Evaluator Award in 2002.

Scot has published more than 60 journal articles in every major business communication and business education journal and is the author or coauthor of nine textbooks in the areas of business communication, keyboarding, shorthand, and software applications. In addition, he has served as the senior author of *Gregg College Keyboarding and Document Processing* for the past 30 years. Scot has spoken or presented papers at hundreds of conferences and training sessions in 43 states as well as Canada, Mexico, Puerto Rico, England, and Greece. Several of his presentations have won the "Best Paper Award" at professional conferences.

Scot and his wife live in Tucson, Arizona, and have five sons.

Contents

Appendix

Welcome to ISAK!

Improving Speed and Accuracy in Keyboarding (ISAK) is a 60-lesson individualized skill-building system designed to provide students the level of keyboarding speed and accuracy needed to meet acceptable standards for employment. ISAK can be used in a stand-alone course or as part of another keyboarding course. The only requirement is a touch-keyboarding speed of at least 20 wpm.

ISAK features these innovations:
1. Web-based software
2. Filling the documented need for keyboarding speed
3. MAP+(Misstroke Analysis and Prescription)
4. Separate practice for accuracy, technique, and speed
5. Flexibility in scheduling

Web-Based Software

Because there is no software to install, students (and instructors) can work from any computer that has an Internet connection. The software's intuitive interface is easy to understand and use. All exercises in the text are completed from within the ISAK software. The software keeps track of student progress and provides automatic scoring for all of the lesson exercises. When students open the software, it automatically opens where the student left off the last time. Students will continue to have access to the ISAK software even after their course ends—for additional skill development.

Filling the Documented Need for Keyboarding Speed

Even institutions that don't offer separate keyboarding courses recognize the need for students to increase their keyboarding speed and accuracy before they graduate, apply for a job, and are required to pass a typing speed test. A recent analysis of online job postings for administrative positions (posted at http://www.gdpkeyboarding.com/Word_Files/Required_Typing_Speeds.pdf) found the following:

1. The most common speed requirement (mode) was 60 wpm, accounting for 43 percent of the listings. The average speed requirement (mean) was 58 wpm. The middle speed requirement (median) was 60 wpm.
2. Job applicants who type at least 40 wpm would qualify for 10 percent of the positions that listed minimum typing speeds, those typing 50 wpm would qualify for 18 percent of the positions, and those typing 60 wpm would qualify for 80 percent of the positions.

The action-research report concluded by stating,

> Regardless of their competence in word processing, students need high-level typing speeds (typically, at least 60 wpm) in order to even be hired for office positions. Achieving this level of speed requires extensive and systematic skillbuilding practice at every level of keyboarding instruction.

"Extensive and systematic skillbuilding practice" is exactly what ISAK is designed to provide!

MAP+ (Misstroke Analysis and Prescription)

MAP+ is a diagnostic component within the ISAK software that analyzes each student's pretest misstrokes and prescribes individualized remediation drills based on the student's misstrokes. Each time the student accesses a drill, all new drill lines appear—thus providing *unlimited new drill lines* for 80 different kinds of keystroking problems.

ISAK Provides Separate Practice for Accuracy, Technique, and Speed Improvement

It is a well-proven fact that students cannot work to improve speed and accuracy simultaneously. After an initial three-lesson keyboard review, each subsequent three-lesson unit in ISAK builds skill in these three areas in separate lessons.

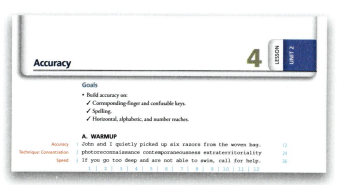

First, every lesson begins with the goals for that lesson—so that students always know exactly what they're trying to achieve in that lesson.

The goals are followed by a three-line Warmup. Line 1 contains all letters of the alphabet—to improve *accuracy*. Line 2 contains various types of drills—to improve *technique*. And Line 3 comprises a sentence made up of short, easy-to-type words—to improve *speed*.

Accuracy Lessons

Lesson 1 of each unit provides systematic practice on these types of accuracy-improvement exercises:

1. **MAP+:** Each accuracy lesson provides one MAP+ exercise in improving keystroking accuracy on the alphabet keys and one MAP+ exercise on either the number or symbol keys—for individualized practice.

2. **Corresponding-Finger Practice:** Students often type a letter using the corresponding finger of the wrong hand. Therefore, ISAK provides practice in distinguishing between F and J reaches, D and K reaches, S and L reaches, and A and Sem reaches.

Note the Pretest-Practice-Posttest (P/P/P) format of this drill. This routine was developed by Dr. Fred Winger of Oregon State University, based upon his extensive body of keyboarding research. The Pretest comprises a 1-minute timed writing passage that is filled with examples of the reach being practiced (in this case, words requiring extensive use of the F and J fingers—to help students distinguish between the two fingers. Finally, students take a Posttest to measure improvement.

3. **Contusable Keys:** Research shows that three types of reaches cause confusions for typists. First, reaches using *consecutive fingers* are problematic—for example, typing *rt* or *tr,* both letters of which are typed with the same finger. So ISAK systematically provides exercises designed to eliminate these confusions. The other types of confusable reaches systematically practiced in ISAK are reaches using *adjacent fingers* (such as *oi* and *as*) and common *substitution* errors (such as typing *g* for *h,* and vice versa). All are practiced in ISAK.

PRACTICE
Consecutive Fingers

rt-tr	28	try trot trifle ort tramp apart art tract cart trial trudge
	29	tragic trip wart triad trim divert truth unhurt troop train
	30	dart true tried retort trowel skirt trick tree exhort shirt
	31	resort quart tremor tray trance desert report oxcart travel
mn-nm	32	entertainment inmost unmask alumni firmness nonmetal unmade
	33	hymnal gymnast alumna Denmark unmet column unmoving remnant
	34	unmelted damned calmness columnist hymn abandonment chimney
	35	autumnal detainment condemned circumnavigate unmade unmined
vb-bv	36	believe vagabond absolve obviated visibly invisible abusive
	37	adverb removable overbite riverboat bevel abusive observant
	38	combative vibrant livable bivouac overbuilt variable viably
	39	bereave overblown riverbank vibes voluble behoove vestibule

4. **Business Spelling.** Most keyboarding instructors agree that competent spelling skills are a critical component of competent keyboarding skill. Dr. Scot Ober's published spelling research has identified vocabulary words that both (a) occur frequently in typical business writing and (b) are frequently misspelled by typical students. Words from his list of the 1,000 most frequently occurring and most frequently misspelled words in business writing are practiced in each accuracy lesson.

C. BUSINESS SPELLING

These spelling words are from a list of the most used and most misspelled words in business writing. Study the words that cause you problems.

20	accounted waiver equivalent obvious recommendation trustees
21	commensurate legislative treasurer's appraisal consequently
22	remuneration deferred attributable inconvenience indication
23	unfortunately consultation regards opportunity installation

5. **Reach Drills.** ISAK provides systematic practice on (a) horizontal reaches, which move to a different key on the same row, (b) vertical reaches, which move from one row to the adjacent row, and (c) jump reaches, which move from the upper row to the lower row, or vice versa.

F. REACH DRILLS: HORIZONTAL REACHES

Horizontal reaches move to a different key on the same row.

er and io	40	amnio ionic goer leery jerk oiler legion polio arioso heron
	41	motion era perky erg cheer period biotic mover violet jerky
	42	here tiger rover refer twerp deer pier berth ere derby trio
	43	liner saber brio ferry merge hers paper manioc ration dozer
te and pu	44	quote terabyte punt toted carte water steal taste pup doted
	45	patented tester termite pulse bate oaten stem vote literate
	46	tenor tempter tenet cited purl often emote feted tease Kate
	47	terse put elite test tepee octet punk spurt testy jute pull

Technique Lessons

To achieve higher speeds and accuracy, students must practice good technique, so Lesson 2 of each unit builds proper technique, using these drills:

1. **Nonprinting Keys.** Students often waste much time when reaching for the TAB, ENTER, SPACE BAR, LEFT SHIFT, RIGHT SHIFT, and BACKSPACE keys. They either have to look down to find the keys or often then fail to return the finger immediately to home-row position. ISAK exercises are designed to remedy these weaknesses.

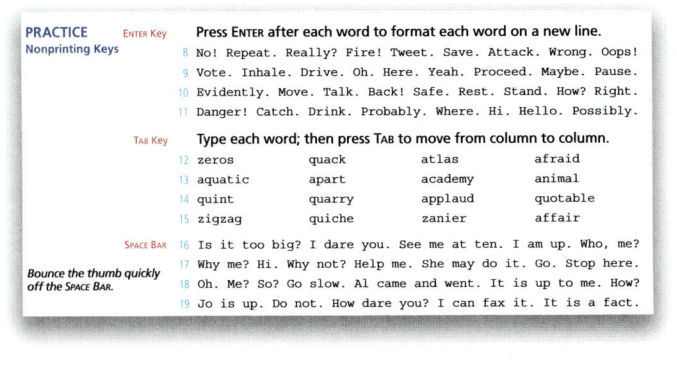

PRACTICE
Nonprinting Keys

ENTER Key — **Press ENTER after each word to format each word on a new line.**

8	No! Repeat. Really? Fire! Tweet. Save. Attack. Wrong. Oops!
9	Vote. Inhale. Drive. Oh. Here. Yeah. Proceed. Maybe. Pause.
10	Evidently. Move. Talk. Back! Safe. Rest. Stand. How? Right.
11	Danger! Catch. Drink. Probably. Where. Hi. Hello. Possibly.

TAB Key — **Type each word; then press TAB to move from column to column.**

12	zeros	quack	atlas	afraid
13	aquatic	apart	academy	animal
14	quint	quarry	applaud	quotable
15	zigzag	quiche	zanier	affair

SPACE BAR

Bounce the thumb quickly off the SPACE BAR.

16	Is it too big? I dare you. See me at ten. I am up. Who, me?
17	Why me? Hi. Why not? Help me. She may do it. Go. Stop here.
18	Oh. Me? So? Go slow. Al came and went. It is up to me. How?
19	Jo is up. Do not. How dare you? I can fax it. It is a fact.

2. **Concentration.** When students don't concentrate, they lose their place in the copy, have to look at the keyboard to find the keys, or make other time-wasting motions. ISAK provides three types of concentration drills: (a) vocabulary words, (b) foreign phrases, and (c) sentences typed from right to left. All are designed to force students to keep their eyes on the copy.

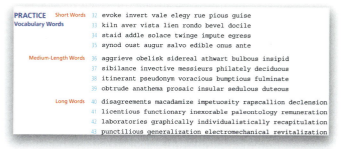

Speed Lessons

Lesson 3 of each unit is designed to build student speed at the keyboard by using these drills.

1. **15-Second Speed Sprints.** Students enjoy these short bursts of speed because they are motivational and show students just how fast their fingers are capable of moving. They are also an excellent vehicle for helping students break the habit of looking at their hands when they type. Tell your students, "You may not be able to go for an entire minute without looking at your hands, but I'll bet you can do it for just 15 seconds."

2. **Common Letter Combinations.** Dr. Scot Ober's published research has identified the most frequently occurring 2-letter, 3-letter, and 4-letter combinations in typical business writing. If students learn to type these frequent combinations quickly (as a "word" as opposed to letter-by-letter typing), their speed will increase.

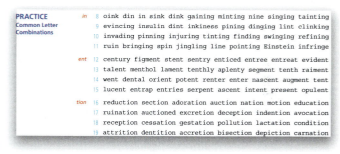

3. **Progressive Practice.** Progressive Practice is an individualized skillbuilding component of ISAK that is designed to build speed and accuracy in short, incremental steps. Thirty-second passages are provided for speeds ranging from 20 wpm to 100 wpm. The ISAK software automatically displays the correct passage for each student. The student practices that passage until he or she can complete it with no uncorrected errors and then moves to the next passage, which is 2 wpm faster. The topics of both the Progressive Practice and Paced Practice relate to grammar and mechanics.

4. **Paced Practice.** Paced Practice is an individualized skillbuilding component designed to build speed by enabling students to speed up—just a little—and then to build accuracy by slowing down—just a little; any gross deviation from normal typing speed is detrimental to skillbuilding. The ISAK software indicates at what point in the timed writing students should be at each 15-second interval. If they're typing too fast, they should slow down a little; if they're typing too slowly, they should speed up a little. Their goal for each timed writing is to be within a character or two of each speed marker when it disappears.

As soon as a student reaches his or her own individualized speed goal, ISAK displays a passage that is 2 wpm slower than the speed goal, and then the student works for accuracy—by slowing down *just a little*.

5. **5-Minute Timed Writing.** Each speed lesson ends with a 5-minute timed writing. All timed writings contain all letters of the alphabet and are the same length, the same level of difficulty (as measured by syllabic intensity), and the same format—to ensure that student differences in speed or accuracy are the result of increased *skill* and not the result of changes in copy difficulty or format. The 40 Supplementary Timed Writings in the Appendix are written to the same standards as the lesson timed writings.

Systematic Skillbuilding

As can be seen from the table on page xiii, all of the above drills are practiced systematically throughout the 60 lessons, because each type of drill builds skill in a slightly different manner. Thus, ISAK is a skillbuilding *system*.

Flexibility in Scheduling

No matter what your course length is, students should complete Lessons 1-3, which comprise a complete keyboard review. Most students need this review in order to be successful in subsequent lessons.

As noted, each unit comprises one accuracy lesson, one technique lesson, and one speed lesson. Lessons 4-60 can be used in any order you think most effective for your students. In other words, one lesson does not depend upon a previous lesson.

In a shorter course, you may opt to have students type each drill 1 time. In a longer course, you may opt to have your students type each exercise 2 or even 3 times. If you do this, remember that having a student type each line two times before moving to the next line promotes speed; having a student type the entire four lines of a drill 1 time and then typing the four lines a second time promotes accuracy. Or, you may opt to have students type all 60 lessons, and then starting over, type all 60 lessons a second time. The choice is yours.

ISAK: A SKILLBUILDING *SYSTEM*

ACCURACY IMPROVEMENT

	Lesson No.	4	7	10	13	16	19	22	25	28	31	34	37	40	43	46	49	52	55	58
WARMUPS																				
1.	**MAP+:**																			
	Alphabet																			
	Number																			
	Symbol																			
2.	**Finger Keys (P/P/P):**																			
	F — J — F and J																			
	D — K — D and K																			
	S — L — S and L																			
	A — ; — A and ;																			
3.	**Confusable Keys (P/P/P):**																			
	Consecutive Fingers:																			
	R-T — M-N — V-B																			
	D-E — O-L — F/R																			
	Adjacent Fingers:																			
	O-I — A-S — S-D																			
	R-E — I-U — W-E																			
	Substitutions:																			
	E-I — G-H — A-E																			
	S-K — Y-T — R-U																			
4.	**Business Spelling:**																			
	Most Frequently Used and Misspelled Business Vocabulary																			
5.	**Reach Drills:**																			
	Horizontal:																			
	er & io, te & pu | fa & up, ad & oi | we & ip, ga & pi | xc & ki, ds & iu																			
	Vertical:																			
	es & li, ra & pl | at & ho, se & il | st & ly, ar & ul | es & li, ra & pl																			
	Jump:																			
	ve & in, cr & on | ce & on, ex & ni | ct & mi, ze & mp																			

TECHNIQUE IMPROVEMENT

	Lesson No.	5	8	11	14	17	20	23	26	29	32	35	38	41	44	47	50	53	56	59
WARMUPS																				
6.	**Nonprinting Keys (P/P/P):**																			
	ENTER Key — TAB Key — SPACE BAR																			
	LEFT SHIFT Key — RIGHT SHIFT Key — BACKSPACE Key																			
7.	**Concentration (P/P/P):**																			
	Vocabulary Words																			
	Foreign Phrases																			
	Reverse Typing																			
8.	**Number Practice**																			
	0 1 2 3 4 5 6 7 8 9																			
9.	**Symbol Practice**																			
	@ # $ % & * ( ) -																			
10.	**Punctuation**																			
	! : ; " ' , . ? /																			

SPEED IMPROVEMENT

	Lesson No.	6	9	12	15	18	21	24	27	30	33	36	39	42	45	48	51	54	57	60
WARMUPS																				
11.	**12-Second Speed Sprints**																			
12.	**Common Letter Combinations (P/P/P):**																			
	in — ent — tion																			
	er — ing — ment																			
	re — ati — able																			
	ti — pro — ther																			
	on — ate — comp																			
	es — con — ance																			
13.	**Special Hand Drills:**																			
	Left-Hand Words — Right-Hand Words — Left- and Right-Hand Words																			
	Alternate-Hand Words — Double-Letter Words — Home-/Upper-/Lower-Row Words																			
14.	**Progressive Practice**																			
15.	**Paced Practice**																			
16.	**5-Minute Timed Writings**																			

A Note About Homework

Students should be able to touch-keyboard at the rate of at least 20 wpm before beginning ISAK. Individualized drills are provided for speeds ranging from 20 wpm to 100 wpm. Each lesson has been developed to require students who type 20 wpm an average of 50 minutes to complete. Using the standard practice of counting 50 minutes of class time as 1 hour (thus allowing for a 10-minute break), these students would typically take 60 hours to type all drills one time in all 60 lessons. You can use this information to determine the amount of homework to assign to fulfill your institution's expectations for homework.

To the Student

Improving Speed and Accuracy in Keyboarding (ISAK) has one purpose: to help you achieve the speed and accuracy skills in keyboarding that will enable you to secure the type of employment position for which you are trained. It is designed to upgrade your keyboarding skills through scientific copy, proven techniques, and individualized practice. You will always be competing against your own previous best effort—not against the class or some arbitrarily set goals.

The drills in this text have been developed based on extensive research regarding how typists learn, what reaches cause them the most problems, and how to remediate those problems so that you become an expert typist. If you complete these drills and follow the practice techniques included, you should see a noticeable improvement in your skill level.

All of your work will be completed through the ISAK software, which is an online program available for use at any computer that has Internet access. The software will either display the copy for you to type or will direct you to the appropriate lesson and page number in the text. Through the software, you will always be able to see which lesson sections you have completed and how you performed on them.

Typing Technique

Position yourself correctly at the keyboard to achieve the best typing results, reduce fatigue, and avoid health problems. Follow these steps:

- Make sure the surface of the monitor is clean. Position the monitor directly in front of you to minimize twisting of the neck, about an arm's length away, and tilt the top of the monitor back a little.
- Use "dynamic seating"—that is, don't sit in the same position for long periods of time.
- Sit slightly reclined (greater than 90 degrees) in the chair, with the lower back against the backrest and your feet flat on the floor. Center your body in front of the keyboard, with the text on one side and the mouse on the other, both at the same level as the desk.
- Raise your hands slightly when typing so that your wrists do not touch the keyboard. There should be a straight line between your lower arms, wrists, and back of the hands (this is called the *neutral* position of the wrist).
- Curve your fingers naturally, with the finger tips lightly touching the home-row keys. Make quick, light strokes, operating all keys by touch and using the correct fingering.

Tension-Reducing Exercises

- Hold your shoulders with your palms and rotate your elbows ten times clockwise, then ten times counterclockwise.
- Keeping your head stationary, rotate your eyes to form a circle, both eyes focusing together, five times clockwise and five times counterclockwise.
- Let your hands hang loosely at your side; rotate your right hand clockwise in a circle, then counterclockwise. Repeat with the left hand.
- Lock your hands behind your head, bring elbows back as far as possible, inhale deeply and hold for 20 seconds. Exhale and relax.
- Roll your shoulders forward in a big circle; then roll them backward in a big circle—the larger the circle, the better.
- Shut your eyes tightly for 3 seconds; then open them wide and blink rapidly; doing so produces tears that moisten and lubricate the eyes.

- Sitting back, raise your right foot slightly and rotate it clockwise in a big circle, then counterclockwise. Repeat with the left foot.
- Standing at attention, breathe in while you bend backward and then breathe out as you return to the normal position. Then repeat, bending forward.
- Tilt your neck to one side (ear toward shoulder), hold for 10 seconds, relax; then tilt your neck to the other side and repeat. Using the same steps, tilt your neck forward and backward.
- While in a relaxed position, place one hand on the abdomen and the other hand on the chest; inhale slowly through the nose and hold for 4 seconds; exhale slowly through the mouth.
- With eyes closed, slowly move the eyes up to the ceiling, down to the floor, to the left, and then to the right.
- With your elbows on the desk and leaning forward, cup your hands over your eyes, close your eyes, and inhale deeply through the nose; hold for 4 seconds and then exhale through the mouth.

Entrance and Exit Timed Writing

Begin your study by taking the following timed writing so that ISAK can chart your beginning performance. At the end of the course (or at any point during the course), take the same timed writing and note your skill gains.

```
 1        If you don't remember the location of a key when you    11
 2  are typing, first look at your keyboard to find it, but       22
 3  then look back at the copy before you strike the key; then    34
 4  say the letter abruptly to yourself while striking the key.   46
 5  Doing this will help fix the key's location in your memory.   58
 6        Initially, you may be able to type a little faster      68
 7  when looking at your fingers. But take the longer view:       79
 8  Looking at your fingers frequently will prevent you from      91
 9  reaching your speed potential, because it takes time away    102
10  from typing and also increases your errors since you lose    114
11  your place in the text and tend to either repeat or omit     125
12  words, thus decreasing your accuracy.                        133
13        Only you can break yourself of this habit. No person   144
14  is looking over your shoulder. But making the effort to      155
15  break this habit will surely pay dividends in this course    167
16  and in the future, when you realize just how many hours you  179
17  will spend daily in front of a keyboard. I'm confident you   191
18  can do it if you set this as an important goal.              200
      1 |  2 |  3 |  4 |  5 |  6 |  7 |  8 |  9 | 10 | 11 | 12
```

Keyboard Review—A

Goal

• Improve accuracy on the alphabet keys.

A. WARMUP

<table>
<tr><td>Accuracy</td><td>1</td><td>We quickly examined very pale azure flowers in the big jar.</td><td>12</td></tr>
<tr><td>Technique: Punctuation</td><td>2</td><td>Cox? peg; Manchu? (lab) dep't y-axis Mac. yes-no pie; Whew!</td><td>24</td></tr>
<tr><td>Speed</td><td>3</td><td>When the day is very hot, we like to swim in the cold pool.</td><td>36</td></tr>
</table>

1 | 2 | 3 | 4 | 5 | 6 | 7 | 8 | 9 | 10 | 11 | 12

B. PRETEST-PRACTICE-POSTEST: ALPHABET KEYS

Take a 1-minute timed writing, pushing moderately for speed.

PRETEST

Strike each key quickly and immediately return to home-row position or to the next character.

<table>
<tr><td>4</td><td>Kevin quickly planted a dozen aqua jonquils and six</td><td>11</td></tr>
<tr><td>5</td><td>white zinnias next to a brown shed. I believe he purchased</td><td>22</td></tr>
<tr><td>6</td><td>them from a major market when he began his current duty on</td><td>34</td></tr>
<tr><td>7</td><td>Friday. They are extremely large and just very pretty.</td><td>45</td></tr>
</table>

1 | 2 | 3 | 4 | 5 | 6 | 7 | 8 | 9 | 10 | 11 | 12

PRACTICE
Home-Row Keys

F 8 fff fff fifth buffer tiff baffle tipoff differ guffaw cliff
   9 rebuff duffle effort puffy runoff stiff offer effect fitful

J 10 jjj jjj jilt Jerry jinx job judo jelly Jake joist jam jewel
  11 juke Jane jock eject banjo join rajah Jack joust jolt jumbo

D 12 ddd ddd eddied iodide doped ruddy devoid bided dodge addend
  13 wedded udder candid dated added addict deduct demand paddle

K 14 kkk kkk woke cork teak skew soak eke king zonk key know ilk
  15 knob skunk kick dank ink Mack Jake funk conk kink sink Jack

S 16 sss sss seas sash dress sues subs Swiss essay skis sis hiss
  17 loss sits stress salsa less sans brass buss sums boss abyss

L 18 lll lll hello quell cull jolly spill allot holly lulu lilac
  19 dwell lawful loyal jello hall alley kill willful alloy hill

A 20 aaa aaa banana saliva larva aha cabana aqua data salsa Anna
  21 llama papaya patina iguana mania Abba Alma Panama aqua casa

semicolon (;) 22 ;;; ;;; thin; jump; able; join; bath; upon; drag; best; ad;
              23 pie; win; vary; bad; are; made; Lucy; edge; stow; Roy; fat;

F and J Fingers

G 24 fgf ggg gorge zigged grog gargle ragtag grudge going wiggle
  25 urging gauge grunge gargle grudge edging gadget gang haggle

H 26 jhj hhh shah hash heh though hush huh rhythm shh health hah
  27 hither whoosh thrush sheath thrash eighth hash harsh thresh

	R	28	frf rrr remarry furry rural array hurry carrier drear radar
		29	furrier burro err ardor arrow briar armor rider arbor ruler
	U	30	juj uuu hum nut subdue sue tumult nun dugout hue guy cut us
		31	out tug gut suture gun unsure guru mucus unhurt bun pug but
	T	32	ftf ttt tattle hottest stilt tutor treat tote attempt titan
		33	tithe ratatat otter Matt putty witty trout tooth stint tart
	Y	34	jyj yyy racy spryly heyday eye Eddy play Rudy Amy toy dryly
		35	Boyd yip yes clay your stay joy Amy Mayday pray any yam yaw
	V	36	fvf vvv oven wave veto verve have vase navy verb over savvy
		37	vase velvet valve volt vibe vain ivy votive Volvo save rave
	M	38	jmj mmm summed yummy summit memoir rammed mom embalm mayhem
		39	commit memo member summon moment medium mammal whammy comma
	B	40	fbf bbb bubble bamboo bulb bumble bomb gobble bobcat cobble
		41	shabby abbey Barbie crabby pebble nabbed bebop nubby ribbed
	N	42	jnj nnn neon intent Anna unsnap uneven unsung wanton bonnet
		43	annual sunken banana Wynn engine indent funny intern zoning

D and K Fingers

	E	44	ded eee wee Peter excel agree scene steel refer breed verve
		45	peek eagle verge venue cheap elate sleeve expel fence erode
	I	46	kik iii bikini idiot digit bigwig crisis bionic idiom alibi
		47	vivid ziti idiot distil licit iris clinic civic midi dioxin
	C	48	dcd ccc cacti crunch occupy cancan croc chuck accuse acacia
		49	scenic church civic concur cuckoo cynic caucus critic coach

S and L Fingers

	W	50	sws www show own how glow stew mown sow word swam whom fowl
		51	claw want wear woe wine wool wing wrap winnow spew brew wit
	O	52	lol ooo pool ozone bongo booboo logo hobo rodeo oleo voodoo
		53	blood coo food gogo Romeo oho rotor odor cook goop took woo
	X	54	sxs xxx oxtail Cox exile expend annex fax oxen twixt exhale
		55	Nixon vex pox extend affix Apex sextet Borax relax fox ibex

A and ; Fingers

	Q	56	aqa qqq equate unique quartz quay quiver quid sequel quarry
		57	quasi squab quail equate bisque quiche squint quaint clique
	P	58	;p; ppp puppet pigpen apply papal pump moppet appear sloppy
		59	prepay supple appall pimple papa upper pamper copper pickup
	Z	60	aza zzz Lizzie geezer brazen Ozark zanier doze woozy Amazon
		61	Bizet zeta stanza zippy zombie Zeus zither Zurich Zulu bozo

POSTTEST

Repeat the Pretest. *Goal*: Improve speed and accuracy.

ISAK says ...

TECHNIQUE TIP

Position the monitor directly in front of you to avoid excessive twisting of the neck—about an arm's length away.

By the power that is vested in me as President by the 11
laws of the United States, I hereby order as follows: 22
We have a unique bond with the American Indian and 32
Alaska Native tribes that are found throughout our land, as 44
shown in the Constitution of the United States, treaties, 56
and executive orders. 61
For many hundreds of years, our bond with these tribes 72
has been guided by a trust, a long-standing pledge on our 83
part to protect the unique rights of these tribes and to 95
ensure the well being of all of our nation's tribes, while 107
respecting their tribal rule. To recognize that commitment, 119
and to fulfill the solemn duties it entails, all agencies 130
must help to improve the educational prospects of tribal 142
students. 144
This is an urgent need, because studies show these 154
students drop out of school at a shocking rate, our nation 166
has made little or no progress in attempting to close the 177
achievement gap between tribal students and other students, 189
and major native languages are on the verge of dying. 200

1 | 2 | 3 | 4 | 5 | 6 | 7 | 8 | 9 | 10 | 11 | 12

This week marked an historic moment in the life of 10
our country and of our military. 17
For nearly nine years, our nation has been at war in 28
Quom. More than one and one half million Americans have 39
served in Quom with honor, skill, and bravery, and tens 50
of thousands of them have been wounded. Military families 62
have sacrificed greatly, none more so than the families 73
of those Americans who made the ultimate sacrifice. Our 84
troops, veterans, and their families will always have the 96
thanks of a grateful nation. We can never minimize their 107
contributions. 110
The colors our armed forces fought under were cased in 122
a ceremony before beginning their journey back home. Our 133
troops are now making their march across the border and out 145
of the country. Quom's future will be in the hands of its 157
own people. Our war there will be over. All of our troops 168
will be out of Quom. This is an extraordinary achievement, 180
one made possible by the hard work and sacrifice of the men 192
and women who had the courage to serve. 200

1 | 2 | 3 | 4 | 5 | 6 | 7 | 8 | 9 | 10 | 11 | 12

Keyboard Review—B

Goal

• Improve accuracy on the number and symbol keys.

A. WARMUP

Accuracy 1 A few of the new stores quickly provided amazing jukeboxes. 12
Technique: One-Hand 2 pony saves nook serve monopoly rewarded onion dates pumpkin 24
Speed 3 The boys and girls all sat in a ring to hear the wild tale. 36

1 | 2 | 3 | 4 | 5 | 6 | 7 | 8 | 9 | 10 | 11 | 12

B. PRETEST-PRACTICE-POSTTEST: NUMBER KEYS

PRETEST

Take a 1-minute timed writing, pushing moderately for speed. Press TAB to move from column to column in each row.

4	792 pads	397 ads	412 jars	408 yams	204 mops	9
5	776 lads	321 gyms	49 guns	904 bars	876 tips	18
6	831 vans	556 logs	552 men	34 pals	235 ears	26
7	539 hoes	679 bins	146 moms	400 cuts	808 bums	35

PRACTICE

Number Keys

5	8	f5f 555	385 bits	575 cuts	159 bums	155 pigs
	9	815 bays	15 gems	515 bars	505 buds	956 bags
6	10	j6j 666	166 men	46 bars	546 tons	656 wars
	11	364 cues	604 cubs	566 ends	376 cups	169 axes
4	12	f4f 444	54 gems	864 ways	624 acts	643 toes
	13	474 jays	742 zoos	214 eels	940 rows	44 bows
7	14	j7j 777	177 ribs	727 acts	878 gaps	762 days
	15	73 pets	677 cabs	727 nods	77 gems	847 bits
3	16	d3d 333	513 pigs	613 pubs	363 vows	836 hens
	17	753 dams	363 vans	373 jays	134 cues	123 cars
8	18	k8k 888	83 pets	868 laps	418 hogs	188 bays
	19	188 seas	8 laws	180 bees	568 ends	868 cuts
2	20	s2s 222	512 nuts	232 tips	532 moms	712 acts
	21	372 cups	712 zoos	27 ages	482 dots	122 boys
9	22	1l1 999	959 oaks	294 dens	199 ants	969 vows
	23	319 nets	399 fads	93 bins	693 toes	799 zoos
1	24	a1a 111	13 pets	110 bees	212 boys	111 rags
	25	101 buds	111 kits	131 gags	19 bugs	416 ears
0	26	;0; 000	360 vans	500 keys	406 ears	502 lots
	27	309 nets	300 fads	640 imps	700 ribs	900 rows

TIMED WRITING 37
Topic: Government

Resolved, that upon the adoption of the resolution it 11
shall be in order to consider the conference report to go 23
with the bill to authorize funds for the fiscal year for 34
all military actions of the Department of Defense, for all 46
military construction, and for all joint defense actions 57
of the Department of Energy, to set all military personnel 69
strengths for such fiscal year, and for other aims of this 81
bill. 82

All points of order against the conference report and 93
against its consideration are waived. The report shall be 105
considered as read. The previous question shall be deemed 116
as ordered on this report to its adoption without other 128
motions except for one hour of debate and one motion to 139
recommit if such is deemed to be valid. 147

It shall be in order at any time through the rest of 158
the first session of the Congress for the Speaker to accept 170
motions that the House suspend the rules, if the text of 181
the measure proposed in a motion is made open to members 192
at least one day before consideration. 200

1 | 2 | 3 | 4 | 5 | 6 | 7 | 8 | 9 | 10 | 11 | 12

TIMED WRITING 38
Topic: Government

The United States Code is a compilation of most public 11
laws that are currently in force; the Code is organized by 23
subject matter. When a law is printed, it tells where it 34
can be found in the Code. 40

When a law has been changed by a newer law, the Code 51
reflects this change. The Code collates the original law 62
with subsequent amendments, and it deletes language that 73
has later been repealed or changed. The Code is organized 85
by subject area into fifty titles. These titles are further 97
broken down by chapter and section. 104

There are more than a few ways to learn where a law 115
is codified, that is, to learn where the law can be found 127
in the Code. A law may be codified in more than one title 138
of the Code, and a law is often codified in more than one 150
section. Although the Code is divided into fifty titles by 162
broad subject area, it is easier to use the Code's general 173
index. The index is detailed and convenient. Another way to 185
determine where a law is located is by looking it up by its 197
popular name. 200

1 | 2 | 3 | 4 | 5 | 6 | 7 | 8 | 9 | 10 | 11 | 12

POSTTEST   Repeat the Pretest. *Goal:* Improve speed and accuracy.

C. PRETEST-PRACTICE-POSTTEST: TOP-ROW SYMBOL KEYS

PRETEST

Take a 1-minute timed writing, pushing moderately for speed. Press TAB to move from column to column in each row.

28 `$448`	`Ha-Ha!`	`82%-85%`	`8# of ore*`	7
29 `following*`	`ole@aol.com`	`Dye & Lee`	`T-shirt`	17
30 `Coe & Coe`	`(sic)`	`119%`	`Slow down!`	25
31 `gli@nc.gov`	`$76`	`#4 ranking`	`(2012)`	33

PRACTICE   percent (%)
Symbol Keys

32 `f5f f%f 973% 506% 57.2% 440% 94.6% 624% 874% 451% 932% 942%`
33 `538% 4.2% 53% 415% 984% 212% 628% 942% 124% 800% 94.6% 369%`

Press the   ampersand (&)
SPACE BAR when
you see the | symbol.

34 `j7j j&j|Hsu & Tan|Ely & Foy|Rea & Nix|Ivy & Dye|Olson & Han`
35 `Dern & Chos|Van & Lau|Wells & Webb|Woods & Gil|Loy & Turner`

dollar sign ($)

36 `f4f f$f $4.98 $30 $9.33 $414 $7.36 $9.89 $5.78 $10 $8.75 $2`
37 `$7.48 $318 $5.57 $5.16 $9.85 $6.09 $5 $5.54 $9.33 $3.40 $30`

asterisk (*)

38 `k8k k*k Bonilla* Bishop* Kennedy* Itou* Santos* Zhao* West*`
39 `Xu* Alvarado* Bishop* Hasan* Salazar* Payne* Okada* Nakano*`

number (#)

40 `d3d d#d|5# of ribs|1# of rock|#8 bus|6# of rice|2# of mulch`
41 `#3-01|#1 concern|24# of flour|3# of sand|#761|#7 box|#9 cab`

parentheses ( )

42 `l9l l(l ;0; ;); (oar) (lag) (lean) (law) (less) (old) (own)`
43 `(olio) (lore) (lisp) (load) (otic) (one) (lap) (oust) (lay)`

Press TAB to move   at (@)
from column to column.

44 `s2s s@s    svan@msn.com    jlam@acics.org    whan@ipa.net`
45 `art@cs.com  cday@att.net    hyu@gmail.com     kgay@bsu.edu`

exclamation mark (!)

46 `a1a a!a Box! Hide! Before! Bad! Chew! Bark! Choose! Better!`
47 `Turn! Exciting! Oops! Run! Air! Swallow! Taxi! Cold! Clean!`

hyphen (-)

48 `;-; --- mix-up follow-up H-bomb play-offs walk-in grown-ups`
49 `slip-ons tune-up deep-six baby-sit come-on also-ran cop-out`

POSTTEST   Repeat the Pretest. *Goal:* Improve speed and accuracy.

D. NUMBER AND SYMBOL PRACTICE

Type the entire paragraph 2 times, concentrating on accuracy and on keeping your eyes on the copy as you type.

50   `Wow! I just learned that 100# of #28 insulation cost`
51 `the firm of Ely & Ray* $76.98 (wholesale). E-mail them at`
52 `sales@e&r.com as a follow-up to my call (824-555-7493) and`
53 `let them know we can offer insulation to them @ $63.43, a`
54 `savings of 16% to 20%, without any mix-ups.* Do it now!`

ISAK says ...

TAKE A BREAK!

While in a relaxed position, place one hand on the abdomen and the other hand on the chest; inhale slowly through the nose and hold for 4 seconds; exhale slowly through the mouth.

All ballots shall be printed and displayed in a format | 11
of such uniform size as will fit the ballot frame and will | 23
be in as plain and clear a type or display as the space | 34
will permit. | 37

The names of parties which contain more than fifteen | 48
letters may be printed on the ballot in a shortened form. | 59
In printing the names of such candidates whose full names | 71
contain more than fifteen letters, only the surname must | 82
be printed in full. The board charged with preparing the | 94
ballots shall request each such candidate to indicate the | 105
shortened form in which his name shall be printed. When | 117
no such indication is received, such board shall make the | 128
adjustment. | 131

The party name and a letter or number shall be fixed | 141
to the name of each candidate or, in case of a presidential | 153
elector, to the names of the candidate for president and | 165
vice president of such party. The titles of offices may be | 177
arranged horizontally, with the names of candidates for an | 188
office arranged vertically under the title of the office. | 200

1 | 2 | 3 | 4 | 5 | 6 | 7 | 8 | 9 | 10 | 11 | 12

The request for a ban that was presented to Justice Carlton | 11
and by him referred to the Court is denied. Justice Smith took | 23
no part in this hearing. | 30

The Court rejected a test of the law that allows the | 41
release of the names of the petitions, but it assured the | 52
petitioners that the release could be blocked if a proper | 64
party could show that the release of the names would result | 76
in threats, harassment, and revenge. | 83

On remand, the District Court rejected this challenge, | 94
relying on a doubtful reading of our precedents. In fact, | 106
the District Court reasoned that only a select few groups | 118
may challenge the disclosure of the names of persons who | 129
sign a petition. If a ballot item succeeds, then, per the | 141
Court, disclosure of the names of the citizens who signed | 152
the petition may not be shielded no matter how strong the | 164
proof of revenge and how severe the nature of the threats. | 176

Whether this is a correct reading of our case presents | 187
an important question that merits serious exam by appellate | 199
court. | 200

1 | 2 | 3 | 4 | 5 | 6 | 7 | 8 | 9 | 10 | 11 | 12

Keyboard Review—C

Goal

• Improve accuracy on punctuation and nonprinting keys.

A. WARMUP

Accuracy	1 The jars prevented the brown mixture from freezing quickly.	12
Technique: Alternate Hands	2 shape amendment idle world right maid cork island rush idle	24
Speed	3 She has a torn seam on the right cuff of her new suit coat.	36

1 | 2 | 3 | 4 | 5 | 6 | 7 | 8 | 9 | 10 | 11 | 12

B. PRETEST-PRACTICE-POSTTEST: PUNCTUATION KEYS

PRETEST

Take a 1-minute timed writing, pushing moderately for speed.

4 Who's going to the marketing department's 2:30 p.m.	11
5 meeting on 3/1/14? The topic is "New Sales Goals." Let's	23
6 send these managers: Mr. Ross, Ms. Pugh, and Mr. Hidalgo;	34
7 Ms. Harrington could also go. Does that sound reasonable?	46

1 | 2 | 3 | 4 | 5 | 6 | 7 | 8 | 9 | 10 | 11 | 12

PRACTICE
Punctuation Keys

comma (,)	8 k,k ,,, Max, cane, wag, tank, band, face, have, gave, bars,	
	9 pack, boa, jog, beg, Abe, baby, avid, slab, wax, big, race,	
period (.)	10 l.l ... a.m. Sat. gov. Mar. Sept. acct. Inc. Aug. Ltd. Apr.	
	11 doz. Dr. i.e. Jan. c.o.d e.g., mdse. Enc. Ph.D. B.S. U.S.A.	
semicolon (;)	12 ;;; ;;; luck; Rome; from; bare, stem; step; back; vary; it;	
	13 head; film; come; pine; diet; navy; join; acre; year; have;	
apostrophe (')	14 ;'; ''' you're let's don't doesn't could've o'clock haven't	
	15 Jim's 'puck' he'd 'plug' 'pork' cont'd 'purr' 'pump' 'putt'	
colon (:)	16 ;:; ::: knew: milk: true: real: read: walk: zero: loop: Hi:	
	17 same: sang: weed: talk: bias: safe: are: trip: pole: saves:	
quotes (")	18 ;"; """ "pope" "pew" "pock" "plum" "o" "plow" "plus" "peso"	
	19 "prod" "poll" "push" "ply" "psi" "peek" "pool" "pied" "art"	
slash (/)	20 ;/; /// bad/badly 1/2 A.D./B.C. http:// 10/16/2013 24/7 c/o	
	21 ac/dc 2014/15 on/off read/write either/or input/output 1/16	
question mark (?)	22 ;?; ??? Again? All? Angry? Before? Better? When? But? Call?	
	23 Empty? Yes? Why? Where? Busy? Who? How? Open? Outside? Who?	

POSTTEST

Repeat the Pretest. *Goal*: Improve speed and accuracy.

Whereas the Governor has just issued a declaration of   11
emergency for the City of New York; and whereas the City   22
has taken steps to carry out these orders to protect the   34
public from harm and continues to do so during this time   45
of recovery from the extreme weather; and whereas there is   57
still risk to the public health and safety that requires   68
the adoption of these steps, then by the power vested in   80
me by the laws of the State of New York and the City of   91
New York, I hereby declare a state of emergency.   101

This state has been declared because of last week's   112
hazardous weather, which has caused flooding, power outage,   124
property damage, and other disruption of vital services,   135
and these conditions risk injury to the public.   145

All state boards are directed to take all actions and   156
steps that are needed to protect life and property and to   167
bring the emergency under control. This Order will take   178
effect immediately and will remain in effect for five days   190
unless it is ended or changed at some prior date.   200

1 | 2 | 3 | 4 | 5 | 6 | 7 | 8 | 9 | 10 | 11 | 12

There is hereby formed a New Hampshire state board of   11
elections, hereinafter referred to as the state board of   22
elections, made up of four qualified citizens named by the   34
governor: two members, one each from among two people named   46
by the head of the state committee of each of the political   58
parties; and two other, one upon the joint recommendation   70
of the legislative leader of one political party in each   81
house of the legislature and one upon the recommendation of   93
the leader of the other political party in each house of   105
the legislature.   108

Each board member shall be named for a term of two   119
years. A member named to the board to fill a vacancy shall   131
serve for the rest of the term. In the event that there is   142
a vacancy in the office of the member who was named on the   154
recommendation of such legislative leaders, these leaders   166
shall jointly name a member to fill the unexpired term, and   178
the governor shall make the appointment in no less than ten   190
days of having received this joint recommendation.   200

1 | 2 | 3 | 4 | 5 | 6 | 7 | 8 | 9 | 10 | 11 | 12

C. PRETEST-PRACTICE-POSTTEST: NONPRINTING KEYS

Take a 1-minute timed writing. Press TAB to move from column to column. Backspace and correct all errors as you type.

Return your finger to home-row position immediately after making each reach to the nonprinting key.

24	Al and Bev	Cal and Dee	Fay and Gus	7
25	Hal and Ida	Jin and Ken	Lev and Mei	14
26	Nat and Ola	Pam and Quin	Rex and Sue	22
27	Ty and Uta	Val and Wes	Yul and Zoe	28

PRACTICE **Nonprinting Keys**

LEFT SHIFT KEY

```
28 Nell Macy Hals Iggy Jedi Long Kern Maya Mari Lacy Ochs Hart
29 Yves Magi Uday Kral Lett Kean Ursa Kent Lent Owen Page Oslo
30 Lama Kane Nast Matt Peru Iraq Paul Jesu Hamm Ubay Yale Neal
31 Pele Mays Mali Hays Liam Ovid Hahn Lena Hadj Kelt Lear Kazu
```

RIGHT SHIFT KEY

```
32 Quan Wise Sims Ahab Quon Ritz Wood Boyd Bond Aida Glen Byrd
33 Alan Elks Thom Wouk Tojo Alma Gina Amur Bull Dior Rita Ryan
34 Guam Zuni Rico Coke Riga Shaw Zola Roma Suez Toby Rolf Alps
35 Cole Burr Quin Ruby Fuji Fish Soto Ames Todd Bonn Cuba Tony
```

BACKSPACE KEY

When you reach the BACKSPACE sign (←), backspace 1 time and then type the letter that follows, thus changing *tea* to *ten*.

```
36 tea←n met←n elf←k hot←p pad←l rag←m hoe←g spa←y get←m ill←k
37 gas←p hid←m box←y jar←y nub←n dim←p kid←n vat←n dig←m zig←p
38 pat←y fad←n wig←n her←n wow←n max←y wag←n pit←n she←y per←p
39 mob←m aid←l dab←y sag←p pub←n tie←p nag←p rig←m art←m add←o
```

ENTER KEY

Type each sentence on a separate line.

```
40 I am. Tom is on the job.  Help me. Who knows? I know. What?
41 I am up. See Mr. Dye. Let me have it. Go. Why is he so mad?
42 What do you want? I have had it. We do. Be here. Hi. He is.
43 Now you can do it. I go. Mark it in red. Why me? We are up.
```

TAB KEY

Type each word; then press TAB to move from column to column in each row.

44	Same	He	Information	Those	School	Section
45	Within	Plan	Insurance	No	Data	Both
46	Work	Up	Department	These	Been	Over
47	Center	Is	Necessary	As	Us	Letter

SPACE BAR

Bounce the thumb quickly off the SPACE BAR.

```
48 Is it true? Help me. I dare you. Of course. Mark it in red.
49 Now you can do it. Who knows? I can fax it. Who? Do it now.
50 Who, me? I am fine. Step on it. What time is it? We are up.
51 The ox may die. I go. Al came and went. How much? Says who?
```

POSTTEST

Repeat the Pretest. *Goal:* Improve speed and accuracy.

ISAK says ...

TECHNIQUE TIP

Sit so that your lower back touches the back of the chair.

During the panel's review of its park-naming rules,   11
Mr. Smith made reference to copies of the current rules. He   23
requested a review of the rules with regard to potential   34
changes or rewording to make the meaning clearer. He added   46
that the types of new parks and the number of signatures   57
required for various-sized parks should be reconsidered   68
since the types as listed no longer exist in accordance   80
with the Strategic Services Plan. Perhaps the numbers of   91
signatures required for the size of each park should be   102
adjusted as well as the service area. There may be other   114
changes members may want to consider as well.   123

Members may wish to form a subcommittee to conduct   133
this review since this is a chance to look at these rules   145
since they are not current. Staff should also review the   156
rules and come back with proposed changes and amendments   168
at the next meeting.   172

This item should be placed on next month's agenda.   182
Naming rights as a potential source of revenue should also   194
be considered for discussion.   200

1 | 2 | 3 | 4 | 5 | 6 | 7 | 8 | 9 | 10 | 11 | 12

As governor of this great state, I am disappointed   10
that agreements could not be reached that would require   22
teacher performance assessments at some of our troubled   33
school districts across the state. There is no excuse for   44
this inaction, and I urge everyone to make his or her voice   56
heard on this issue.   61

Our citizens and students lose twice because of this   71
failure. First, the failure to reach agreements on teacher   83
assessment will force these schools to continue to operate   95
without true accountability, a process which would ensure   107
that students receive a high-quality education from high-   118
quality teachers. Second, these schools may also jeopardize   130
millions of dollars in much-needed federal aid.   140

I urge all of those involved to get back to the table   151
now, put all differences aside, and put the kids first for   162
a change. They must agree on an assessment plan that will   174
raise performance and that will prevent the loss of more   185
than one hundred million dollars a year for our schools   197
across the state.   200

1 | 2 | 3 | 4 | 5 | 6 | 7 | 8 | 9 | 10 | 11 | 12

Accuracy

Goals

• Build accuracy on:
  ✓ Corresponding-finger and confusable keys.
  ✓ Spelling.
  ✓ Horizontal, alphabetic, and number reaches.

A. WARMUP

Accuracy   1   John and I quietly picked up six razors from the woven bag.   12

Technique: Concentration   2   photoreconnaissance contemporaneousness extraterritoriality   24

Speed   3   If you go too deep and are not able to swim, call for help.   36

1 | 2 | 3 | 4 | 5 | 6 | 7 | 8 | 9 | 10 | 11 | 12

B. PRETEST-PRACTICE-POSTTEST: CORRESPONDING FINGERS

Take a 1-minute timed writing, pushing moderately for speed.

PRETEST

Strike each key quickly and immediately return to home-row position or to the next character.

4   John and Ruby must name all of the nouns and verbs on   11
5   the forms just to be sure they are correct. Mr. Hyde gave   23
6   them five minutes to do the job, even though they did not   34
7   need all of that time to finish it. Hooray for those two.   46

1 | 2 | 3 | 4 | 5 | 6 | 7 | 8 | 9 | 10 | 11 | 12

PRACTICE   F Finger
Corresponding Fingers

8   tot vat but Jeff gate gulf goof debt Bob fate roof vote rig
9   egg flag grab rub rug rob urge rot bare tear lift veer belt
10   frog robe tug bet fat Viv tree free verb vary vast tomb fog
11   tab glob rest rage gift bomb gut tube Bev brag big ebb gang

J Finger

12   numb hub Ann shy hay mug fun menu dun jay July bum nine hen
13   Jane Hyde June drum inn huge gnu Hugh menu jug jam name Jim
14   harm jut must urn hem Nan they mind joy hand hymn your envy
15   ugly may horn hut Fuji Josh man hug busy hour hum bush noun

F and J Fingers

16   rightly rusty typify fought rupture granary glutton turmoil
17   buttery rusting gluten barley toughen faulty beauty borough
18   return thatch bygone bashful twangy bulging tankful foundry
19   throng tenth thermal gusting fraught bough Ruby thrash burn

POSTTEST

Repeat the Pretest. *Goal:* **Improve speed and accuracy.**

C. BUSINESS SPELLING

These spelling words are from a list of the most used and most misspelled words in business writing. Study the words that cause you problems.

20   accounted waiver equivalent obvious recommendation trustees
21   commensurate legislative treasurer's appraisal consequently
22   remuneration deferred attributable inconvenience indication
23   unfortunately consultation regards opportunity installation

Whereas the firm has need to utilize the consulting   11
services of those who have the skills to act as a council   22
agent on a frequent basis and whereas the contractor states   34
that he or she has the background and skills to perform   45
these jobs, now therefore, in consideration of the promises   57
contained herein, the parties do hereby agree to all of the   69
terms that are set forth below.   76

This agreement may be ended by either party with or   86
without cause by giving written notice to the other party   98
at least one month in advance. The services to be performed   110
shall be to provide assistance in the course of on-site   121
assessment visits and special help as agreed to by both   132
parties. Such help shall be performed as per the standards   144
and policies of the firm.   149

Payment to the contractor for the services rendered   160
will be based on the daily rate of six hundred dollars for   172
each full day scheduled. Expenses of the contractor fairly   184
incurred in performance of services under this agreement   195
will be paid by the firm.   200

1 | 2 | 3 | 4 | 5 | 6 | 7 | 8 | 9 | 10 | 11 | 12

This license agreement is made effective between Liza   11
D. Banks of New York City, New York, and Gail C. Bush of   22
Tell Me a Story, Inc. In the agreement, the party who will   34
be granting the right to use the licensed property will   45
be referred to as the licensor and the party who will be   57
receiving the right to use the licensed property will be   68
referred to as the licensee.   74

The licensor owns a unique series of children's books   85
sold as Let's Read. In accordance with this agreement, the   97
licensor grants J. Renee an exclusive license to sell Let's   109
Read in the State of Kansas. The licensor retains title and   121
ownership of the Let's Read series of her books.   131

If the licensee fails to abide by the duties of this   141
agreement, including the duty to make all royalty payments   153
on time, the licensor shall have the option to cancel this   165
agreement by providing thirty days' written notice to the   177
licensee. The licensee shall have the right to prevent the   188
end of this agreement by taking action that cures default.   200

1 | 2 | 3 | 4 | 5 | 6 | 7 | 8 | 9 | 10 | 11 | 12

D. MAP+: ALPHABET
Follow the software instructions for this exercise to improve accuracy.

E. PRETEST-PRACTICE-POSTTEST: CONFUSABLE KEYS

PRETEST

Pay special attention to these consecutive-finger reaches that often get confused.

Take a 1-minute timed writing, pushing moderately for speed.

24   For entertainment, let's try to travel to that famous   11
25 resort in Bolivia by the riverbank. I believe I have heard   24
26 good reports about the vibrant atmosphere, and everybody   35
27 raves about the vegetables and beverages available there.   46

    1 | 2 | 3 | 4 | 5 | 6 | 7 | 8 | 9 | 10 | 11 | 12

PRACTICE
Consecutive Fingers

rt-tr
28 try trot trifle ort tramp apart art tract cart trial trudge
29 tragic trip wart triad trim divert truth unhurt troop train
30 dart true tried retort trowel skirt trick tree exhort shirt
31 resort quart tremor tray trance desert report oxcart travel

mn-nm
32 entertainment inmost unmask alumni firmness nonmetal unmade
33 hymnal gymnast alumna Denmark unmet column unmoving remnant
34 unmelted damned calmness columnist hymn abandonment chimney
35 autumnal detainment condemned circumnavigate unmade unmined

vb-bv
36 believe vagabond absolve obviated visibly invisible abusive
37 adverb removable overbite riverboat bevel abusive observant
38 combative vibrant livable bivouac overbuilt variable viably
39 bereave overblown riverbank vibes voluble behoove vestibule

POSTTEST

Repeat the Pretest. *Goal*: Improve speed and accuracy.

F. REACH DRILLS: HORIZONTAL REACHES

er and io
40 amnio ionic goer leery jerk oiler legion polio arioso heron
41 motion era perky erg cheer period biotic mover violet jerky

Horizontal reaches move to a different key on the same row.

42 here tiger rover refer twerp deer pier berth ere derby trio
43 liner saber brio ferry merge hers paper manioc ration dozer

te and pu
44 quote terabyte punt toted carte water steal taste pup doted
45 patented tester termite pulse bate oaten stem vote literate
46 tenor tempter tenet cited purl often emote feted tease Kate
47 terse put elite test tepee octet punk spurt testy jute pull

G. MAP+: NUMBERS
Follow the software instructions for this exercise to improve accuracy.

TAKE A BREAK!

ISAK says ...

With your elbows on the desk and leaning forward, cup your hands over your eyes, close your eyes, and inhale deeply through the nose; hold for 4 seconds and then exhale through the mouth.

TIMED WRITING 27
Topic: Legal

This confidentiality agreement, hereafter called the	11
contract, is between Juan Dye, ex-owner of Prime, Inc., and	23
Quinton Kidd, current owner of Prime, Inc. In the contract,	35
the party who owns the confidential data, hereafter called	47
data, will be referred to as the data owner, and the party	58
to whom the data will be disclosed will be referred to as	70
the recipient.	73

Data refers to any material that is proprietary to 83
Prime, whether or not owned or developed by Juan Dye, which 95
is not generally known other than by Juan Dye or Quinton 107
Kidd, and through which Juan Dye may obtain through any 118
contact with Prime. Data includes without limits all plans 130
and business records. 134

Juan Dye understands that this data will have been 145
obtained by Prime through the investment of major time, 156
effort, and expense, and that the data is a special and 167
unique asset to the organization. Each employee to whom 178
such data is disclosed shall sign a contract much like this 190
one before such data is disclosed to him or her. 200

1 | 2 | 3 | 4 | 5 | 6 | 7 | 8 | 9 | 10 | 11 | 12

TIMED WRITING 28
Topic: Legal

Each spouse shall repay any and all debts incurred 10
in his or her own name prior to the date of this marriage 22
unless otherwise stated in this agreement. Each spouse will 34
also repay any debts incurred in his or her own name during 46
the course of this marriage. 52

The parties recognize that neither of them shall ever 63
receive spousal support from the other, and each waives any 75
and all claims against the other for alimony, maintenance, 87
or spousal support. The parties also agree that the court 98
will not retain jurisdiction in this matter and that this 110
waiver ends any and all rights each party may have held to 122
such support. Prior agreements are void once this agreement 134
is executed. 136

The parties agree that if any dispute, question, or 147
change occurs affecting the terms of the agreement, they 158
will work together to negotiate with each other in good 169
faith, with the aim of reaching a resolution that is of 181
benefit for both of the parties. If the parties fail in 192
this, they agree to first seek mediation. 200

1 | 2 | 3 | 4 | 5 | 6 | 7 | 8 | 9 | 10 | 11 | 12

Technique

Goals

- Improve technique on the nonprinting, number, symbol, and punctuation keys.
- Improve concentration.

A. WARMUP

Accuracy	1 Peter moved very quickly and seized the big jar of old wax.	12
Technique: Alternate-Hand	2 shape amendment idle world right maid cork island rush idle	24
Speed	3 She uses gold and blue a lot in her art; it will sell well.	36

1 | 2 | 3 | 4 | 5 | 6 | 7 | 8 | 9 | 10 | 11 | 12

B. PRETEST-PRACTICE-POSTTEST: NONPRINTING KEYS

PRETEST

Take a 1-minute timed writing, pushing moderately for speed. Type each sentence; then press TAB to move from column to column.

4 See me soon.	Oh, not him.	Run quickly.	So be quiet.	10
5 Add me, too.	Who knew it?	How goes it?	Why not you?	21
6 What was it?	When was it?	He is tired.	I like them.	31
7 I can do it.	I am so hot.	I see a cat.	I may do it.	41

PRACTICE
Nonprinting Keys

ENTER Key

Press ENTER after each word to format each word on a new line.

8 No! Repeat. Really? Fire! Tweet. Save. Attack. Wrong. Oops!
9 Vote. Inhale. Drive. Oh. Here. Yeah. Proceed. Maybe. Pause.
10 Evidently. Move. Talk. Back! Safe. Rest. Stand. How? Right.
11 Danger! Catch. Drink. Probably. Where. Hi. Hello. Possibly.

TAB Key

Type each word; then press TAB to move from column to column.

12 zeros	quack	atlas	afraid
13 aquatic	apart	academy	animal
14 quint	quarry	applaud	quotable
15 zigzag	quiche	zanier	affair

SPACE BAR

16 Is it too big? I dare you. See me at ten. I am up. Who, me?
17 Why me? Hi. Why not? Help me. She may do it. Go. Stop here.
18 Oh. Me? So? Go slow. Al came and went. It is up to me. How?
19 Jo is up. Do not. How dare you? I can fax it. It is a fact.

Bounce the thumb quickly off the SPACE BAR.

POSTTEST

Repeat the Pretest. *Goal:* Improve speed and accuracy.

C. NUMBER PRACTICE

Press TAB to move from column to column in each row.

Eyes on copy!

20 496	290	439	855	782	697	436	351	574	914
21 329	545	799	549	989	987	826	187	363	330
22 518	387	341	784	842	347	126	757	979	791
23 162	428	512	612	807	267	588	398	281	109

It is now the duty of the court to instruct you as to 11
the law. Under our legal system, this court decides all 22
questions of law and procedures that may arise during the 34
trial, and it is the duty of the members of the jury to 45
follow the instructions of the court in every respect and 57
in all cases. 59

On the other hand, the jury is the sole judge of the 70
facts and of the reliability of the evidence. The power of 82
the jury is not arbitrary, and if the court instructs you 94
as to the law on a particular subject or how to judge the 105
evidence, you shall follow these instructions. 115

Evidence refers to testimony and exhibits. In deciding 126
this case, you are to analyze and weigh all of the evidence 138
you find worthy of belief. The statements or arguments that 150
you have heard from the attorneys are not evidence. They 161
are intended to be helpful to you, but if your recollection 173
of the evidence differs from the attorneys', depend upon 185
your own memory. Thank you for your service. Please proceed 197
to the jury room. 200

1 | 2 | 3 | 4 | 5 | 6 | 7 | 8 | 9 | 10 | 11 | 12

If I, Jan Q. Lazar, am in a terminal state or am in 11
an irreversible coma or am in a permanent vegetative state 22
that my doctors feel to be not reversible or not curable, I 34
don't want my life to be prolonged, and I don't want life 46
sustaining treatment, beyond comfort care, that would serve 58
only to delay the moment of my death. If I have a condition 70
that is stated above, it is my wish to receive artificially 82
administered food and fluids until my death. 91

If I am pregnant and the fetus has a good chance of 102
surviving at birth, I want life sustaining treatment as 113
well as food and fluid. 118

I name my husband, Max J. Lazar, as my agent for all 128
matters relating to my healthcare, which includes, without 140
limits, the power to give and refuse consent to healthcare, 152
including the provision of life sustaining treatment. I 163
make this power of attorney while I am healthy, aware, and 175
of sound mind. This power of attorney is effective upon 186
the inability to make or to communicate my own healthcare 198
decisions. 200

1 | 2 | 3 | 4 | 5 | 6 | 7 | 8 | 9 | 10 | 11 | 12

D. SYMBOL PRACTICE

Keep your eyes on the copy as you type these top-row symbols.

```
24  (lad) qli@bsu.edu West & Little boo-boo Ngo & Ely bad-badly
25  Han & Hsu $1.14 697% $1 cli@bsu.edu 157.2% (lady) Noe & Ray
26  932% (laid) 958%  sngo@az.gov 233% (lace) Owens & Young 12%
27  729% 6% Shan* Mills & Ham $1.68 also-ran aorr@cs.com Berry*
```

E. PRETEST-PRACTICE-POSTTEST: CONCENTRATION
Take a 1-minute timed writing, pushing moderately for speed.

PRETEST

Concentrate on keeping your eyes on the copy as you type these vocabulary words. How many of these terms do you know?

```
28      The voracious disagreements between the two municipal     11
29  departments under the guise of attempting to further the      22
30  revitalization of the city were an anathema to the crew       34
31  who recalled the invective of earlier similar arguments.      45
        1 | 2 | 3 | 4 | 5 | 6 | 7 | 8 | 9 | 10 | 11 | 12
```

PRACTICE
Vocabulary Words

Short Words

```
32  evoke invert vale elegy rue pious guise
33  kiln aver vista lien rondo bevel docile
34  staid addle solace twinge impute egress
35  synod oust augur salvo edible onus ante
```

Medium-Length Words

```
36  aggrieve obelisk sidereal athwart bulbous insipid
37  sibilance invective messieurs philately deciduous
38  itinerant pseudonym voracious bumptious fulminate
39  obtrude anathema prosaic insular sedulous duteous
```

Long Words

```
40  disagreements macadamize impetuosity rapscallion declension
41  licentious functionary inexorable paleontology remuneration
42  laboratories graphically individualistically recapitulation
43  punctilious generalization electromechanical revitalization
```

POSTTEST

Repeat the Pretest. *Goal*: Improve speed and accuracy.

F. PUNCTUATION PRACTICE

Eyes on copy!

```
44  pine; "peg" net; lack, room; ash: lab, amt. pin; kid, axed,
45  rust; pile; Hot! seat; Break? rain; dep't flag's elk, face,
46  one; load; "peep" tag; cans, 1/7 Ph.D. loom; nine; it, Mrs.
47  Phil! onto; sat; i.e. Aug. beg, jack, Candy? am, lace, But?

48  pie; approx. sky; Burglar? Lucy; caps, aid, pat; How? pace;
49  pull; sink; balk: flea's Drive! att. mart; road; led, neat;
50  ear, bail, our; Yea! www.cnn.com/ Danger! Sell! div. Where?
51  be, Asia: Help! Ltd. shall/will cars, Carl, elf, able, dig,
```

TECHNIQUE TIP

ISAK says ...

Adjust the height of your chair so that your feet rest flat on the floor and your thighs are parallel to the floor.

I, William Z. Freeman, do make, publish, and declare   11
this my last will, hereby revoking all former wills and   22
codicils. I am married to Eloise Z. Freeman, hereinafter   33
referred to as my spouse. We are now the parents of three   45
presently living children. As used in this will, children   57
shall mean my children listed in Exhibit A and any other   68
children adopted by me or born to me either before or after   80
my death.   82

If my spouse does not survive me, I then nominate as   93
guardian of any child or children of mine who have not yet   105
reached majority, Lois R. Smith, if willing and able to   116
serve. If a conservator is required for the estate of any   127
child of mine, I nominate the same person as that nominated   139
as guardian.   142

I nominate my spouse as personal representative of my   153
estate and of this, my last will. If my spouse is unwilling   165
to serve, I nominate my brother, Matthew R. Freeman, as my   177
personal representative. I direct that any and all of the   188
above named people shall be allowed to serve without bond.   200

1 | 2 | 3 | 4 | 5 | 6 | 7 | 8 | 9 | 10 | 11 | 12

The undersigned natural person, who is on this date   11
more than eighteen years of age, hereby establishes a new   22
corporation pursuant to the laws of Maine and adopts these   34
articles of incorporation. The name of this corporation   45
shall be Living Words, Inc. The purpose of the new firm   56
shall be to edit magazine articles, textbook chapters, and   68
other text on a freelance basis.   75

To further the above purpose, the corporation shall   85
have all of the rights now or in the future conferred on   97
the corporation organized under the laws of Maine. It may   108
also do everything required or proper for the achievement   120
of its purpose.   123

The number of shares that the corporation shall have   134
power to issue is one hundred shares of common stock, each   146
having a par value of one dollar. At all meetings of the   157
shareholders, at least one half of the shares entitled to   169
vote at such meeting shall make up a quorum. When a quorum   181
is present, an affirmative vote of a majority of the shares   193
shall be the act of the shareholders.   200

1 | 2 | 3 | 4 | 5 | 6 | 7 | 8 | 9 | 10 | 11 | 12

Speed

Goals

- Build speed on:
  - ✓ 15-Second Speed Sprints and 30-Second Progressive Practice drills.
  - ✓ Common letter combinations and special hand drills.
- Assess speed and accuracy on a 5-minute timed writing.

A. WARMUP

Accuracy	1 Alphabetizing the new index forms will be a very quick job.	12
Technique: Transpositions	2 on no|Alec lake|ant nap|led elk|err Rex|anus nary|Edie deny	24
Speed	3 Her dad puts the new oil in the car to keep it in top form.	36

1 | 2 | 3 | 4 | 5 | 6 | 7 | 8 | 9 | 10 | 11 | 12

B. PRETEST-PRACTICE-POSTTEST: COMMON LETTER COMBINATIONS

PRETEST

Take a 1-minute timed writing, pushing moderately for speed.

4 After finding that the new stent in a section of the	11
5 invading cancer was evidently injuring the patient, the	22
6 doctor offered to include nine additional procedures to	33
7 help bring the patient some cessation of his pain.	43

1 | 2 | 3 | 4 | 5 | 6 | 7 | 8 | 9 | 10 | 11 | 12

PRACTICE
Common Letter Combinations

in
8 oink din in sink dink gaining minting nine singing tainting
9 evincing insulin dint inkiness pining dinging lint clinking
10 invading pinning injuring tinting finding swinging refining
11 ruin bringing spin jingling line pointing Einstein infringe

ent
12 century figment stent sentry enticed entree entreat evident
13 talent menthol lament tenthly aplenty segment tenth raiment
14 went dental orient potent renter enter nascent augment tent
15 lucent entrap entries serpent ascent intent present opulent

tion
16 reduction section adoration auction nation motion education
17 ruination auctioned excretion deception indention avocation
18 reception cessation gestation pollution lactation condition
19 attrition dentition accretion bisection depiction carnation

POSTTEST

Repeat the Pretest. *Goal*: Improve speed and accuracy.

C. 15-SECOND SPEED SPRINTS

Goal: Increase your speed on each retyping of the same sentence.

20 Soon this snow will melt; then we will find what lies here.
21 Save some now so that you may spend it a few days from now.
22 The sea was cold, but she was too keen to surf to stay out.
23 When we meet, I will ask you to read the mail they sent us.

This contract is made between James R. King and Ann A. | 11
King, who are husband and wife, their heirs and assigns, | 23
hereinafter referred to as seller, and Wayne Q. Tobin, a | 34
single person, his heirs and assigns, hereinafter referred | 46
to as buyer. | 48

Seller agrees to sell and buyer agrees to buy from | 59
seller for the price and on the terms and conditions set | 70
forth below that certain real property that is located in | 82
Pima County, State of Arizona, as described in Exhibit A | 93
that is attached. | 97

The purchase price of the property, that seller agrees | 108
to pay, will be the sum of ninety five thousand dollars and | 120
no cents, which shall consist of five thousand dollars that | 132
has been paid as earnest money and ninety thousand dollars, | 144
which shall be paid on execution hereof. | 152

Seller agrees to keep the building on said premises | 163
insured against loss by fire or other means in an amount | 174
not less than the fair market value, with any loss payable | 186
to the parties as their interest shall appear at the time | 198
of the loss. | 200

1 | 2 | 3 | 4 | 5 | 6 | 7 | 8 | 9 | 10 | 11 | 12

Landlord hereby warrants that it and no other person, | 11
form, or organization has the right to lease the premises | 23
as hereby demised. | 26

So long as tenant shall perform each and all covenants | 38
to be performed by tenant hereunder, tenant shall enjoy the | 50
quiet and exclusive use and possession of the said premises | 62
without hindrance on the part of the landlord, and landlord | 74
shall defend tenant in such peaceful and quiet possession | 85
and use under landlord. | 90

Tenant's rights under this lease are and shall always | 101
be subordinate to the terms of any mortgage, deed of trust, | 113
or other security means now and in the future placed on the | 125
structure or any part or parts thereof, by landlord. In | 136
confirmation thereof, tenant shall execute such further | 148
pledge as may be required by landlord at any points in the | 159
future. | 161

Tenant shall pay upon execution of this agreement a | 172
security deposit in the amount of the monthly rent that may | 184
be used as the last month's rent, so long as tenant is not | 195
in default of any kind. | 200

1 | 2 | 3 | 4 | 5 | 6 | 7 | 8 | 9 | 10 | 11 | 12

D. SPECIAL HAND DRILLS

Left-Hand Words

Maintain the nontyping hand in home-row position.

24 tracer afterward greatest waves rates tree acts cat streets
25 bears Eve reserved creates exceeded staff Sara faster safes
26 acres sweater base greeted bases card eats get Baxter state
27 eraser deed gate bet secret deserve stages Everett regarded

Right-Hand Words

28 phony honk noon oilily nil monopoly mum oink onion him join
29 mil Jon poplin inn ink hunk opinion uphill imp pin pill hip
30 plunk loin uplink Yukon pop noun pull lymph phylum Kim Milo
31 upon limp poi lop minimum phi linkup Phil junk pumpkin loom

Left- and Right-Hand Words

32 sad Yukon arrears are ilk fear area Lynn sat puppy Fred tax
33 sever greet Polly deeds deserves oink reserved waste stated
34 taste inn set red race kill lymph scattered wears jolly raw
35 kilo addresses Jimmy arrest revert deserve vast kimono deed

E. 30-SECOND PROGRESSIVE PRACTICE

Follow the software directions for this exercise to improve keystroking speed and accuracy.

F. 5-MINUTE TIMED WRITING

Take two 5-minute timed writings.

Goal: Push moderately for speed while keeping your accuracy under control.

If you finish typing the passage, press ENTER and start again.

36 Secretaries and administrative assistants have now	10
37 assumed duties that were once reserved for managers and	22
38 their staff. In spite of this, their core duties have not	33
39 changed much over the years. They are still in charge of	45
40 most of the functions of the office and create, store, and	56
41 analyze documents for their clients and for their staff.	68
42 Most of these jobs are full-time in an office, even	78
43 though some secretaries now work from home. Typing, word	90
44 processing, and communication skills are required for these	102
45 positions. Most of these workers have at least a two-year	113
46 degree, and most legal secretaries have a four-year degree.	125
47 These positions make up one of the largest type of	136
48 occupations in industry and are found throughout the world.	148
49 The future job outlook for such positions is excellent,	159
50 especially for those workers who can use the most common	170
51 software programs. Promotions often come with experience	182
52 and involve more complex tasks. As with all types of jobs,	194
53 the work is constantly changing.	200

1 | 2 | 3 | 4 | 5 | 6 | 7 | 8 | 9 | 10 | 11 | 12

TAKE A BREAK!

ISAK says ...

Shut your eyes tightly for 3 seconds; then open them wide and blink rapidly.

Mitch, a large male, checked himself into the hospital 11
this morning at nine. He told us that his right big toe was 23
swollen, hot, and very tender to the touch. His wife came 35
with him, and she stated that in the past, his father had 46
suffered from gout on several occasions. 55

The joint at the base of his right big toe was swollen 66
and red. His heart rate, blood pressure, and breathing were 78
all normal; however, he was running a high fever. These 89
symptoms are consistent with acute gout, but to be certain, 101
I had a joint fluid sample analyzed. Urate crystals were 113
found in the fluid. While this analysis was being done, we 124
attempted to reduce the fever and swelling by applying ice 136
to the toe and treating him with naproxen. 145

His gout is most likely caused at least in part by 155
genetics. Mitch's high body mass index is equally a risk 167
factor. To prevent future episodes, I counseled the patient 179
to limit his intake of meat and alcohol, maintain a low- 190
calorie diet, and take an ascorbic acid supplement. 200

1 | 2 | 3 | 4 | 5 | 6 | 7 | 8 | 9 | 10 | 11 | 12

Zoe is a patient of ours whose father brought her into 11
our office six weeks ago. Then she had a runny nose, a mild 23
sore throat, and nasal congestion. The physician diagnosed 35
her with a viral cold and suggested her father administer 47
some over-the-counter meds to treat the symptoms. 57

Her father brought her back today. Over the last few 67
weeks, her ailment had gone up and down, and she has now 79
developed a bad cough. She evidenced no fever at her visit 91
today, but last night she woke with a high fever that her 102
father treated with ibuprofen. 109

Her lungs sounded fairly clear, though her cough was 119
quite productive. Her father stated that her mucous is dark 131
green in the morning but clear during the day. I think she 143
has bronchitis and that it is likely bacterial. I wrote her 155
a prescription for penicillin and advised her father to 166
continue administering the same medicines for her symptoms. 178
Just to be sure, I also had a nurse take a sample of her 190
sputum, which we will stain and check for bacteria. 200

1 | 2 | 3 | 4 | 5 | 6 | 7 | 8 | 9 | 10 | 11 | 12

Accuracy

Goals

- Build accuracy on:
  - ✓ Corresponding-finger and confusable keys.
  - ✓ Spelling.
  - ✓ Vertical, alphabetic, and symbol reaches.

A. WARMUP

Accuracy	1	Pete had to move quickly to seize the big jar of bee's wax.	12
Technique: Concentration	2	anticonservationist intellectualization disenfranchisements	24
Speed	3	The math test will be hard, but I am sure she will pass it.	36

1 | 2 | 3 | 4 | 5 | 6 | 7 | 8 | 9 | 10 | 11 | 12

B. PRETEST-PRACTICE-POSTTEST: CORRESPONDING-FINGER KEYS
Take a 1-minute timed writing, pushing moderately for speed.

PRETEST

Strike each key quickly and immediately return to home-row position or to the next character.

4	Dickie had a date with Erica and drove to a deli in	11
5	Waikiki; they had a pickle, Coke, and chips. Then he asked	22
6	her to go hiking and skiing with him in the evening. The	34
7	weather was brisk, and they had a wild and carefree time.	45

1 | 2 | 3 | 4 | 5 | 6 | 7 | 8 | 9 | 10 | 11 | 12

PRACTICE
Corresponding Fingers

D Finger

8 cad puce odd herd dove acme Ted end doe feed Eric edit aide
9 coke cage date dime nice deck idle lead died jade wade made
10 cud clef led once ode mace bed Eve vice Chet cued cote mend
11 dyed chew idea lice dive care peck cell Dave heed ride pace

K Finger

12 ski mink pickle napkin frisk Mickey fickle king sink sickle
13 Waikiki wick kiln brisk kid pick skit disk Nike ilk kin kit
14 kid, Minsk Kiev wok, knit like kiddy ark, Erika Jackie skim
15 heck Kim, smirk trick skirt flick Dick chink pick Rick ask,

D and K Fingers

16 slick iodine Dick victim stick suicide pick disdain thicken
17 icky flick licked chick idiotic deficit bicker chicken lick
18 Rick wicked thick indict indigo kick flicked knocked sicken
19 Mickey quicken idolize wick kiddie idiom picked quick knack

POSTTEST

Repeat the Pretest. *Goal:* Improve speed and accuracy.

C. BUSINESS SPELLING

These spelling words are from a list of the most used and most misspelled words in business writing. Study the words that cause you problems.

20 facilities suite reimburse associated derived entry alleged
21 priority capacity variance discussing hereinafter existence
22 bargaining vendor quarterly consultants yield establishment
23 unique function secretaries advisory identification maximum

The patient is a male infant, four days old, who was   11
brought to the newborn intensive care ward when his parents   23
noticed that his skin had taken on a yellow tint. His vital   35
signs were normal. The color extended from his face to his   47
chest, and his sclera were also yellowed. We analyzed his   58
bilirubin levels, which were high, but that is not unusual   70
for newborn jaundice.   74

We explained that jaundice is a very common condition   85
in infants, and it is generally not a cause for concern.   97
We are having the patient undergo light therapy at home,   108
and we will check his bilirubin levels in three days to see   120
if treatment in the ward is required. No symptoms of a more   132
serious form of jaundice were detected.   140

The parents reported few bowel movements, and I think   151
the infant has breast-feeding jaundice. He was delivered   163
via cesarean section, so it may be that the mother's milk   174
production is not adequate as a result. More regular breast-   186
feeding sessions stimulates this and also increases bowel   198
movements.   200

   1 | 2 | 3 | 4 | 5 | 6 | 7 | 8 | 9 | 10 | 11 | 12

Sandra arrived today for her six-month teeth cleaning.   11
When asked if she had any concerns or any questions, she   23
stated that one of her mandibular molars had become more   34
sensitive to cold lately. I performed her dental exam after   46
prophylaxis by the hygienist and then discovered that the   58
enamel on both her left and right mandibular first molars   69
was abraded on the left side.   75

I showed the abrasions to the patient, and asked if   86
she were aware of clenching her teeth. She said that she   97
has been under some stress at work and will sometimes wake   109
in the morning with a sore jaw but that she does not recall   121
clenching. I explained to her that she was suffering from   133
nocturnal bruxism and that without treatment, it would at   144
best result in dental decay and-at worst dental fracture.   156

I recommended to her that we schedule an appointment   167
to replace the crown on the left side due to the size and   178
depth of the abrasions but that the right side crown did   190
not yet show enough wear to warrant a replacement.   200

   1 | 2 | 3 | 4 | 5 | 6 | 7 | 8 | 9 | 10 | 11 | 12

D. MAP+: ALPHABET

Follow the software instructions for this exercise to improve accuracy.

E. PRETEST-PRACTICE-POSTTEST: CONFUSABLE KEYS

PRETEST

Take a 1-minute timed writing, pushing moderately for speed.

Pay special attention to these consecutive-finger reaches that often get confused.

24   A lot of older folks frown upon debt. They love to
25 fret about the side effect of loans from loose lenders and
26 the loan lobby. Often, they have cool logic on their side.
27 Keep your debt load low and under control all of the time.
    1 | 2 | 3 | 4 | 5 | 6 | 7 | 8 | 9 | 10 | 11 | 12

PRACTICE
Consecutive Fingers

de-ed
28 debt yodel creed adder mode aside node deep reed decal dude
29 deli depth side wide delta anode defy decoy under ode delay
30 abode devil chide oxide dyed sped aide dew deer elude hazed
31 derby dear deaf bred Ted eked dell iced zoned edge deft deb

ol-lo
32 yolk loin golf folk lot solar tool holy poll lobo mold lost
33 loath lord lone lout loupe viol olden loyal spool molt load
34 loan droll loose polka loam love logic low login whole cool
35 colt lobby loch Colin stole roll loll Volvo pool viola loom

fr-rf
36 frog airflow frail friend frizzy scarf frolic frill defrost   10
37 affront fourfold from fry colorful perfume earful fret serf   22
38 frame friar franc frailty defraud frenzy frozen fro carfare   34
39 fridge refrain surf front fretful frosh fringe curfew frown   46

POSTTEST

Repeat the Pretest. *Goal*: Improve speed and accuracy.

F. REACH DRILLS: VERTICAL REACHES

es and li
40 eases slide dozes lib loess ides resin clip mesa pesky lira
41 lion glib liar reset vest dries flip chili link bliss blink
42 best lied live fixes blimp slip alien essay geese less does
43 limp calix Dali yes oozes life rest west lisp lid limo lime

Vertical reaches move from one row to the adjacent row.

ra and pl
44 ramp apply bra grave braid plume draw grace brake aura rage
45 Kraft plot split plank plum crazy graze trap Ray graph ploy
46 grand plea razz ample rare fraud raid maple borax wrap grab
47 crawl plead rake drag crack plane oral mural rash irate rad

G. MAP+: SYMBOLS

Follow the software instructions for this exercise to improve accuracy.

TECHNIQUE TIP

Sit so that all body angles are slightly more than 90 degrees: (a) shoulders, hips, and knees; (b) shoulder, elbow, and wrist; and (c) hips, knees, and feet.

ISAK says ...

The patient is a homeless man who looks to be in his   11
sixties. A friend of his brought him to the emergency room,   23
saying that he had been vomiting. The patient's speech was   35
slurred, and he seemed unsteady on his feet. We put him on   46
a drip to replace fluids and electrolytes. A blood test   58
indicated no alcohol in his system.   65

The patient complained of a headache, dizziness, and   76
nausea. I asked if he had been injured recently, but he   87
seemed confused and could not remember. His friend reported   99
that the patient had slipped on the ice, fallen, and lost   110
consciousness for a few seconds. No external injury was   122
visible, and his pupils were equal in size.   130

I ordered a computer tomography scan to ensure   141
there was no trauma. The patient was advised of his conditions   153
and that the only treatment is sufficient rest. He will   164
remain here for twenty-four hours, and after that I have   175
requested that he return in two to three days for further   187
medical care and to check that his symptoms have not gotten   199
worse.   200

1 | 2 | 3 | 4 | 5 | 6 | 7 | 8 | 9 | 10 | 11 | 12

Diane came in today for an annual eye exam. She is a   11
new patient, fifty-seven years old. She has no history of   22
eye disease, except for a lazy left eye that was corrected   34
with surgery when she was a child. She reports being myopic   46
since she was in her twenties, and she wears glasses to   57
correct this. In the past year, she has noticed a change   69
in her ability to focus on close objects.   77

Based upon the external exam, her corneas, irises,   88
sclera, eyelids, and the tissues around the eyes were all   99
typical. I confirmed the myopia with an eye-chart test and   111
measured the refractive error with the phoropter. I think   123
from her recent eye strain that her eyes are farsighted. We   135
discussed the condition, and I urged her to get bifocals   146
this year.   148

Her left pupil was half a millimeter larger than her   159
right, which is not abnormal, and both are of regular shape   171
and react normally to light. Her eye motility, both quick   183
and slow, was fine. The visual fields of both eyes were   194
checked and found to be normal.   200

1 | 2 | 3 | 4 | 5 | 6 | 7 | 8 | 9 | 10 | 11 | 12

Technique

Goals

- Improve technique on the nonprinting, number, symbol, and punctuation keys.
- Improve concentration.

A. WARMUP

Accuracy	1	Ask Jo to quit being lazy and come with Riva to fix a post.	12
Technique: Double Letters	2	cell took heed dress Eddie alley hall Allen bass bill carry	24
Speed	3	We will not win this game if only half of the team is here.	36

1 | 2 | 3 | 4 | 5 | 6 | 7 | 8 | 9 | 10 | 11 | 12

B. PRETEST-PRACTICE-POSTTEST: NONPRINTING KEYS

PRETEST

Backspace to correct all errors as you type.

Take a 1-minute timed writing, pushing moderately for speed.

4	Alma Jean and Pete Hart went to Oslo, and Mark Rose	11
5	and Mara Cody went to Iran. Before Hedy Boyd retires, she	22
6	and Jean Quin want to visit Cuba and also to see the Ural	34
7	Mountains. I want to see the Cook Islands sometime in May.	45

1 | 2 | 3 | 4 | 5 | 6 | 7 | 8 | 9 | 10 | 11 | 12

PRACTICE
Nonprinting Keys

	8	Yale Jesu Mack Hank Jess Leif Levi Lake Mach Jean Lacy Owen
	9	Hart Palu Lego Hale Jack Oahu Mara Haru Kent Hugh Marx Ives
LEFT SHIFT Key	10	Lama Ursa Mead Kate Isis Peke Pete Nazi Nast Yank Mark Maya
	11	Mays Parr Iggy Mesa Ural Oran Iran Hahn Oslo Hedy Nell Paul
RIGHT SHIFT Key	12	Alma Cuba Chen Bond Enid Gigi Quan Boyd Aldo Quin Rose Dona
	13	Rosa Anne Shui Ruth Cody Ames Fisk Chad Anna Zola Bush Rowe
	14	Todd Tory Gish Glen Ross Togo Bonn Riga Suez Finn Alan Soto
	15	Emma Suva Cohn Duma Cook Gina Rita Emil Siam Elks Burt Elia

BACKSPACE Key

When you reach the Backspace sign (←), backspace 1 time and then type the letter that follows.

16 pot←p she←y sot←y egg←o ill←k box←y hex←y oaf←k gym←p pub←n
17 box←n big←n wag←y dim←p woe←k tee←n tie←p pit←n has←m gut←m
18 zig←p raw←y tea←n gag←y sag←p hug←m pie←n rid←p her←n sin←p
19 nub←n rug←m cue←p are←k leg←i rag←m aid←l cab←n jag←m inn←k

POSTTEST

Repeat the Pretest. *Goal*: Improve speed and accuracy.

C. NUMBER PRACTICE

Press TAB to move from column to column in each row.

Eyes on copy!

20	321	437	560	747	224	242	729	790	137	454
21	246	520	264	366	719	569	301	231	243	604
22	842	914	330	791	109	661	186	105	402	438
23	826	290	365	868	848	322	694	487	604	196

Alex's mother brought him in this morning, saying he   11
was having pain in his left ankle. She stated that over the   23
weekend, he was at a playmate's house jumping on a large   34
trampoline, when he fell off and landed poorly on his left   46
foot. While he was able to walk, she stated he had a limp   58
and was in quite a lot of pain.   64

The area around the ankle is red and swollen. I asked   75
Alex if he recalled hearing any sound at the time of the   86
injury, and he didn't. There was no tenderness along the   98
distal portions of his tibia and fibula, and the joints   109
could bear his weight in the office. As such, I am ruling   121
out a fracture. Based on the location of this patient's   132
tenderness, he has an inversion ankle sprain.   141

I advised his mother to practice basic first aid for   152
the ankle, including getting plenty of rest, applying ice   163
to the injury, and elevating the joint above heart level.   175
Due to the severity of the patient's discomfort, I have   186
immobilized the joint with an air cast and recommend he   197
use crutches.   200

1 | 2 | 3 | 4 | 5 | 6 | 7 | 8 | 9 | 10 | 11 | 12

Ruth is a new patient who had an appointment at our   11
office today. Her primary-care doctor referred her to us   22
after she expressed concern over still having acne at the   34
age of thirty. I discussed with her the hormonal and the   45
genetic causes of acne, as well as the way pimples form.   56

Ruth has mild acne on her face. I noted blackheads on   67
the base of her nose and also pustules on her forehead. She   79
had a small number of scars on her forehead. I advised that   91
she use a face wash with benzoyl peroxide once per day, and   103
I also spoke to her about lifestyle changes that can reduce   115
acne, in particular frequent exercise and a diet with a low   127
glycemic load.   130

During her exam, I also noticed an atypical mole on   141
her back, just below the neck. It is five millimeters in   152
diameter, and it has an uneven border and coloration. Due   164
to her having a family history of melanoma, I excised it   175
and am sending it to our lab for analysis. I am also having   187
the patient schedule a visit for a full screening of her   199
moles.   200

1 | 2 | 3 | 4 | 5 | 6 | 7 | 8 | 9 | 10 | 11 | 12

D. SYMBOL PRACTICE

Keep your eyes on the copy as you type these top-row symbols and return your fingers immediately to home-row position.

24 Parker* $1 #8 nut (lad) Santos* #1-20 (lag) also-ran (lack)

25 212% Fuentes* imply-infer Sokolov* 268% A-frame $1.09 57.2%

26 $0.34 Han & Hsu sngo@az.gov $2 233% 697% Owens & Young 932%

27 aorr@cs.com (lain) 958% Mills & Ham add-on Ely & Foy Shan*

E. PRETEST-PRACTICE-POSTTEST: CONCENTRATION

Take a 1-minute timed writing, pushing moderately for speed.

PRETEST

Pay attention to what you're typing.

28   If you are in Northern Spain, you may greet the locals   11

29 by saying, "Egunon," whereas in East Africa, you may say,   23

30 "Habari za asubuhi." The French greet each other by saying,   35

31 "Bonne matin," and the Italians say, "Buon giorno."   45

    1 | 2 | 3 | 4 | 5 | 6 | 7 | 8 | 9 | 10 | 11 | 12

PRACTICE   Short Phrases
Foreign Phrases

32 Basque: Egunon.

33 Finnish: Huomenta.

34 Latin: Bonum mane.

35 Danish: God morgen.

Medium-Length Phrases

36 French: Bonne matin.

37 Portuguese: Bom dia.

38 Italian: Buon giorno.

39 English: Good morning.

Long Phrases

40 Indonesian: Baik pagi.

41 Estonian: Tere hommikust.

42 Filipino: Magandang umaga.

43 Swahili: Habari za asubuhi.

POSTTEST

Repeat the Pretest. *Goal*: Improve speed and accuracy.

F. PUNCTUATION PRACTICE

Eyes on copy!

44 pain; back, so/so that Sara; Wed. max. egg, Pete; ea. luck;

45 1/7 jog, par; Thu. sack; Walk? Dale's out; pat; pump; stub;

46 Whew! i.e. pull; road; Fri. cars, att. Bart: 4/10 Gas? set;

47 Mark; loud; tag; star; sing; e.g. So? bldg. "pear" 3/4 Sun.

48 neat; don't P.O. Mr. Leon; Alone? Luis; navy; Follow? bays,

49 pack; maybe/may be Safe! roar; Hear? pond; qty. Here! size;

50 Where? go, our; by, Ed.D. Lucy; bars, raise/rise Why? link;

51 Dec. div. art: beg, he, 1/9 in, 7/10 sink; ear, barn, gave,

ISAK says ...

TAKE A BREAK!

With eyes closed, slowly move your eyes up to the ceiling, down to the floor, to the left, and then to the right. Repeat.

The patient is a female in her thirties. She came to 11
the emergency room at eight at night in distress, and she 22
complained of difficulty when she spoke and of an acute 34
itching sensation over her whole body. She reported taking 45
a vitamin this morning and a painkiller at lunch, as well 57
as having eaten two slices of a plain pizza at a cafe for 69
dinner in the past too. 75

She was cogent but seemed to speak with an impediment. 86
Her tongue and throat were both swollen. An epidermal exam 98
showed no rash or abrasions, aside from mild redness due to 110
her having been scratching. Her heart rate was slightly 121
raised, and while a nurse took her blood pressure, she 132
complained of having trouble breathing. She was quickly 143
injected with four hundred micrograms of adrenaline. Five 155
minutes later, her breathing returned to normal. 164

She was advised to stay in the hospital for the night 175
for further tests. Also, she was counseled on additional 187
allergy treatment, such as over-the-counter medications 198
and shots. 200

1 | 2 | 3 | 4 | 5 | 6 | 7 | 8 | 9 | 10 | 11 | 12

The patient is a short, thin male, who is forty-two 11
years old. He was out of breath and felt pressure on his 22
chest, and he believed himself to be having a heart attack. 34
He was brought to the coronary care unit. We put him on 45
oxygen and gave him two aspirin, and I ordered an exam to 57
check the troponin levels in the patient's blood. He was 68
upset and got into an argument with the nurse. 78

The final results of the troponin test showed that his 89
levels were not increased. We also ordered a cardiogram, 100
and I saw zero changes in serial leads. Once he understood 112
that he was not having a heart attack, he let us administer 124
a mild sedative. I think the patient was just in the midst 136
of a panic attack. 140

He asked to be permitted to remain in the coronary 150
unit for the evening to have his condition monitored. We 161
needed the space for critical patients, but I transferred 173
him to the general medical floor for tonight. Please permit 185
him the opportunity to ask questions prior to administering 197
any more tests. 200

1 | 2 | 3 | 4 | 5 | 6 | 7 | 8 | 9 | 10 | 11 | 12

Speed

Goals

- Build speed on:
  - ✓ 15-Second Speed Sprints and Paced Practice drills.
  - ✓ Common letter combinations and special hand drills.
- Assess speed and accuracy on a 5-minute timed writing.

A. WARMUP

Accuracy	1	Zelda just bought six printers very quickly from two malls.	12
Technique: Upper Row	2	ere tepee wept yet tot tore weeper pet pirouette pore quite	24
Speed	3	The fish tank has a leak; I knew we did not set it up well.	36

1 | 2 | 3 | 4 | 5 | 6 | 7 | 8 | 9 | 10 | 11 | 12

B. PRETEST-PRACTICE-POSTTEST: COMMON LETTER COMBINATIONS

PRETEST

Take a 1-minute timed writing, pushing moderately for speed.

4	Did the clerk infer that the apartment easement and	11
5	the cover of the wire were going to lead to a deferment	22
6	here in our department? If so, the sheer size of a merger	33
7	may be taking too long to complete, and we may defer it.	45

1 | 2 | 3 | 4 | 5 | 6 | 7 | 8 | 9 | 10 | 11 | 12

PRACTICE
Common Letter
Combinations

er

8 skier infer fiber paper mower deter anger pager serif verse
9 sever merrier mover avert exert timer heron beret pert over
10 edger verger merge joker clerk here voter alert wiper perch
11 overt boxer sheer rerun dozer cover ruler laser herder user

ing

12 zinging naming owning wading boxing fixing sing toting zing
13 wing towing living hiking dingy biking lacing fringe dining
14 wiring asking lazing eying tiring aging fling aching mining
15 acing pinging during going engulf making trying ring aiming

ment

16 momentum mental cement adornment easement apartment pimento
17 sediment pavement implement element mentor foment placement
18 determent deferment amendment condiment amazement abasement
19 segment armament movement basement ferment ailment rudiment

POSTTEST

Repeat the Pretest. *Goal:* Improve speed and accuracy.

C. 15-SECOND SPEED SPRINTS

Goal: Increase your speed on each retyping of the same sentence.

20 If you hold tight to an ice pack, it will help you so much.
21 Just face the fact that you did miss a very nice boat trip.
22 Put that pen to a pad if you want to tell her how you feel.
23 She does love to cook; too bad she does not do it too well.

Wouldn't it be nice if we lived in a world where no 11
one ever complained? Well, maybe it would not be, because 22
sometimes complaints are justified. For example, if someone 34
were deliberately rude to you, you would not want to just 46
let that pass. That would not be good for your self-esteem. 58

When making a complaint, go directly to the person 68
most directly involved in the problem. Without assigning 80
blame, tell that person exactly how his or her remarks made 92
you feel. Also, explain what techniques might have been 103
more effective for the person to have used. 112

When complaining about a product or service, go to the 123
person who is most likely to get you the results you want. 135
It is only fair to let that person have the first chance to 147
correct the problem. Then, if you do not get satisfaction 158
at that level, go up that person's direct supervisor. 169

Finally, do not apologize for making a complaint and 180
avoid making it personal. If you feel that a complaint is 191
justified, there is no reason to apologize. 200

1 | 2 | 3 | 4 | 5 | 6 | 7 | 8 | 9 | 10 | 11 | 12

Too many students go the whole school term without 10
ever meeting with their instructors during their office 22
hours. Talking to an instructor before or after class may 33
help you to get quick, specific questions answered, but 44
there is just not enough time then to help build a true 56
relationship. 58

Most of your instructors will have posted office hours 70
during which you can either make an appointment or just 81
walk in. Many instructors may add extra hours during exam 92
times. Use these times to talk about class assignments, 104
as well as to talk about more difficult subjects such as 115
grades, personality conflicts, attendance policies, and 126
lectures. 128

Plan to maximize your time at these sessions by coming 139
prepared. Instead of complaining about a grade on a term 151
paper, come prepared to discuss exactly how you went about 163
preparing the paper and ask for specific comments on what 174
you could have done differently to improve the grade. Then, 186
use this feedback to improve your performance on the next 198
assignment. 200

1 | 2 | 3 | 4 | 5 | 6 | 7 | 8 | 9 | 10 | 11 | 12

D. SPECIAL HAND DRILLS

Alternate-Hand Words

24 forms ant foam wit soak Pamela kept hair Bob civic fir pair
25 Diane blend coal title usual sight amend theme chairmen Jay
26 fish mama element endowment lend Dick Janeiro Blanche Claus
27 worn for of Laurie England she duck Helen apt flap bus maid

Double-Letter Words

28 Scott odd butte Ross Tommy fussy Billy apple hall affix all
29 Kelly happy dress Betty quill fee feel bill Ann Sally Hyatt
30 kill buzz Harry book keep Isaac shook cliff loose too teeth
31 Polly sorry Terry access arrow Danny sweet door hello cross

Home-Row Words

32 elks dash age: jade flaked Dahl saga lake: sakes lead: lead
33 ask shade: shakes Hadj sled "dad" hag "ask" desks shad sale
34 heal leaf less shads lass addles fled fall kegs lades safes
35 shelf fake ads galls sags sash false gala: salad dad adages

E. PACED PRACTICE

Follow the software directions for this exercise to improve keystroking speed and accuracy.

F. 5-MINUTE TIMED WRITING

Take two 5-minute timed writings.

Goal: Push moderately for speed while keeping your accuracy under control.

36   Business reading is not a spectator sport. To learn   11
37 what they need to know to do their jobs better, business   22
38 managers spend a third of their time reading. That makes   33
39 reading an important skill; yet reading is not a skill that   45
40 may come automatically. It requires your direct attention.   57
41   The main thing to do if you want to improve your skill   68
42 in reading is to examine your attitude toward reading. Do   80
43 you think of it as a passive task? Your reading skills will   92
44 increase if your reading is active, that is, if you put   103
45 your own thinking and ideas in charge of the process.   114
46   First of all, take a minute to look through the report   125
47 just to get the main idea and size of the topic. Then go   137
48 through the report a second time, reading for details. Ask   148
49 yourself questions to help you evaluate the writer's ideas.   160
50   Unfortunately, most people read no faster today than   171
51 their ancestors did a hundred years ago. Reading faster   182
52 helps you keep an active mind frame and helps you retain   194
53 all of the desired information.   200

    1 | 2 | 3 | 4 | 5 | 6 | 7 | 8 | 9 | 10 | 11 | 12

ISAK says ...

TECHNIQUE TIP

Tilt the top of the monitor back a little, with the screen at eye level.

Do you often find that you get bored when reading an assigned chapter in a textbook or feel you do not remember the important points in the chapter? Here are some tips for more effective reading.

First, skim the chapter to get its overall meaning. Scan all the headings and subheadings before you read the chapter itself. Turn these headings into questions, which will serve as a hook to focus your attention as you read. Study the introduction and summary. Most textbooks have comprehension questions at the end of each chapter. Scan these before reading and, as you read, see which of them you can answer.

As you read the actual chapter, stay involved in the process. Don't let your mind wander. Pay special attention to key terms that are italicized or in bold; the author probably considers them essential to your understanding. Take notes or underline, but just of the important points. After reading a chapter, take the time to try to recall in your own words the high points of the chapter.

11
23
35
39
50
62
73
85
96
107
119
122
133
145
156
167
179
190
200

1 | 2 | 3 | 4 | 5 | 6 | 7 | 8 | 9 | 10 | 11 | 12

Do you believe everything that you read or hear? Of course you do not, so you are already engaged in some form of critical thinking, which is defined as a process that questions your assumptions and attempts to overcome your own biases by carefully judging what you read and hear. Here are some useful methods for polishing your thinking skills.

First, try to be as objective as you can be. Check your emotions at the door because emotions only confuse critical thinking. Try to clarify the issue that is being discussed. Seek examples or ask questions until you are sure that you truly understand the issue. Try to suspend judgment until you are sure that you have all the facts. Also, recognize that different people may have different cultural traditions.

Consider the source. Even if a speaker has a vested interest in what he or she is saying, that does not mean that what the person is saying is not true. It just means that you should seek out other opinions to verify what you are hearing.

11
22
34
45
56
68
69
80
91
103
114
125
137
148
152
163
174
186
198
200

1 | 2 | 3 | 4 | 5 | 6 | 7 | 8 | 9 | 10 | 11 | 12

Accuracy

10

Goals

• Build accuracy on:
✓ Corresponding-finger and confusable keys.
✓ Spelling.
✓ Alphabetic, jump, and number reaches.

A. WARMUP

Accuracy	1 Cy's jet black box was quite filled with proven topaz gems.	12
Technique: SHIFT Keys	2 Albert Burns typed. Chico Duarte listened. Eugene Ford sat.	24
Speed	3 It is too hot in the sun, so I will sit near the tall tree.	36

1 | 2 | 3 | 4 | 5 | 6 | 7 | 8 | 9 | 10 | 11 | 12

B. PRETEST-PRACTICE-POSTTEST: CORRESPONDING-FINGER KEYS

PRETEST

Take a 1-minute timed writing, pushing moderately for speed.

4 Lola and Flo wore woolen shells to the six global art	12
5 shows in Hilo. They drooled when they say the gold medal	23
6 winners, whom they knew well; they now own two new works	35
7 in oil and one in wax. They loaded them into a nearby taxi.	46

1 | 2 | 3 | 4 | 5 | 6 | 7 | 8 | 9 | 10 | 11 | 12

PRACTICE
Corresponding Fingers

S Finger

8 webs slew shows sows taxes waits Wes muss assist sibs swims
9 awes swap skews pass sets sixths sums fuss suds wasps mixes
10 wish moss sixth exist wares axis owns exams saps axles subs
11 swig swat walks buss swim saw ewes spew skis sins wises wax

L Finger

12 Lou plot slop loaf oblong jell. lotion droll Laos Oct. lope
13 look global load oil volt lowly poorly sold Lola sloop bloc
14 loin told glob Flo cold gold holy hello slog loony lore old
15 golly slowly fold loot blot Olga folk wallop oral loop Hilo

S and L Fingers

16 silos rolls drools woolens slots slopes wolves spells looks
17 swallow widows spoons knolls sorrows loosens scrolls stalls
18 salsas wells lowbrow wool shells shows snows glosses boosts
19 lawless oodles oleos dowels pillows closes slews wows loons

POSTTEST

Repeat the Pretest. *Goal:* Improve speed and accuracy.

C. BUSINESS SPELLING

These spelling words are from a list of the most used and most misspelled words in business writing. Study the words that cause you problems.

20 attended negative maturity bearing dividends recommendation
21 ledger accidents criteria herein jewelers supplement solely
22 position approximately discrepancies immediately percentage
23 consistent efficiency enrollment sense monitors established

There is power in positive thinking. If you expect 10
good things to happen, they will, so it is important that 22
you visualize only what you want to happen. Find reasons 33
to smile more often, read inspiring stories, and surround 45
yourself with happy people. 51

The easiest way to achieve positive thinking is simple 62
and basic: be nice. Be nice to other people no matter what. 74
Tell people they look nice today or that they did a great 85
job on that presentation. Remember that there is a positive 97
aspect in everything. In each person and in each situation, 109
there is something good. Sometimes we may have to look hard 121
for it, but it will be there. 127

When we are stressed, certain hormones spread through 138
our body. If they are released infrequently, these hormones 150
are harmless. But stress hormones can cause our bodies much 162
long-term damage. So, for better health, think positive 174
thoughts. You'll feel better, you will be more creative, 185
and others will like you better this way. It really is a 196
win-win situation. 200

1 | 2 | 3 | 4 | 5 | 6 | 7 | 8 | 9 | 10 | 11 | 12

You may have come to believe that one of the biggest 11
differences between high school and college is the amount 22
and depth of research papers that are required for your 34
courses. College instructors expect students to be quite 45
familiar with how to locate and analyze data, whether it 56
comes from books, journals, or online sources. 66

Today's librarians are trained explorers. They know 76
how to search out data from many different sources. Their 88
purpose on the job is to help you, so do not be afraid to 100
ask for this help. It can save you hours of work. As you 111
are getting help from a librarian, you are also learning 122
how a trained professional gathers needed information, so 134
the next research project will probably go much smoother. 146

Also, keep in mind that the best resource may not be 156
in paper form. It may be online instead. Since anyone can 168
publish whatever he or she wants online, one of the most 179
basic research skills you will need to acquire is how to 191
evaluate the quality of the data you collect. 200

1 | 2 | 3 | 4 | 5 | 6 | 7 | 8 | 9 | 10 | 11 | 12

D. MAP+: ALPHABET
Follow the software instructions for this exercise to improve accuracy.

E. PRETEST-PRACTICE-POSTTEST: CONFUSABLE KEYS

PRETEST

Pay special attention to these adjacent-finger reaches that often get confused.

Take a 1-minute timed writing, pushing moderately for speed.

24	The point is that she said we are going to build a new	12
25	studio in the eastern region to avoid paying rent. We need	24
26	this asset as soon as possible, and it will not be an easy	35
27	task. The other odds and ends can be saved for next week.	47

1 | 2 | 3 | 4 | 5 | 6 | 7 | 8 | 9 | 10 | 11 | 12

PRACTICE
Adjacent Fingers

oi-io
28 droid region nation joist wooing vision barrio biotic point
29 iodine toil void heroic loin potion studio soil scion audio
30 biopsy avoid violet doily olio diode boil viola going kiosk
31 junior memoir koi broil idiot mooing prior radio iota idiom

as-sa
32 sang crash save saint clash okras bask teas base east Judas
33 comas areas sawn rasp laser sand asset mask coast said lash
34 salt fleas sack task abase amass lasso abash easy sale lass
35 gash as salad Degas samba last haste satin sauce grasp gasp

sd-ds
36 girds fads finds misdone adds odds ends pods bauds ads rods
37 studs bids wards scads plods moods misdeed bends wads beads
38 maids sleds mends curds vends melds eavesdrop misdial woods
39 grads binds goods lids sudsy misdeal rends lads cards funds

POSTTEST

Repeat the Pretest. *Goal*: Improve speed and accuracy.

F. REACH DRILLS: JUMP REACHES

ve and in
40 venom veal event in leave oven grave revel lever suave veil
41 vet give verb even dive vex inane save hive ink shave novel
42 rave delve lave vend pave veto aver seven fever valve ingot
43 brave Vera crave inn inset veer nerve solve liven info wove

Jump reaches move from the upper row to the lower row or vice versa.

cr and on
44 crunch crepe decree crow crown creek crude online crumb cry
45 ecru credit craw screen Ono scribe crick on creep onyx crux
46 sacred create secret onyx acre crag crease crop crib cringe
47 Velcro craven crouch onto crab scrap cried crack craft crew

G. MAP+: NUMBERS
Follow the software instructions for this exercise to improve accuracy.

TAKE A BREAK!

ISAK says ...

Tilt your neck to one side (ear toward shoulder), hold for 10 seconds, relax; then tilt your neck to the other side and repeat. Using the same steps, tilt your neck forward and backward.

Effective note-taking skills are a major help if you 11
want to succeed in college. No student can be expected to 22
remember everything that the instructor says, so you should 34
get directly involved in the process. 42

When you are taking notes, do not try to write down 53
everything. Instead, look for signals that the instructor 64
is making an important point, such as when the instructor 76
pauses, repeats a concept, or writes it on the board. Use 88
your own words, because doing so involves you more intently 100
in the process. Avoid using complete sentences because they 112
are a waste of time. Be brief, writing down only the major 123
points. In other words, analyze what you are hearing and 135
determine its importance. 140

Develop your own technique for taking notes. Decide 151
whether you prefer an outline form, jotting down the main 162
ideas, or the like. And remember that studies have shown 174
that students who sit near the front of the class often get 186
better grades. They can see and hear better and have fewer 197
distractions. 200

1 | 2 | 3 | 4 | 5 | 6 | 7 | 8 | 9 | 10 | 11 | 12

The human brain is quite a bit more complex than a 10
computer, so you cannot just add a chip to increase your 22
memory. Memory is like a muscle: the more you use it, the 33
better it gets. The less you use it, the worse it gets. 45

Memory works by making links between data, that is, by 56
fitting facts into mental frameworks. Just as your muscles 68
need exercise and sleep, so does your brain. Also, remember 80
that you are able to retain more information when you are 91
relaxed. And, because humans are social animals, healthy 103
relationships stimulate our brain power. Capitalize on this 115
by expanding your social circle. 121

Use charts, cartoons, and other pictures to connect 132
facts and illustrate relationships. The reason that this 143
works is that visual facts and verbal facts are stored in 155
different parts of the brain, so, in effect, you're placing 167
those facts in two parts of the brain, thus increasing your 179
chance of recall. And don't forget that two short study 190
sessions are more effective than one long session. 200

1 | 2 | 3 | 4 | 5 | 6 | 7 | 8 | 9 | 10 | 11 | 12

11

Technique

Goals

- Improve technique on the nonprinting, number, symbol, and punctuation keys.
- Improve concentration.

A. WARMUP

Accuracy	1	Darlene quickly spoke to five women dozing in the jury box.	12
Technique: Substitutions	2	d-s ads sold adds dash sand desks send sod used dusts sodas	24
Speed	3	It was not very wise to skip her last big exam of the year.	36

1 | 2 | 3 | 4 | 5 | 6 | 7 | 8 | 9 | 10 | 11 | 12

B. PRETEST-PRACTICE-POSTTEST: NONPRINTING KEYS

PRETEST

Take a 1-minute timed writing, pushing moderately for speed. Type each sentence; then press TAB to move from column to column.

4	Help me out.	Let me stay.	He is tired.	Is it alive?	10
5	I am up now.	How goes it?	Run quickly.	Who does it?	21
6	I say I can.	I saw a man.	He is tardy.	We all knew.	31
7	How are you?	Why not her?	When was it?	She says so.	41

PRACTICE
Nonprinting Keys

ENTER Key

Press ENTER after each word to format each word on a new line.

8 Walk. Choose. Oh. Ready? Save. Wrong. Here. Press. Goodbye.
9 Translate. Bark. Hit. Ugh! Super. Guess. Pull. Down. Let's.
10 Gross! Hey! Now. Amen. Who? Pause. Gee. Evidently. Release.
11 Slow. Proceed. How? Sit. Hi. Heck. Drink. Italicize. Write.

TAB Key

Type each word; then press TAB to move from column to column.

12	adage	quilt	zooms	algae
13	zapper	areas	zealot	award
14	quartz	always	quill	airbag
15	attach	amaze	alpha	apathy

SPACE BAR

Bounce the thumb quickly off the SPACE BAR.

16 Do it now. Tom is on the job. Who knows? Buy a map for me.
17 Is it true? How are you? Help me. Now is the time. Go slow.
18 Go up to the top. I think so. Stop here. I do. Why? Do not.
19 Hi. I may just do it. Don't do it now. I may go to bed. Oh.

POSTTEST

Repeat the Pretest. *Goal*: Improve speed and accuracy.

C. NUMBER PRACTICE

Press TAB to move from column to column in each row.

20	437	543	780	430	382	358	896	464	521	947
21	530	305	942	914	276	679	737	887	879	606
22	330	548	496	968	630	294	767	573	794	811
23	282	718	279	401	490	563	957	882	176	553

Supplementary Timed Writings

All 40 Supplementary Timed Writings are of equivalent difficulty and length and are written to the same specifications.

Cultural differences exist not only among nations but	11
within a country or region itself. No matter if you ever	22
leave this country, you will live and work with people who	34
are different from you. We must learn to respect and value	46
people, regardless of the language they speak, the color of	58
their skin, their physical abilities, or their gender. In	70
fact, we should value people because of their uniqueness.	81
Diversity among people means that we can gain access to	92
other viewpoints and ways to solve problems.	101
Each of us must be able to reach for our dreams and	112
feel that whatever goals we want to accomplish in life are	124
possible. We should feel loved and included and never have	136
to suffer the pain of rejection or exclusion. We should all	148
realize that discrimination hurts and leaves scars that can	160
last a lifetime.	163
We should never let racist or harmful remarks go by	174
without stepping in. It is important to let others know	185
that name-calling of any kind is hurtful and wrong. It can	197
also be illegal.	200

1 | 2 | 3 | 4 | 5 | 6 | 7 | 8 | 9 | 10 | 11 | 12

Most students experience some form of anxiety when	10
taking a test. The first thing you need to remember is that	22
grades do not measure your creativity, your intelligence,	34
or even your ability to contribute to society. The only	45
thing grades measure is your ability to take tests.	56
View the exam as a chance to show how much you have	66
learned and a chance to be recognized for your studying.	78
Most tests are announced ahead of time, so don't wait until	90
the last minute to begin studying. Budget your time so that	102
you will not be faced with one jumbo cram session the night	114
before the test. Plan instead for several frequent shorter	126
study sessions at least a week ahead of the test.	136
While taking the test, be sure to read the directions	147
carefully and budget your test-taking time. If you do go	158
blank on one question, simply skip it for the time being.	170
Do not get spooked when students begin turning in their	181
papers early. And remember that some test anxiety helps to	193
sharpen our brain and keep us alert.	200

1 | 2 | 3 | 4 | 5 | 6 | 7 | 8 | 9 | 10 | 11 | 12

D. SYMBOL PRACTICE

Keep your eyes on the copy as you type these top-row symbols and return your fingers immediately to home-row position.

24 Batista* Parker* Noe & Ray imply-infer $1.68 add-on 697% $1
25 (lake) Riley & Dow $1.68 57.2% 3# of sand $0.34 sngo@az.gov
26 A-frame baby-sit 212% rorr@ua.edu Santos* Shane* $1.09 958%
27 rho@cs.com 6% (lag) Ely & Foy #9 jib Harrison* (lamb) $1.14

E. PRETEST-PRACTICE-POSTTEST: CONCENTRATION

Take a 1-minute timed writing, pushing moderately for speed.

PRETEST

Type the Pretest exactly as shown, but type the Practice sentences below from right to left.

28   Below is an exercise in concentrating on keeping your   11
29 eyes on the copy as you type unfamiliar lines. Type each   22
30 sentence from right to left. Thus, the sentence ".ylesicnoc   34
31 etirW" will appear as "Write concisely." when you type it.   46

    1 | 2 | 3 | 4 | 5 | 6 | 7 | 8 | 9 | 10 | 11 | 12

PRACTICE
Reverse Typing   *Short Sentences*

32 .ylesicnoc etirW
33 .snoisserpxe ydrow diovA
34 .snoisserpxe gnilgnad diovA
35 .tseuqer etilop a retfa doirep a esU

Medium-Length Sentences

36 .ecnetnes a fo drow tsrif eht ezilatipaC
37 .dnammoc ro tnemetats a retfa doirep a esU
38 .tcejbus ralugnis a htiw brev ralugnis a esU
39 .noitatouq tcerid a retfa dna erofeb sammoc esU

Long Sentences

40 .noitnetta laiceps rof esarhp ro drow a ezicilatI
41 .nehpyh a tuohtiw sexiffus dna sexiferp tsom etirW
42 .saedi ralimis rof erutcurts lacitammarg ralimis esU
43 .enola sdnats taht noitcarf a etanehpyh dna tuo llepS

POSTTEST

Repeat the Pretest. *Goal*: Improve speed and accuracy.

F. PUNCTUATION PRACTICE

Eyes on copy!

44 did, Rome; Tue. Call? back, bog, sink; fog, Mack; 2/10 Mar.
45 fig, bare: lazy, Sign! Alone? Who? 13/24 Aug. he, pat; par;
46 that/which dept. Start? Again! lion; Mark; mgt. path; acct.
47 pink; sky; qty. Dance? cave, Funny? Sara; Taxi? must; don't

48 Nothing! aid, Why? M.D. bank, Nov. "peek" Angry? Now? main;
49 pp. beg, are: know, pack; in, bail, by, avg. Fire? qtr. go,
50 Yes? 8/10 ax, gal's Ltd. Mr. No? pile; 1/5 Fast? Stay! 7/10
51 ask: size; stop; rain; Where? "peer" Whew? out; noun; Asia:

ISAK says ...

TECHNIQUE TIP

Position the mouse at the same height as the keyboard. Move the mouse with the forearm rather than your wrist.

98

    An abbreviation is a shorter form of a word or phrase. Use them sparingly in business writing. Many abbreviations are appropriate only for technical writing, statistical material, tables, and other situations where space is at a premium. Consult a dictionary for the correct form for abbreviations, and remember the rule: when in doubt, write it out. If there is any possibility of confusion, spell out the word the first time it is used and follow it with the abbreviation in parentheses.

100

    When a whole dollar amount occurs within a sentence, it is not necessary to add a decimal point and two zeros unless the amount occurs in the same context with a number consisting of dollars and cents or you want to give special emphasis to the exact amount. In a column of figures, if any amount contains cents, add a decimal and two zeros to all whole dollar amounts to maintain a uniform appearance. In a column, when an item consists only of cents, do not place two zeros before a decimal point.

Speed

Goals

- Build speed on:
  - ✓ 15-Second Speed Sprints and 30-Second Progressive Practice drills.
  - ✓ Common letter combinations and special hand drills.
- Assess speed and accuracy on a 5-minute timed writing.

A. WARMUP

Accuracy	1	The five dozen jugs of liquor were packed in my box by Jan.	12
Technique: Home Row	2	salad: jell deaf; sad shakes dell flea's glad; salads gal's	24
Speed	3	It is a bold move to turn down any job at a time like this.	36

1 | 2 | 3 | 4 | 5 | 6 | 7 | 8 | 9 | 10 | 11 | 12

B. PRETEST-PRACTICE-POSTTEST: COMMON LETTER COMBINATIONS
Take a 1-minute timed writing, pushing moderately for speed.

PRETEST

4	We are sure to be able to acquire a sizable amount of	11
5	stable and readable code without the creation of a totally	22
6	new program. Matilda says we can just disable or redo the	33
7	unusable sections that require any new coding language.	43

1 | 2 | 3 | 4 | 5 | 6 | 7 | 8 | 9 | 10 | 11 | 12

PRACTICE
Common Letter Combinations

re
8 rare require wren rein acre rehire revere are freeware dare
9 prefired free reread redo retire rent regret hare reef Bren
10 yore rendered bare reed referred respire tire recreate prep
11 bore here drew crew reel refresh rely sure repaired referee

ati
12 Matilda satire satirize sedative nation mating eating patio
13 beatify dilating dating vocation creation rebating volatile
14 station sedation stating rotation sweating donating heating
15 platinum clematis ovation citation ration curative dilation

able
16 mailable tenable culpable washable stable erasable voidable
17 bribable deniable sellable parable curable salable sizeable
18 disable huggable quotable usable readable adorable fordable
19 amicable reliable likeable laudable tamable livable towable

POSTTEST

Repeat the Pretest. *Goal:* Improve speed and accuracy.

C. 15-SECOND SPEED SPRINTS

Goal: Increase your speed on each retyping of the same sentence.

20 We all love when you tell us all you did with your own day.
21 Go to your bank at the end of the day if you need the cash.
22 Get over to the dock on time and the boat may wait for you.
23 Toss the rocks back into the pond for the frog to sit upon.

90

Use figures, rather than spelling the numbers out, for all numbers that have technical significance or that need to stand out for easy comprehension.[1] The all-figure style should be used in tables, in statistical material, and in expressions of dates, clock time, proportions and[2] ratios, academic grades, money, percentages, sports scores,[3] and votes. Also use the all-figure style for periods of time, highway numbers, measurements, and page numbers.[4]

92

Proper nouns (such as company names and the titles of publications) are considered singular and require singular verbs, even when they appear to be plural in form.[1] It helps to remember that in each case, we are referring to just[2] one item. A collective noun is a word that is singular in form but that represents a group of people or things.[3] Collective nouns, in general, are singular and take singular verbs. Thus, you would say that the committee is meeting.[4]

94

You may have heard from the grammar police that, as in Latin, a sentence in English cannot end in a preposition. But[1] English is derived from German--not from Latin. The real rule should be to write your sentences in a logical and natural manner.[2] If you do, most of the time you will see that your sentences will not end with a preposition. However, there[3] is nothing wrong with sentences that end with a preposition, and often, rewording them creates an awkward passage.[4]

96

Capitalize the first word of each sentence and of each expression that is used as a sentence. Also capitalize a quoted[1] sentence and an independent question that occurs within a sentence. Capitalize the first word in a displayed list or in[2] an outline. You must also capitalize each line in a poem and only the first word of the salutation and the complimentary[3] closing of a letter. Do not capitalize the first word of a sentence enclosed in parentheses inside of another sentence.[4]

D. SPECIAL HAND DRILLS

Left-Hand Words

Maintain the nontyping hand in home-row position.

24 brass breeze safes addresses beaver grader attracted crafts
25 best revert stated great Webster defect bear average better
26 fact Dave stars base rated Ted beverages agrees adverbs bed
27 cars age vast beg grades reader feet crew raw exceeds treat

Right-Hand Words

28 Lynn John monk July pony milk p.m. opinion Johnny upon noun
29 lip nil unhook Kohl ink nip pool minimum mom oink imply ump
30 punk pull kiln pun ply nylon pink you'll hypo hip yon nymph
31 uplink kill pump only unpin moon homily inn him pop Jon hop

Left- and Right-Hand Words

32 bar tracer oily yip acre stage agrees cards mill text jolly
33 Barbara streets noun p.m. get pill draw caves jumpy cartage
34 pumpkin case loop pull save affected deed Webster Phil Ohio
35 oink drafts nil tract lump greatest taxes vase regard Texas

E. 30-SECOND PROGRESSIVE PRACTICE

Follow the software directions for this exercise to improve keystroking speed and accuracy.

F. 5-MINUTE TIMED WRITING

Take two 5-minute timed writings.

Goal: Push moderately for speed while keeping your accuracy under control.

36	Most of us can use all the help we can get when it	10
37	comes to our writing, and that's where grammar and style	22
38	checkers come in. These programs analyze a passage and then	34
39	identify all possible examples of awkward writing, jargon,	46
40	mismatched punctuation marks, and the like. They will then	57
41	propose alternatives that you can accept, reject, or mark	69
42	for subsequent fixing.	74
43	A few of these programs use artificial intelligence to	85
44	spot misused or omitted words, mismatched verb tenses, and	97
45	the like. These programs go far beyond spelling checkers.	108
46	How well do such programs work? Many are rather slow	119
47	and nit-picking. A large number of words marked are, in	130
48	fact, correct. Most of these programs will also flag any	142
49	use of the passive voice when, in fact, the passive voice	153
50	is the preferred method of constructing some sentences,	164
51	such as when you are conveying bad news.	173
52	Grammar and style checkers may be far from perfect,	183
53	but we can use the help they provide, so they might be	195
54	worthwhile for you to buy.	200

1 | 2 | 3 | 4 | 5 | 6 | 7 | 8 | 9 | 10 | 11 | 12

ISAK says ...

TAKE A BREAK!

Roll your shoulders forward in a big circle; then roll them backward in a big circle—the larger the circle, the better.

82

Because italic type is available in word processing programs, it is the preferred means of stressing[1] a word or term, rather than underling it. Italicize a word that is referred to as a word. Such words[2] are often introduced by the expression "the term" or "the word." You should also italicize a letter if it[3] is referred to as a letter. Using italics is preferred to putting these terms in all-capital letters.[4]

84

You should italicize the titles of complete works that are published as separate pieces. Such publications as[1] books, newspapers, magazines, pamphlets, and long poems should be italicized. Also italicize the titles[2] of movies, plays, musicals, operas, television and radio shows, and pieces of art or sculpture. You[3] should also italicize the names of subtitles of these works. Do not italicize the titles of video games.[4]

86

The asterisk should be used to refer the reader to a footnote that is placed at the bottom of a page, table,[1] or diagram. When some other mark of punctuation and the asterisk come together within a sentence, the asterisk[2] goes after that mark of punctuation, with no intervening space. Similarly, in the footnote itself, leave[3] no space after the asterisk. You may also use an asterisk to replace words that are considered obscene.[4]

88

You should abbreviate units of measure whenever they occur frequently, for example, for technical and scientific[1] writing, on forms, and in tables. Type them in lowercase letters without periods. Insert a space between the number[2] and the abbreviation and between abbreviations. Use figures for all numbers and do not insert a comma between the parts[3] of a single measurement. Finally, use the same abbreviation for singular and plural forms.[4]

Accuracy

Goals

- Build accuracy on:
  - ✓ Corresponding-finger and confusable keys.
  - ✓ Spelling.
  - ✓ Alphabetic, horizontal, and symbol reaches.

A. WARMUP

Accuracy 1 Exquisite opal jewels made the big funky buyers very crazy. 12

Technique: Lower Row 2 connecting coning coven Macon? can, manner combining manned 24

Speed 3 My home is now on the edge of town, just past the old mill. 36

1 | 2 | 3 | 4 | 5 | 6 | 7 | 8 | 9 | 10 | 11 | 12

B. PRETEST-PRACTICE-POSTTEST: CORRESPONDING-FINGER KEYS

PRETEST Take a 1-minute timed writing, pushing moderately for speed.

4   Ava Poe and Dana Pope ate a pizza and salad ahead of 11

5 receiving their award for meeting their quota in Asia; Pam 23

6 ate part of an apple pie. Did she share the quart of ale? 34

7 All of them may attend an awards gala in Zurich in April. 46

1 | 2 | 3 | 4 | 5 | 6 | 7 | 8 | 9 | 10 | 11 | 12

PRACTICE
Corresponding Fingers

A Finger 8 kazoo Anna mamma agate afar quiz quaff mafia Asia natal Nat

9 mezzo qualm Aqaba data quake aroma Nana pizza zit Aswan Ava

10 balsa Aida anal salad canal laze razor papa hazy gala award

11 panda mama macaw buzz quart parka avian java aqua Sara Quit

; Finger 12 peg pod on/onto lap hip yep pan pen zap lay/lie yap ape phi

13 sip rip sap pen; pug pit; pin cap tip; lip ump Peg? Arp dop

14 hop Poe; pea pod; Pamela's pro pry Pia pop pep paw Poe? amp

15 Pop? Tip? Alp may/can "Pepsi" fop lop pet: asp pix type/key

A and ; Fingers 16 pug lop nasal manna madam amass avian Diaz anal of/have opt

17 map Tip? ahead pap lap qualm rap basal pry top pub; set/sit

18 quaff pen zap who/that aim pus balsa pix Ada; zeal Ajax sap

19 saga; panda Pip? zip pal ahead saga pew ups azure quota sip

POSTTEST Repeat the Pretest. Goal: Improve speed and accuracy.

C. BUSINESS SPELLING

These spelling words are from a list of the most used and most misspelled words in business writing. Study the words that cause you problems.

20 asbestos closing achievement principal universities breaker

21 economy similar voluntary capabilities disclosure violation

22 affects considerable confirmed referral statutes separately

23 executives substantial procedure lesson procedural academic

72

If a misreading might otherwise occur, use a semicolon to separate independent clauses that contain any internal commas: Stephanie ordered soup, salad, and macaroni and cheese; and a shrimp cocktail and baked chicken breast were served instead. Jerome ordered chicken wings, a steak, and a baked potato, and Lisa ordered just a bowl of soup and a house salad.

74

Use commas before and after a state or a country that follows a city. Do not, however, insert a comma between a state name and a zip code: Mr. Harold Meyers now serves as our marketing representative in Toulon, France, but will soon be moving to our Little Rock, Arkansas, office when he takes the new position of assistant director of marketing in August or September.

76

Use quotation marks around the title of a newspaper or magazine article, chapter in a book, report, conference, and similar items: Janice wrote an article titled "Six Keys to Success" that discussed ways to increase the success of your sales calls; the article was included in the chapter titled "Marketing Strategies" of a very successful college textbook on consumer marketing.

78

Spell out a number that begins a sentence, indefinite numbers, ordinal numbers, indefinite amounts of money, and fractions that stand alone: Twenty-four of the contestants were in their mid-thirties, and three-fourths of them were invited to take part in a panel discussion on the fortieth floor of our headquarters building; in total, they received about a million dollars for their work.

80

Capitalize a title that precedes a person's name but not one that follows a name or one that is followed by an appositive: Mayor Anne Richardson and Governor Benjamin Gardner welcomed visitors to the ribbon-cutting ceremony for the new assembly plant; J. Willard Andrews, president of the company, acted as the master of ceremonies and was the one who in fact cut the ribbon at the end of the event.

D. MAP+: ALPHABET
Follow the software instructions for this exercise to improve accuracy.

E. PRETEST-PRACTICE-POSTTEST: CONFUSABLE KEYS

PRETEST

Pay special attention to these adjacent-finger reaches that often get confused.

Take a 1-minute timed writing, pushing moderately for speed.

24   Louis drew the fewest conclusions to ensure they were   11
25 all built on facts and not in error. The multiuse devices   23
26 he recommends are equipped with scores of new features we   34
27 are sure to use in our new stores and factories in Zaire.   46

     1 | 2 | 3 | 4 | 5 | 6 | 7 | 8 | 9 | 10 | 11 | 12

PRACTICE

Adjacent Fingers

re-er

28 dire were mature wire core spore before chore satire rewire
29 are ire scare cure mare score erotic erode chore here snore
30 ensure erase share pore store hare squire flare dare entire
31 aware where sure erupt desire beware erne ware errant Zaire

iu-ui

32 annuity arguing squirm quick juice anguish quit quaff equip
33 guide quiver guild multiuse guitar quip penguin Louis build
34 liquify quiet aquarium calcium fluid cruise pursuit suiting
35 quid titanium suing quiz cuing opium guilt guiding emporium

we-ew

36 lower Lowe sewer fewest grew Swede anew jewel rewind showed
37 newbie sweep wedge answer reworn weirdo dwelt sewage wealth
38 skewer weep few cashew tower swerve twelve weak weave weigh
39 newer dowel beware prewar towel wear we power new crew weed

POSTTEST

Repeat the Pretest. *Goal*: Improve speed and accuracy.

F. REACH DRILLS: HORIZONTAL REACHES

fa and up

Horizontal reaches move to a different key on the same row.

40 prefab farm facts facial supply faucet factor couple abrupt
41 fall fan up super cup fanjet upon holdup famous infant fail
42 faith recoup faze fabric pickup uphold defame backup cupful
43 affair nonfat occupy upend lineup loupe facet uptown upshot

ad and oi

44 squad ready lady hoist bread grad toilet oil pad oink glade
45 madam coin shad voice doing addle bad moist plead adore sad
46 dead adage join sadly road mad glad point egoism fad poison
47 recoil stead ado doily loin wad choice lad head evade radar

G. MAP+: SYMBOLS
Follow the software instructions for this exercise to improve accuracy.

TECHNIQUE TIP

ISAK says …

Curve your fingers naturally, with the finger tips lightly touching the home-row keys.

62   Hyphenate a compound job title when it describes dual functions and a compound noun that contains a prepositional phrase: The secretary-treasurer of the board proved to be a jack-of-all-trades by agreeing to serve as an ambassador at-large on a temporary basis for the new government being formed in Brisbane.

64   Capitalize organization and brand names but do not capitalize any common nouns that follow these names. Treat organizational names as the organization prefers: When I worked at Disney World, I used a Dell computer, but now that I work for the Centers for Disease Control, I use an iMac, which is made by Apple Computer.

66   When establishing agreement between the subject and verb, disregard words that come between the subject and verb: The leader of the Boy Scouts was busy, and he, as well as three of his assistants, has to attend a make-up session of the training workshop that taught the new types of merit badges that was held in Reno last month.

68   Use a semicolon between two independent clauses that are not connected by a coordinate conjunction: Mrs. Sarah G. Richardson was elected to the position of program chair; she will be responsible for securing speakers for each of the monthly meetings of the society and will also have to make sure that the television stations are notified.

70   Use parentheses to enclose explanatory material that is not essential, but that is still important enough to include: The three steps (backing up your data regularly, keeping your software up to date, and always running virus protection software) are always important in any computing but are critical when working in our Flagstaff (Arizona) office.

Technique

Goals

- Improve technique on the nonprinting, number, symbol, and punctuation keys.
- Improve concentration.

A. WARMUP

Accuracy	1	Few helped deliver odd-sized oxygen equipment back in June.	12
Technique: Transposition	2	atop tail|item tile|Alec lake|unit null|alit last|Esau send	24
Speed	3	She made her best pal feel sad, but what she said was true.	36

1 | 2 | 3 | 4 | 5 | 6 | 7 | 8 | 9 | 10 | 11 | 12

B. PRETEST-PRACTICE-POSTTEST: NONPRINTING KEYS

PRETEST

Take a 1-minute timed writing, pushing moderately for speed.

Backspace to correct all errors as you type.

4	Andy Rolf served in Iraq and Jack Ford served on Oahu,	11
5	while Jess Wauk was stationed in Bonn. Lena Rice went from	23
6	Cuba to Guam, but she had a short layover at Orly Airport	35
7	in Paris, where she bought an Izod blouse and a Dior suit.	46

1 | 2 | 3 | 4 | 5 | 6 | 7 | 8 | 9 | 10 | 11 | 12

PRACTICE
Nonprinting Keys

LEFT SHIFT Key

8 Lent Kent Hall Hahn Mari Jane Ural Lapp Peru Nell Macy Lett
9 Otos Marx Owen Jack Manx Lena Jena Palu Mack Yank Matt Newt
10 Magi Nero Kane Orly Mars Oslo Herb Kern Hamm Urdu Nast Hays
11 Mara Yang Yves Izod Mali Oahu Jean Hugh Iraq Ives Mann Jess

RIGHT SHIFT Key

12 Aldo Quon Elam Alma Andy Bull Rolf Wise Guam Fuji Rice Amex
13 Ahab Ross Rose Rome Zola Alps Fish Goya Buck Cola Wouk Bonn
14 Gish Tina Cork Shui Ford Shaw Cuba Byrd Boyd Bill Siam Chen
15 Dior Rowe Coke Roma Rios Tojo Rita Tory Goth Fido Duma Aida

BACKSPACE Key

When you reach the Backspace sign (←), backspace 1 time and then type the letter that follows.

16 tad←n pot←p lad←p bud←m egg←o she←y put←p cog←n wig←n cow←p
17 was←y bat←y kid←n tag←m mow←p nub←n flu←y box←n dim←p zig←p
18 lie←p rig←m has←y and←y jag←m hex←y oaf←k mar←p fig←n her←n
19 aid←l inn←k bus←y ale←l big←n cow←y hot←p fad←n dab←y dug←n

POSTTEST

Repeat the Pretest. *Goal*: Improve speed and accuracy.

C. NUMBER PRACTICE

Press TAB to move from column to column in each row.

20	429	896	898	430	614	825	131	390	243	173
21	446	370	304	312	681	844	755	732	419	955
22	460	524	125	357	257	392	577	443	819	869
23	509	917	527	201	914	521	656	833	336	965

52   Use a colon to introduce explanatory material that is preceded by an independent clause: This is the situation that our company will soon face: we will soon outgrow our current location but will not be able to move into our new facility until the end of fall.

54   Use parentheses to enclose numbers or letters that precede items in a series within a sentence: My new duties will include (a) making flight and hotel reservations, (b) scheduling the conference room, and (c) seeing that all of our guests feel comfortable and welcomed.

56   Hyphenate most compound adjectives that come before the noun; do not hyphenate them when they come after the noun: Watching the first-day activities was a never-to-be-forgotten experience. Watching the activities on the first day would never be forgotten by the English visitors.

58   Use a plural verb with a plural subject and a singular verb with a singular subject: The president wants to double our annual shipments of oil, but the board members are not willing to do that unless they get an agreement that each shipment can maintain our present level of gross revenue.

60   Capitalize the name of a particular person, language, race, nationality, and religion: I heard that Ivan Ivanov, who is Russian but speaks fluent English, recently put on an intercultural workshop attended by Hindu and Buddhist programmers who were working as interns in New York City for ten weeks.

D. SYMBOL PRACTICE

Keep your eyes on the copy as you type these top-row symbols.

24 Naser* rorr@ua.edu Santos* West & Little (lace) 932% (lady)
25 (lamb) Ngo & Ely uely@az.gov 958% boo-boo 268% $1.71 (lags)
26 cli@bsu.edu add-on $1.04 Naser* (lack) sngo@az.gov Batista*
27 $1.14 bad-badly add-on imply-infer $0.34 aho@cs.com all-day

E. PRETEST-PRACTICE-POSTTEST: CONCENTRATION
Take a 1-minute timed writing, pushing moderately for speed.

PRETEST

Concentrate on keeping your eyes on the copy as you type these vocabulary words. How many of these terms do you know?

28 We should approach the recommendations to rewrite the	11
29 codicil to our will enthusiastically and with amity. You	22
30 cannot refute the fact that our affairs are now in a state	34
31 of flux and that some simplification is now in order.	45

1 | 2 | 3 | 4 | 5 | 6 | 7 | 8 | 9 | 10 | 11 | 12

PRACTICE   Short Words
Vocabulary Words

32 tyro prate mete refute cede laud recede
33 causal pommel writhe grotto akin apiary
34 blithe brogue cajole pyre elicit finite
35 amity fete qualm flux skiff wile infest

Medium-Length Words

36 codicil mordant panacea osculate ignoble bibulous
37 peccant doleful concerto mawkish epicure verbiage
38 cognate inveigh invidious bullock hydrous redound
39 panegyric redolence facetious rapacious reprobate

Long Words

40 fastidious uncommunicativeness renegotiable recommendations
41 enthusiastically equalization discountenance specifications
42 simplification reprehensible deindustrialization iconoclast
43 inglorious sequestrate beneficent accomplishment diffusible

POSTTEST

Repeat the Pretest. *Goal*: Improve speed and accuracy.

F. PUNCTUATION PRACTICE

Eyes on copy!

44 most; acre: ax, But? sat; 1/7 Corp. Dale's Now! lost; "peg"
45 rare; Start. Sit! pine; Finish? must; Ohio; Fri. tab, labs,
46 noun; 2/10 pond; dep't Ms. Leon; kid, Mon. cont. skin; Sun.
47 gave, Ed.D. art: Sat. pp. balk: bank, axis, You? Ida, Stop!

48 8/10 No! neat; tact; Lucy; came, New? load; So? song; rain;
49 lace, Funny? 13/24 babe, "peak" bldg. don't son; Esq. Busy?
50 onto; Give? Fire! acid, able, led, set; Better? stay; Whew!
51 bail, What? "peek" can, enc. size; See? net; Knox, Morning:

TAKE A BREAK!

ISAK says ...

Lock your hands behind your head, bring your elbows back as far as possible, inhale deeply and hold for 20 seconds. Exhale and then relax. Repeat two times.

38   Use dashes to set off an expression that you wish to emphasize: The convention of the International Association of Administrative Professionals--especially the speakers-- was very exciting.

40   Use a comma between two adjacent adjectives if they modify the same noun: It was a long, difficult trip from San Jose to Panama, but the trip back was a quick, easy one because of the nonstop flight.

42   Use quotation marks around an expression that needs special attention; note that periods and commas go inside the closing quotation mark, but colons and semicolons go outside: Please mark my package "Fragile."

44   Use commas before and after the year when it follows the month and day; do not use a comma with a partial date: I need to apply to college sometime in March and let them know my decision by June 15, 2013, at the latest.

46   Use a comma between two independent clauses joined by a coordinate conjunction: I just received my associate's degree in medical assisting, and I am now looking for a position in a private practice in the greater Sacramento area.

48   Use dashes to set off an expression that already has internal commas: Some of the furniture to be auctioned--for example, the Murphy bed, the Victorian dining table, and the cherry chest of drawers--are quite beautiful and a bit expensive.

50   Use a semicolon after each item in a series if any of the items already contain a comma: The compliance workshops will be held in Winston-Salem, North Carolina; Manchester, New Hampshire; and San Jose, California, in late December and early January.

Speed

Goals

- Build speed on:
  - ✓ 15-Second Speed Sprints and Paced Practice drills.
  - ✓ Common letter combinations and special hand drills.
- Assess speed and accuracy on a 5-minute timed writing.

A. WARMUP

Accuracy	1	Zack waxed eloquently about the big jump over fake candles.	12
Technique: SPACE BAR	2	One at a time. What time is it? Who does? Go. I am up. Who?	24
Speed	3	The old man has such a sad tale; she wept when he told her.	36

1 | 2 | 3 | 4 | 5 | 6 | 7 | 8 | 9 | 10 | 11 | 12

B. PRETEST-PRACTICE-POSTTEST: COMMON LETTER COMBINATIONS
Take a 1-minute timed writing, pushing moderately for speed.

PRETEST

4	We are proud to approve the new contract for the most	11
5	prolific author in the entire nation. His ratings promise	23
6	to generate further profits for us. We should plan a book	34
7	tour for him in either northern or southern major cities.	46

1 | 2 | 3 | 4 | 5 | 6 | 7 | 8 | 9 | 10 | 11 | 12

PRACTICE
Common Letter Combinations

ti
8 tipsy tirade Latina timid eating sting emetic gratin cities
9 noting attire potion tiring stilt tizzy Latino rating tibia
10 pitied tide mating hating ratio nation exotic notion tidier
11 lentil entity tinsel tied stint ration lotion tilting tithe

pro
12 prorate propjet apropos province repro prologue prone apron
13 promise pro uproar prowl proviso proxy propel proud probate
14 prolific probable proton approve prospect prof proper prong
15 prophet promo promote probe approach profit prosper prosaic

ther
16 southern smoother breather northern slither neither another
17 thereon thereto Heather soother bather tither tether father
18 rather hither slather either loather wither whether thermos
19 therapist therewith further feather blather thereupon other

POSTTEST

Repeat the Pretest. *Goal*: Improve speed and accuracy.

C. 15-SECOND SPEED SPRINTS

Goal: Increase your speed on each retyping of the same sentence.

20 As you knew it was to be, you must not make a fuss over it.
21 The cute dogs ran fast to get a ball to give it back to me.
22 The rain is wet on my feet, but the sun will soon dry them.
23 We can beat the heat of the day if we go swim at that pond.

20   Use a period after a polite request: Would you please[1] sign the letter before the end of next month[4].[2][3]

22   Use a period after an indirect question: The question[2] is how we can fix the problem before our next deadline.[1][3][4]

24   Use a comma after an introductory expression: As a[1] matter of fact, he is planning to do the very same thing[2][3] quite soon.[4]

26   Use quotation marks around a direct quotation: "What[1] we need to know," Ms. Washborne said, "is how to handle[2][3] the matter at hand."[4]

28   Use commas before and after interrupting expressions:[1] Jean may, for example, decide to take her entire payout[2][3] on her sixty-fourth birthday.[4]

30   Use commas before and after nonessential expressions:[1] My youngest sister, who is three years my junior, will be a[2][3] freshman at Bard College next year.[4]

32   Use commas before and after a name that is used in[1] direct address: Thank you, Mrs. McDonald, for taking the[2] time out of your schedule to see me this afternoon.[3][4]

34   Use a comma between each item in a series of three or[1] more: I typed the monthly status report, proofread it, and[2] then gave it to Fernando to collate and make the copies.[3][4]

36   Use commas before and after a direct quotation in a[1] sentence: The consultant said, "My job is to make several[2] recommendations," and added, "then your task will be to[3] assess them."[4]

D. SPECIAL HAND DRILLS

Alternate-Hand Words
24 rocks big panel men risks if Lakeland fir duck visit rub us
25 ancient ruby do turkey Dick Helen Diana she towns own shelf
26 fish held did such Burns aid woe got Glen firm buck dug sod
27 Claus cow hand Blair Rufus bush them pays enrich eight lake

Double-Letter Words
28 hook keep wood buzz funny Mann Nelly glass brass cross loop
29 bee Betty jell shall pool bull sheep broom door greet Scott
30 Lee worry egg queen knee proof hobby Jill gross Quinn speed
31 carry fall poor petty call three Billy sheet hurry Emma zoo

Upper-Row Words
32 pewter pro pie pet utter woo rep torque prow puree row pity
33 rote potty pyre rite tip tow root tier wet teeter epee yeti
34 roe repute potter purity put our quieter tower pier weepier
35 Tory troop quote outwit ort otter witty pout typewrite were

E. PACED PRACTICE

Follow the software directions for this exercise to improve keystroking speed and accuracy.

F. 5-MINUTE TIMED WRITING

Take two 5-minute timed writings.

Goal: Push moderately for speed while keeping your accuracy under control.

36	Many executives do not like memos, whether sent by	10
37	e-mail or on paper. A recent study showed that four out of	22
38	five executives think memos are a major waste of time in	34
39	this era when social media exists. Many executives also	46
40	criticize memos for being too self-serving or too long or	56
41	sent to too many employees.	62
42	Of course, many memos can be written for the wrong	72
43	reasons, such as to avoid making difficult decisions or to	84
44	place blame elsewhere. But a memo has much to offer. For	96
45	one thing, a memo offers its author a chance to carefully	107
46	organize his or her thoughts and to think through his or	119
47	her position. If the position is a hostile one, writing a	130
48	memo gives the writer the time to cool off and to compose	142
49	criticism that will likely be more constructive than would	154
50	a verbal tirade.	157
51	From a practical standpoint, a memo is still a good	168
52	way to inform a large number of people without holding a	179
53	meeting. And a written note of appreciation still carries	191
54	quite a bit more weight than passing remarks.	200

1 | 2 | 3 | 4 | 5 | 6 | 7 | 8 | 9 | 10 | 11 | 12

ISAK says ...

TECHNIQUE TIP

Sit back from the keyboard, reposition your feet, and rest your hands in your lap when not keyboarding.

Paced Practice

Paced Practice is an individualized skillbuilding program designed to build speed by enabling you to speed up—*just a little*—and then to build accuracy by slowing down—*just a little*. The ISAK software tells you at what point in the timed writing you should be at each 15-second interval. If you're typing too fast, slow down a little; if you're typing too slowly, speed up a little. Your goal for each timed writing is to be within a character or two of each speed marker when it disappears.

This section contains 1-minute timed writings ranging from 20 wpm to 100 wpm. Before beginning the timed writings, take a 1-minute Placement timed writing. If you make more than 3 uncorrected errors, repeat the Placement timed writing.

Based on your performance on this Placement timed writing, the ISAK software will display a timed writing that is 1-2 words higher than your current speed. You will use a two-step process—first working to achieve your speed goal and then working to achieve your accuracy goal.

1. **Speed Goal:** Take up to four 1-minute timed writings on the displayed passage. Your speed goal is to complete the passage without regard to the number of errors made, so don't take time to correct typos.

2. **Accuracy Goal:** When you reach your speed goal, ISAK then displays a timed writing that is 2 wpm slower than your speed goal (remember, the key to accuracy is to slow down—just a little). Your accuracy goal is to complete the passage with no more than 1 uncorrected error. When you have met your accuracy goal, ISAK displays a passage that is 2 wpm higher than your speed goal in Step 1, and the process continues.

3. When you have completed a total of four 1-minute timed writings, ISAK moves you to the next exercise in the current lesson.

4. ISAK keeps track of your progress and will display the appropriate passage to type each time you access the Paced Practice routine.

Placement Timed Writing

```
    Marks of punctuation serve as a roadmap to help guide    11
the reader through the twists and turns of what he or she    23
reads and writes. They help to make clear the meanings of    34
written words by organizing the words into clear phrases,    46
clauses, or sentences. You must acquire excellent knowledge  58
of basic punctuation and rules of grammar in order to be     69
successful on the job and to make sense of what you read.    81
   1 | 2 | 3 | 4 | 5 | 6 | 7 | 8 | 9 | 10 | 11 | 12
```

16

Accuracy

Goals

- Build accuracy on:
  - ✓ Corresponding-finger and confusable keys.
  - ✓ Spelling.
  - ✓ Alphabetic, vertical, and number reaches.

A. WARMUP

Accuracy	1 Forty women quickly gave the six prizes back to the judges.	12
Technique: Punctuation	2 Pop? cub. "pig" pop; "per" (lice) Ore. tap; lake's How? Go!	24
Speed	3 He must get some of this work done now, but it is not easy.	36

1 | 2 | 3 | 4 | 5 | 6 | 7 | 8 | 9 | 10 | 11 | 12

B. PRETEST-PRACTICE-POSTTEST: CORRESPONDING-FINGER KEYS

PRETEST
Take a 1-minute timed writing, pushing moderately for speed.

4 Greg gave much attention to the free incentives to	10
5 buy big home improvements. In a memo, he should urge many	22
6 homeowners to make their main purchases in June or July.	33
7 There is much he can do in the short term to help them.	44

1 | 2 | 3 | 4 | 5 | 6 | 7 | 8 | 9 | 10 | 11 | 12

PRACTICE   F Finger
Corresponding Fingers

8 bang gag lift rig aft Bev rot flag beef rest tube iffy Greg
9 free Viv buff tug Gobi vast rift gear gave vet rub rag fate
10 vat tact rug form gray goof raft Cobb tar urge bulb tub gut
11 veto golf fib ebb belt boor fig trap grab ogre bar big term

J Finger

12 much jump fund army joy buy gnu noon hum nine hump mug chin
13 many man mom home onyx must hymn harm main Nan snub hub nun
14 shy bush mum Mary you bum him ham hem high inn June may any
15 hug gum hay July norm fun horn Juan just dumb undo memo Amy

F and J Fingers

16 buffoon fraught thirty buttery tenth tangent fantasy bubbly
17 fluffy turbine burden trough theory fudging gunnery touting
18 fury guru tyranny tangy tutu gourmet burley burning tankful
19 rematch gusting rubbing therapy turnout bury butane burgeon

POSTTEST
Repeat the Pretest. *Goal*: Improve speed and accuracy.

C. BUSINESS SPELLING

These spelling words are from a list of the most used and most misspelled words in business writing. Study the words that cause you problems.

20 modifications authorized league vacuum satisfaction entered
21 pursuant procurement appreciate initial identifying premium
22 deferred implementing cited acquisition addition structures
23 surveillance prior judgment scheduling inquiry representing

WPM	Passage
82	A secondary source is a source with information derived from the study of primary sources or other secondary sources. Textbooks journal articles, or encyclopedia articles are examples of secondary sources.
84	Plagiarism is the use of anyone else's words, ideas, or other original work without acknowledging its source. Plagiarism is, in effect, the stealing of someone else's intellectual property and must not be used.
86	A direct quotation is the reproduction of the exact words someone else has spoken or written. In academic writing, direct quotations are enclosed in quotation marks or, if long, set off in a different block of text.
88	Parallelism is the presentation of equal ideas in the same grammatical forms; individual terms with individual terms, phrases with phrases, and clauses with clauses. The use of parallelism results in parallel structure.
90	A portfolio is a collection of one's writing to show others, such as to show potential employers. An electronic portfolio is a portfolio in electronic form and will include video, audio, and image files as well as text files.
92	Tense is the form of the verb that indicates its time of action. There are three simple tenses: present, past, or future. The perfect tenses indicate actions that were or will be accomplished by the time of another action or time.
94	A conclusion is the closing section of a report. It briefly reviews the problems and the procedures used to solve the problem and provides an overview of the major findings. It also gives the reader a sense of completion of the report.
96	An argument is an effort to persuade others to accept a point of view or a position on a contentious issue through logic and the marshaling of evidence. In your writing, reasoned positions are more important than opinions based on feelings.
98	Inductive reasoning is one method of reasoning that involves deriving a general conclusion from specific facts. When using inductive reasoning, a writer presents evidence to convince reasonable people that the writer's argument is probably true.
100	Comparison is the form of an adjective or adverb that indicates its degree or amount. The positive degree is the simple form and involves no comparison. The comparative degree compares two things. The superlative degree compares three or more things.

D. MAP+: ALPHABET
Follow the software instructions for this exercise to improve accuracy.

E. PRETEST-PRACTICE-POSTTEST: CONFUSABLE KEYS

PRETEST

Pay special attention to these keys that are often substituted for each other.

Take a 1-minute timed writing, pushing moderately for speed.

24   Eric caught a slight cold in spite of his having taken   11
25 his vitamins. He lost his voice and is quite weak. He isn't   23
26 used to being sick, so we bought him some medicine and gave   35
27 it to him. We are hoping it might be able to help him.   46

    1 | 2 | 3 | 4 | 5 | 6 | 7 | 8 | 9 | 10 | 11 | 12

PRACTICE
Substitutions

e-i
28 rite medic smile niece guide heir wine wide dike dive crime
29 guile genie ovine bide slide adieu being exist voice guise
30 wise emit tile file Erica bride spine rinse fiend vibe line
31 exit chive miter spite lie prize dries lei wield feign life

g-h
32 having Afghan gather sleigh fought aweigh hug caught slight
33 might laugh gash thigh change Garth bought Goth gush wright
34 shrug gulch hog hoeing hang fight blight thigh sight gusher
35 eight taught enough aghast hiking sought ghost ought dinghy

a-e
36 apse acne aerate pane hare gate Alec are late game sea lame
37 dead lake jade nape age area date abet reap reggae eta ante
38 same Dale weak race base hale rear able pear haze laze raze
39 rake save real rare each earn deal tale gave tape east mean

POSTTEST

Repeat the Pretest. *Goal*: Improve speed and accuracy.

F. REACH DRILLS: VERTICAL REACHES

at and ho
40 pat what gloat hook Honda wombat hot hop cat hoe hold splat
41 spat carat hobo hone stat seat Muscat holly beat caveat hog
42 sweat oat honor howl rat hole pleat hover hobby neat hooray
43 threat mat home flat float tomcat hovel heat hoof moat swat

Vertical reaches move from one row to the adjacent row.

se and il
44 ease grill self seen spill hilt kill poll house whose civil
45 file else milk oily soil obese wilt coil sewer oil sew serf
46 mild peril rile horse agile easel seam till these tile pile
47 sear fuse cause film tail while bilk pilaf kitty sever jail

G. MAP+: NUMBERS
Follow the software instructions for this exercise to improve accuracy.

TAKE A BREAK!

ISAK says ...

Sitting back, raise your right foot slightly and rotate it clockwise in a big circle, then counterclockwise. Repeat with the left foot.

WPM	Passage
56	A predicate is a word or expression in a sentence that tells what the subject does, what is done to it, or how it's identified or described.
58	A polite request is a request, a suggestion, or a command that is placed in the form of a question only out of politeness; it ends with a period.
60	A predicate is a word or phrase in sentences that tells what the subject of a sentence does, what is done to it, or how it is identified or described.
62	A conjunctive adverb is a word which serves the double function of connecting two independent clauses and also showing the kinship between the two clauses.
64	Fair use is the provision of copyright law that permits the reproduction of limited portions of a copyrighted work for news reporting or for scholarly purposes.
66	Gender is the characteristic of nouns and pronouns which indicates the sex; a pronoun that can refer to either a male or female is considered to be of common gender.
68	An elliptical clause is a clause in which one or more grammatically necessary words are omitted because their meaning and function are clear from the surrounding context.
70	Comparison is the manner by which the adjective or adverb expresses a greater or less degree of the same quality; the three degrees are positive, comparative, and superlative.
72	Person is the characteristic of a noun or pronoun that indicates whether a person is speaking (first person), being spoken to (second person), or being spoken about (third person).
74	A sentence is made up of a subject and predicate not introduced by a subordinating word and that fit together to make a statement, ask a question, give a command, or express an emotion.
76	A clause is a group of related words containing a subject and a predicate. An independent clause can stand on its own as a sentence. A dependent clause cannot stand on its own as a sentence.
78	A transitional sentence is one that refers to the previous paragraph and at the same time moves a report on to the next paragraph. Transitions are important because they link one idea to another.
80	A run-on sentence is two or more independent clauses run together without any punctuation between them or with only a comma between them or that would be more effectively stated as separate sentences.

Technique

Goals

- Improve technique on the nonprinting, number, symbol, and punctuation keys.
- Improve concentration.

A. WARMUP

Accuracy	1 David flexed thumbs at work when squeezing the juicy plums.	12
Technique: One-Hand	2 pun degree puny tree hypo rates oily server pump crews hill	24
Speed	3 The map says to turn right when you come upon the oak tree.	36

1 | 2 | 3 | 4 | 5 | 6 | 7 | 8 | 9 | 10 | 11 | 12

B. PRETEST-PRACTICE-POSTTEST: NONPRINTING KEYS

PRETEST

Take a 1-minute timed writing, pushing moderately for speed. Type each sentence; then press TAB to move from column to column.

4 He is tired.	Is it alive?	I dare them.	We think so.	10
5 See Mr. Dye.	I say I can.	How are you?	Here you go.	21
6 I see an ax.	Who is here?	She is sick.	Why not eat?	31
7 Can he help?	Take my bag.	Drive there.	Turn around.	41

PRACTICE
Nonprinting Keys

ENTER Key

Press ENTER after each word to format each word on a new line.

8 Super. Me? Wait. Nope. Here. Certainly. Erase. Hit. Answer.
9 Yikes. Swim. Pay. Move. Bad. Incredible! Bravo! Catch. Who?
10 But? Hi. Draw. Whew! Exactly. Stretch. Whoa! Indeed! Spell.
11 Gosh. Possibly. Okay. Probably. Always! Smile. Lift. Guess.

TAB Key

Type each word; then press TAB to move from column to column.

12 acrobat	quips	arcade	quads
13 ahead	query	awkward	quench
14 quibble	alarm	quaff	quantify
15 quick	queen	alpaca	aviator

SPACE BAR

Bounce the thumb quickly off the SPACE BAR.

16 Who? It is a fact. I can fax it. She may do it. What gives?
17 Can you see him? Don't do it now. I do. Hi. Let me have it.
18 I can do the job. I may. Jo is up. I see. Why is he so mad?
19 What is it for? We are up. See Mr. Dye. I am up. Do it now.

POSTTEST

Repeat the Pretest. *Goal:* Improve speed and accuracy.

C. NUMBER PRACTICE

Press TAB to move from column to column in each row.

20 320	591	472	584	159	342	469	149	184	800
21 773	109	535	361	554	404	520	398	655	478
22 388	530	224	189	177	846	182	381	172	445
23 920	147	150	778	493	709	363	116	229	402

WPM	Passage
20	A pronoun is a word used in the place of the noun.
22	An adjective is a word that modifies a noun or pronoun.
24	A conjunction is a word that joins words or groups of words.
26	An antecedent is a noun or noun phrase that a pronoun stands for.
28	A dependent clause is a clause that doesn't convey a complete thought.
30	An interjection is a forceful word, often ending with an exclamation point.
32	An independent clause is a clause that can stand alone as one complete sentence.
34	A phrase is a group of related words that do not have both a subject and a predicate.
36	A transitive verb is an action verb that requires a direct object to complete its meaning.
38	A simple sentence is a sentence which contains one independent clause and no dependent clauses.
40	A collective noun is a word that is singular in form but that represents a group of people or items.
42	A compound sentence is a sentence that contains two or more independent clauses and no dependent clauses.
44	Grammar is the set of rules that guide writers of standard American English in combining words into sentences.
46	A preposition is a word which shows the relationship between a noun or pronoun and some other word in the sentence.
48	A restrictive expression is an expression which limits and restricts the meaning of the noun or pronoun that it follows.
50	A nonrestrictive expression is a group of words that may be taken out without changing the essential meaning of the sentence.
52	A subject is a word or group of words in a sentence which does something, has something done to it, or is identified or described.
54	The subjunctive mood is the verb mood that states a demand, motion, or necessity or a condition that is improbable or contrary to fact.

D. SYMBOL PRACTICE

Keep your eyes on the copy as you type these top-row symbols.

24 729% Li & Ng, Inc. Fuentes* 212% Ngo & Ely $1.04 aho@cs.com
25 (lair) 932% 57.2% (lady) #1-20 baby-sit also-ran 268% $1.68
26 697% West & Little rho@ac.com $1.09 (lag) $0.34 imply-infer
27 (laid) Berry* (lack) $1.14 (lace) 970% (lake) 958% Sokolov*

E. PRETEST-PRACTICE-POSTTEST: CONCENTRATION

PRETEST

Take a 1-minute timed writing, pushing moderately for speed.

Concentrate on keeping your eyes on the copy as you type these foreign phrases.

28   In France, if they do not understand you, they might   12
29 say, "Je ne comprends pas," and in Spain, they might say,   23
30 "No entiendo." In German, "Ich verstehe nicht" means "I do   35
31 not understand you." In Italian, it would be "Non capisco."   47

   1 | 2 | 3 | 4 | 5 | 6 | 7 | 8 | 9 | 10 | 11 | 12

PRACTICE   Short Phrases
Foreign Phrases

32 Swahili: Sielewi.
33 Italian: Non capisco.
34 Latin: Non intellego.
35 Spanish: No entiendo.

Medium-Length Phrases

36 Lithuanian: Nesuprantu.
37 Afrikaans: Ek verstaan nie.
38 Dutch: Ik begrijp het niet.
39 German: Ich verstehe nicht.

Long Phrases

40 French: Je ne comprends pas.
41 English: I do not understand.
42 Indonesian: Aku tidak mengerti.
43 Filipino: Hindi ko maintindihan.

POSTTEST

Repeat the Pretest. *Goal:* **Improve speed and accuracy.**

F. PUNCTUATION PRACTICE

Eyes on copy!

44 stub; able, Where? chg. bid, none; Escape! dig, "peak" Oct.
45 Dance? near; acre: Here? lab, flea's bog, www.cnn.com/ Jan.
46 Whew! avid, pick; i.e. pin: in, lack, Drink? sad; beg, bed,
47 aid, loom; Give? boa, 8/10 did, Pete; learn/teach do, stem;

48 e.g. pp. Mr. Buy! pine; In? You? only: made; is, sat; lost;
49 song; More? "peat" cont'd Mark; pat; Carl, John! knee, Mon.
50 "peg" Dave, "peer" ring; equally/as room; son; balk: "peel"
51 fed, Cold? Type? See? by, sing; don't 7/10 ax, "peal" long:

ISAK says ...

TECHNIQUE TIP

Keep your elbows relaxed and close to the body. Do not swing your elbows as you are typing.

Progressive Practice

Progressive Practice is an individualized skillbuilding program designed to build speed and accuracy in short, incremental steps. This section contains 30-second timed writings ranging from 20 wpm to 100 wpm. Before beginning the timed writings, take a 1-minute Placement timed writing. If you make more than 3 uncorrected errors, repeat the Placement timed writing.

Based on your performance on this Placement timed writing, the ISAK software will display a timed writing that is 1-2 words higher than your current speed.

1. Take up to six 30-second timed writings on this passage. You goal is to complete the passage with 0 uncorrected errors.

2. When you reach your goal, displays the next timed writing, where your goal is 2 wpm higher, and you repeat the process. When you have completed six total timed writings, ISAK moves you to the next exercise in the current lesson.

3. ISAK keeps track of your progress and will display the appropriate passage to type each time you access the Progressive Practice routine.

Placement Timed Writing

```
    Marks of punctuation serve as a roadmap to help guide    11
the reader through the twists and turns of what he or she    23
reads and writes. They help to make clear the meanings of    34
written words by organizing the words into clear phrases,    46
clauses, or sentences. You must acquire excellent knowledge  58
of basic punctuation and rules of grammar in order to be     69
successful on the job and to make sense of what you read.    81
    1  |  2  |  3  |  4  |  5  |  6  |  7  |  8  |  9  |  10  |  11  |  12
```

Speed

18

LESSON

UNIT 6

Goals

- Build speed on:
  ✓ 15-Second Speed Sprints and 30-Second Progressive Practice drills.
  ✓ Common letter combinations and special hand drills.
- Assess speed and accuracy on a 5-minute timed writing.

A. WARMUP

Accuracy	1	The proud woman quickly bought just five extra zoo tickets.	12
Technique: Transpositions	2	ore row|ark ran|ergo read|oral roar|ink kin|Ann nag|ash say	24
Speed	3	When she sees the time, she will wish she had not slept in.	36

    1 | 2 | 3 | 4 | 5 | 6 | 7 | 8 | 9 | 10 | 11 | 12

B. PRETEST-PRACTICE-POSTTEST: COMMON LETTER COMBINATIONS

PRETEST

Take a 1-minute timed writing, pushing moderately for speed.

4	If the union is prone to be complacent about the rate	11
5	of climate change, we should compel our staff to confront	23
6	them if they violate even one of the clauses in our union	34
7	contract. I trust that this will not have to be done soon.	46

    1 | 2 | 3 | 4 | 5 | 6 | 7 | 8 | 9 | 10 | 11 | 12

PRACTICE
Common Letter Combinations

on   8 hone monk donor arson Macon demon wont honk song conk croon
           9 yon onto sonic blond union prone one onion capon spoon soon
           10 ion tonic Ono among peony confront upon rayon pontoon scion
           11 done shone alone conch lone onyx bony bond clone ebony pone

ate   12 slate curate collate gate agitate grate nitrate sate patent
           13 rebate platen violate emulate latex climate chateau bleated
           14 late senate ate adulate estate actuate citrate rate elevate
           15 prate primate isolate pleated inflate neater testate karate

comp   16 compadre complacent compassion compass comparison complaint
           17 compete comparative compliance compose compassion encompass
           18 compression composition competitor companion compel compost
           19 comprehend computation compunction compact complex comprise

POSTTEST

Repeat the Pretest. *Goal*: Improve speed and accuracy.

C. 15-SECOND SPEED SPRINTS

Goal: Increase your speed on each retyping of the same sentence.

20 Both have a cold but will be all well once they have slept.
21 If she cuts it up in tiny bits for you, you can try a bite.
22 It is such a long way to go in an old car, but we must try.
23 Take the bus away from camp to chop some wood with the axe.

K. NUMERICAL DATA ENTRY

92	851521339	156173622	303553835	
93	795751853	627718456	544984502	
94	652811082	810249587	578861992	
95	815712648	320390036	435261809	
96	858574400	101406550	460947518	111422991
97	564788285	623317612	246827354	166397935
98	924831144	430500600	803170873	594838178
99	234622689	394584548	354225330	602046959

100	734007268	487919211	398848147	748527475	966896229
101	656705555	649901998	162627841	364401119	553365935
102	927105491	219569000	746806156	156457436	316530582
103	591852617	758672326	975873682	897248500	425892540

Take two 1-minute timed writings.

Goal: Stress accuracy rather than speed.

Error notification is turned off in ISAK. Your digit-per-minute (DPM) speed and number of errors will be displayed at the end of each timed writing.

L. 1-MINUTE TIMED WRITING A: DATA ENTRY

Press ENTER after typing the final digit of each number. Type the first column from top to bottom; then move to the next column and continue entering data.

104	35023	63997	24292	10454	53128	14083	85389
105	97386	41123	74324	75912	61277	41164	79647
106	30462	79069	91382	98880	77823	63212	65600
107	89867	84817	49497	89987	52863	21634	24904
108	17848	43691	57240	45139	75491	84580	90343
109	99433	56647	82475	66086	18358	60275	51667
110	71176	88986	46758	70057	40430	60509	30450

Take two 1-minute timed writings.

M. 1-MINUTE TIMED WRITING B: CALCULATIONS

Press the appropriate arithmetic key after each number except the last number in each column. After typing the last number, press ENTER to display the total, move to the next column, and continue entering data.

111	3296+	401911/	878.35−	639793/	922.08−	8.26
112	578.08+	8048−	400*	807.67/	493.57+	7382−
113	1874−	6.17+	675.04*	520*	4155−	4.27/
114	8549−	865.87*	74431−	2612.25+	22−	20293*
115	8438.20*	1405.13+	2964.02/	402236+	3064+	8.88*
116	97+	3700−	4609*	4277−	4590*	75.20/
117	236.89	394.58	330	60.59	.15	4548

D. SPECIAL HAND DRILLS

Left-Hand Words

Maintain the nontyping hand in home-row position.

24 beast grave Sever sets bears create sweeter rewarded seated
25 acre access fares best Warsaw deserves braces east fed bats
26 cassettes weave afterwards dared babe created adverb agrees
27 bet readers verbs Steve Sara ear test acts care areas bases

Right-Hand Words

28 jump onion monk unhook junky linkup oink lop limp hop union
29 ploy nook puny Lynn inn unlink opinion pun plum ink million
30 yon only pull hill Kim ill hypo lump oilily oil kimono look
31 pinky Philip pin pop Honolulu holy Yukon imp Kohl Phil Milo

Left- and Right-Hand Words

32 lump rave cares ill wasted dressed ink crafts deer debt mil
33 drawer Molly nip asset jolly readers July severe edges mill
34 kimono edge bag lop add stressed look p.m. you'll plum link
35 addresses save fear Yukon Fred beat decreased fewer dresses

E. 30-SECOND PROGRESSIVE PRACTICE

Follow the software directions for this exercise to improve keystroking speed and accuracy.

F. 5-MINUTE TIMED WRITING

Take two 5-minute timed writings.

Goal: Push moderately for speed while keeping your accuracy under control.

36   The ability to analyze page after page of difficult   11
37 data, glean the important points, and present this data in   23
38 a clear manner is becoming more important each day. We are   34
39 being bombarded with more data than we can absorb.   44
40   Attempting to process all of this data can cause us to   56
41 have information anxiety, that is, the gap between what we   67
42 know and what we think we should know. It is a myth that   79
43 the more choices you have, the more freedom you have. More   91
44 choices can cause more anxiety.   97
45   The first step in overcoming information anxiety is to   108
46 accept that there is much that you will never understand.   120
47 That is true for all of us. Do not be afraid to ask someone   132
48 to clarify a point. Separate what you are really interested   144
49 in from what you merely think that you should be interested   156
50 in. You should minimize the amount of time that you spend   167
51 reading news that is not required.   175
52   Finally, just reduce your office reading, primarily   185
53 e-mail. These steps will help you to be more comfortable in   197
54 the workplace.   200

1 | 2 | 3 | 4 | 5 | 6 | 7 | 8 | 9 | 10 | 11 | 12

ISAK says ...

TAKE A BREAK!

Let your hands hang loosely at your side; rotate your right hand clockwise in a circle, then counterclockwise. Repeat with the left hand.

F. ARITHMETIC OPERATORS

Note: Depending upon your computer, to perform calculations, you may have to first open Calculator by clicking the Start button, clicking All Programs, clicking Accessories, and then clicking Calculator.

Use the Sem finger.

Plus Key

Press the plus key after each number except the last number in each column. After typing the last number (in line 55), press ENTER to display the total, which is shown in blue.

52	583+	948+	719+	372+	342+	745+	238+
53	735+	592+	705+	330+	112+	486+	201+
54	846+	257+	166+	883+	418+	315+	336+
55	144	782	472	566	174	873	987
	2308	2579	2062	2151	1046	2419	1762

Use the Sem finger.

Minus Key

Press the minus key after the first number and press ENTER after the second number to display the total, which is shown in blue.

56	790−	345−	847−	702−	939−	418−	607−
57	449	268	619	431	329	216	326
	341	77	228	271	610	202	281

58	742−	884−	856−	980−	739−	690−	557−
59	567	381	200	818	238	555	322
	175	503	656	162	501	135	235

Use the L finger.

Multiplication Key

Press the multiplication key after the first number and press ENTER after the second number to display the total, which is shown in blue.

60	571*	868*	771*	352*	978*	420*	187*
61	199	722	262	434	613	342	541
	113629	626696	202002	152768	599514	143640	101167

62	903*	311*	608*	590*	491*	700*	745*
63	335	905	514	699	498	725	963
	302505	281455	312512	412410	244518	507500	717435

Use the K finger.

Division Key

Press the division key after the first number and press ENTER after the second number to display the total, which is shown in blue.

Only two decimal places are displayed in the text.

64	672/	236/	646/	425/	206/	879/	532/
65	611	668	189	120	190	947	588
	1.09	.35	3.41	3.54	1.08	.92	.90

66	976/	383/	483/	538/	450/	768/	988/
67	828	792	655	885	179	603	101
	1.17	.48	.73	.60	2.51	1.27	9.78

TAKE A BREAK!

ISAK says ... Looking away from your screen, stare at a distant object for 5 seconds.

D. MAP+: ALPHABET

Follow the software instructions for this exercise to improve accuracy.

E. PRETEST-PRACTICE-POSTTEST: CONFUSABLE KEYS

Take a 1-minute timed writing, pushing moderately for speed.

PRETEST

Pay special attention to these keys that are often substituted for each other.

24	In two weeks, Tyler knows that our four desks are sure	11
25	to need replacing. He and Ruth will rush out to an office	23
26	store and seek to replace them. Any type of desks will be	34
27	fine so long as they are not too tiny for our work team.	46

1 | 2 | 3 | 4 | 5 | 6 | 7 | 8 | 9 | 10 | 11 | 12

PRACTICE
Substitutions

s-k

28 nooks barks books masks nukes necks skins shark rakes snack
29 peeks skill skew skid seek picks desk dunks inks keys monks
30 weeks banks skirt ducks balks stalk sneak knows knots knobs
31 steak kinds docks leaks sleek swank speck forks ranks jerks

y-t

32 thy booty meaty duty type Tommy sty typed Teddy fatty patsy
33 byte yet city yeast they ritzy stay nasty sooty stony witty
34 entry stray thyme tally party dirty petty tarry aptly ditzy
35 cyst tryst misty toy style Tyler jetty unity tiny arty toys

r-u

36 brush ruder turf rule bury dour burst crush ecru surly purr
37 rural cur sure our blur femur burn run rush drum exurb Ruth
38 rube brute court sour cure rug true humor amour scour outer
39 lurid rust burnt trump runt hour incur pour curd four grunt

POSTTEST

Repeat the Pretest. *Goal*: Improve speed and accuracy.

F. REACH DRILLS: JUMP REACHES

ce and on

Jump reaches move from the upper row to the lower row or vice versa.

40 pone none race bond bicep along place force blond don agony
41 son conch onto shone lone stone onus moon rayon emcee union
42 canon voice honor fence ulcer tenon farce ounce ebony wince
43 colon Donna facet on pounce bonk ozone song won among melon

ex and ni

44 snit bunion hex nippy exile expat denim exhume night excuse
45 exhort Rex denial latex sex mini ibex animus nine nib extra
46 expo Pyrex sexy bionic extort convex banish panic vex exact
47 genie expert Niger expect cynic extend expire expose exempt

G. MAP+: SYMBOLS

Follow the software instructions for this exercise to improve accuracy.

ISAK says ...

TECHNIQUE TIP

Sit about a hand width away from the keyboard. If your keyboard has pop-up legs in the back, do not engage them.

C. ZIP CODES

Press ENTER after typing the final digit of each number. Type the first column from top to bottom; then move to the next column and continue entering numbers.

Eyes on copy!

28	55531	70241	70247	42047
29	77602	20102	16570	26405
30	64657	15851	52653	28224
31	47566	17790	59512	30803
32	53339	59424	74032	78831
33	25477	61880	83397	57864
34	35093	65906	92973	69823
35	52668	68773	51536	50993

D. SOCIAL SECURITY NUMBERS

36	550246242	207571638	513222384
37	725122282	519526793	810892446
38	381624156	629982835	787436617
39	802400952	596874738	482844969
40	970402841	958923775	651732314
41	797527177	342803150	885911249
42	616228429	408630179	730703389
43	471873526	403694722	576512710

E. TELEPHONE NUMBERS

44	6251161386	1928850121	2453614579	5684880262
45	3802374228	6574602639	4751826595	6634653537
46	2388151583	1011983188	1810269012	7659096624
47	7035934523	7148264099	2863270976	5135081430
48	3841164607	8577327551	1620150252	2531545605
49	2473734268	9444990328	6865132381	9664019474
50	1424718667	9535702428	5865574378	5262721894
51	8899495280	9487039490	2067179740	3404078786

ISAK says ...

TECHNIQUE TIP

Adjust the height of your chair so that your feet rest flat on the floor and your thighs are parallel to the floor. If necessary, use either a chair cushion or a footstool.

Technique

Goals

- Improve technique on nonprinting, number, symbol, and punctuation keys.
- Improve concentration.

A. WARMUP

Accuracy	1	Give a big quiz just for a student who expects early marks.	12
Technique: Alternate-Hand	2	chair Nancy dial corps is laid downtown girl Janeiro social	24
Speed	3	Make your bed when you wake up so your mom will not be mad.	36

1 | 2 | 3 | 4 | 5 | 6 | 7 | 8 | 9 | 10 | 11 | 12

B. PRETEST-PRACTICE-POSTTEST: NONPRINTING KEYS

PRETEST

Take a 1-minute timed writing, pushing moderately for speed.

Backspace to correct all errors as you type.

4	Alex Uris is the man with the map of Cuba. Ask Toby	11
5	Parr and Ruby Gore to consult with the law firm of Ochs &	22
6	Elbe for help in getting visas to visit Cuba. Wilt Hayes	36
7	and Jack Hahn can leave in ten weeks to travel to Cuba.	45

1 | 2 | 3 | 4 | 5 | 6 | 7 | 8 | 9 | 10 | 11 | 12

PRACTICE
Nonprinting Keys

LEFT SHIFT Key

8 Isis Hays Haru Hale Otto Mach Maya Oran Meir Levi Mars Ubay
9 Parr Jean Jack Hedy Mace Hahn Lena Mary Ural Lett Uday Nast
10 Paul Nazi Uris Peke Iggy Ochs Lapp Hadj Jess Leon Urdu Herb
11 Owen Nero Oahu Nell Matt Utes Yang Leif Mesa Page Ubon Hart

RIGHT SHIFT Key

12 Cody Rice Giza Dona Wolf Dior Toby Anna Roma Aldo Alex Elbe
13 Siam Sikh Elks Wise Wood Cork Rosa Goya Aida Tiki Boer Sims
14 Amur Goth Elia Shui Duma Buck Quin Fuji Wilt Ruby Gore Cuba
15 Fisk Gina Ahab Gigi Soto Ryan Bull Ames Rita Zion Ford Ruth

BACKSPACE Key

When you reach the Backspace sign (←), backspace 1 time and then type the letter that follows.

16 ash←k tee←n put←p bus←y rug←m dab←m mob←m ash←k spa←y tea←n
17 via←m ale←l her←n ire←k bag←m dig←m sue←m add←o mud←m cot←p
18 cab←n rag←m par←n pug←n tow←y wag←y rat←p gee←m own←l vie←m
19 mar←p box←n the←y log←o art←m bog←o wig←n zig←p rut←n yea←n

POSTTEST

Repeat the Pretest. *Goal:* Improve speed and accuracy.

C. NUMBER PRACTICE

Press TAB to move from column to column in each row.

Eyes on copy!

20	320	591	472	584	159	342	469	149	184	800
21	773	109	535	361	554	404	520	398	655	478
22	388	530	224	189	177	846	182	381	172	445
23	920	147	150	778	493	709	363	116	229	402

Ten-Key Numeric Keypad Practice

Goals

- Build speed and accuracy on the ten-key numeric keypad.
- Assess speed and accuracy on a 1-minute timed writing on the ten-key numeric keypad by calculating the number of digits typed per minute.

A. REVIEW

Ensure that the NumLk key is active.

Press ENTER after typing the final digit of each number. Type the first column from top to bottom; then move to the next column and continue entering numbers.

Home Row (4, 5, and 6)

1	444	646	466	655	645	465	565	546	554	665
2	555	544	454	556	444	456	545	644	656	555
3	666	455	446	464	654	564	665	445	664	566

Upper Row (7, 8, and 9)

4	777	979	799	988	978	798	898	879	887	998
5	888	877	787	889	777	789	878	977	989	888
6	999	788	779	797	987	897	998	778	997	899

Lower Row (1, 2, and 3)

7	111	313	133	322	312	132	232	213	221	332
8	222	211	121	223	111	123	212	311	323	222
9	333	122	113	131	321	231	332	112	331	233

0

10	000	607	406	106	800	604	960	501	210	504
11	204	907	840	150	500	605	760	200	302	805
12	503	205	320	309	706	740	820	260	208	104

Decimal

13	1.9	3.5	9.2	6.8	3.7	4.1	8.0	9.9	1.6	8.2
14	1.1	8.4	5.7	3.4	4.0	1.8	6.4	5.4	6.0	9.1
15	4.7	8.8	1.0	4.9	4.2	9.8	2.4	1.7	5.0	6.2

B. ALL NUMBERS

16	9057	2083	5818	6110	9647	6661	7140
17	6947	7418	8753	4006	4892	3643	9327
18	6878	2357	4019	8574	7017	2200	2976
19	4322	8997	8079	2155	3033	8432	1597

20	5774	5155	5994	5342	8824	7273	5634
21	8232	5698	3753	5641	6071	5890	4516
22	3802	3857	3874	6168	2457	4161	1129
23	2970	5689	2873	6554	7015	4245	9693

24	.514	1.82	53.2	.546	4.41	72.6	.676
25	9.06	84.5	.903	5.78	20.8	.350	1.14
26	91.9	.566	7.03	26.9	.649	4.84	73.9
27	.938	7.40	11.9	.155	2.35	38.8	.318

D. SYMBOL PRACTICE

Return your fingers immediately to home-row position after typing each of these top-row symbols.

24 (lake) Han & Hsu also-ran be-all 932% qli@bsu.edu Harrison*
25 Berry* (lace) $1.04 Ngo & Ely 7# of stew #10 station #9 jib
26 #5 egg Batista* $1.14 $2 #8 nut add-on Owens & Young (lady)
27 729% sngo@az.gov (lag) 233% Mills & Ham Santos* rorr@ua.edu

E. PRETEST-PRACTICE-POSTTEST: CONCENTRATION
Take a 1-minute timed writing, pushing moderately for speed.

PRETEST

Type the Pretest exactly as shown, but type the Practice sentences below from right to left.

28   Why would you need to type sentences from right to   10
29 left? After all, is this ever done in the workplace? Of   22
30 course, not. But many typists still tend to look at their   33
31 keys as they type, and this exercise forces concentration.   45

     1 | 2 | 3 | 4 | 5 | 6 | 7 | 8 | 9 | 10 | 11 | 12

PRACTICE
Reverse Typing   Short Sentences

32 .ycnadnuder diovA
33 .seman reporp ezilatipaC
34 .srebmun etinifedni tuo llepS
35 .evitcepsrep s'redaer eht morf etirW

Medium-Length Sentences

36 .noitseuq tceridni na retfa doirep a esU
37 .yenom fo stnuoma etinifed rof serugif esU
38 .sdrow fo spuorg ro sdrow snioj noitcnujnoc A
39 .brev eht fo noitca eht seviecer tcejbo tcerid A

Long Sentences

40 .gnihtemos sdibrof ro ,sdnamed ,stseuqer dnammoc A
41 .net hguorht orez srebmun eht tuo lleps ,lareneg nI
42 .eurt ton si ro si gnihtemos taht smriffa tnemetats A
43 .nosrep a fo sdrow tcaxe eht dnuora skram noitatouq esU

POSTTEST

Repeat the Pretest. *Goal*: Improve speed and accuracy.

F. PUNCTUATION PRACTICE

Eyes on copy!

44 step; agt. Mrs. Asia: fig, Danger! hog, tact; New? in, mgt.
45 Gas? 1/7 is, Taxi! Angry? Soon? set; caps, made; so/so that
46 Fri. Mar. luck; Pete: fact, bog, acct. Feb. mfg. qty. cave,
47 Ltd. let; cog, cans, balk: Walk! be, axis, shall/will acre,

48 id, bars, Mr. main; onto; sack; ax, M.D. Follow! Ely, big,
49 addl. nine; Now! "peg" gave, am, So? bail, gal's tab; past;
50 Dale's approx. lacy, bring/take "peer" noon; ear, par; beg,
51 Cold? learn/teach asst. sing; line; Ohio; former/first Who?

TAKE A BREAK!

ISAK says ...

Massage each finger of each hand slowly and gently, starting with the space between the finger and moving toward the nail.

Appendix

Goals

- Build speed on:
  - ✓ 15-Second Speed Sprints and Paced Practice drills.
  - ✓ Common letter combinations and special hand drills.
- Assess speed and accuracy on a 5-minute timed writing.

A. WARMUP

Accuracy 1 Have wizards examine a copy of the huge black antique jars. 12

Technique: Concentration 2 interchangeableness counterinflationary electromechanically 24

Speed 3 Run over to the shop by noon so you can buy a roll of tape. 36

1 | 2 | 3 | 4 | 5 | 6 | 7 | 8 | 9 | 10 | 11 | 12

B. PRETEST-PRACTICE-POSTTEST: COMMON LETTER COMBINATIONS

PRETEST Take a 1-minute timed writing, pushing moderately for speed.

4   In this instance, our reluctance is that we may not 11

5 have the votes to convert the condos in compliance with 22

6 current governance control. Tenants may file a grievance; 33

7 without their consent, we do not have the votes we need. 45

1 | 2 | 3 | 4 | 5 | 6 | 7 | 8 | 9 | 10 | 11 | 12

PRACTICE
Common Letter Combinations

es 8 dates toes does eves piles cages bones bites rest zest west

9 jest ales dress pies less eases cases boxes dies woes bikes

10 quest vest cries hies goes pest ires rises saves rests Jess

11 dues votes bales crest best ties ones awes byes Agnes cakes

con 12 abscond concern bacon icon contest contrive deacon constant

13 Macon consent contour iconic contort consign consul console

14 confirm conifer coconut confused control consist conger con

15 convert condo confuse Congo converge conceal falcon convent

ance 16 instance distance dominance appearance abundance governance

17 endurance substance penance tolerance conveyance temperance

18 advanced nuisance cancel trance avoidance compliance glance

19 insurance balanced grievance refinance reluctance annoyance

POSTTEST Repeat the Pretest. *Goal:* Improve speed and accuracy.

C. 15-SECOND SPEED SPRINTS

Goal: Increase your speed on each retyping of the same sentence.

20 His high note was not so off; he jams just like a true pro.

21 Let us sit down and eat the fine pile of food she has made.

22 She does love to pull her big red cart at the farm at dawn.

23 Take one egg and mix it with ham to cook his very top meal.

D. SPECIAL HAND DRILLS

Left-Hand Words

Maintain the nontyping hand in home-row position.

24 wet faster deserve faced regarded screw cartage Egbert save
25 Bert afterward fast facets effect bases stressed stewardess
26 breezes affect streets safe state arrest wage aware degrees
27 text verbs edge server crew rag Barbara reserved bar feared

Right-Hand Words

28 monopoly loom linkup lumpy noun homily poi pop ply mop pill
29 nymph polo jumpy puppy kin homonym I'm hilly uphill lop Kim
30 hook mom Joplin Yukon hypo joy inn loop nylon ump junk Kohl
31 minimum I'll Molly oilily loin holy inky noon mil ilk Polly

Left- and Right-Hand Words

32 hymn holy exceeds punk few caves bed tea great pumpkin hill
33 swears best race rear yon creates stars arts lion pink fare
34 minion grass grace gate hum wave Carter rebate save was fed
35 opinion assessed saved lop verbs defects exceeded Kohl east

E. 30-SECOND PROGRESSIVE PRACTICE

Follow the software directions for this exercise to improve keystroking speed and accuracy.

F. 5-MINUTE TIMED WRITING

Take two 5-minute timed writings.

Goal: Push moderately for speed while keeping your accuracy under control.

36 Your body is the most important machine you will ever	11
37 operate, so treat it with the same care you do with other	23
38 expensive equipment, such as your computer or your car.	34
39 Regular exercise will improve your performance at school,	45
40 at home, and on the job. Your brain functions better when	57
41 you are in shape; regular exercise also decreases tension.	69
42 Our bodies were meant to exercise. Think back to the	80
43 times of the hunters and gatherers and how much time people	92
44 back then had to spend just to put food on the table. Diet	103
45 alone cannot create a healthy body. It takes both proper	115
46 diet and movement to remain healthy.	122
47 Begin by doing something easy, such as walking for	133
48 fifteen minutes a day. Start easy and build up as you feel	144
49 your stamina grow. Then build in some assortment of aerobic	156
50 activity, that is, any activity that raises your heart rate	168
51 to a faster pace. Try using a treadmill or biking. If you	180
52 keep at it, you will be amazed at how much better you look	192
53 and how much better you feel. Try it now.	200

1 | 2 | 3 | 4 | 5 | 6 | 7 | 8 | 9 | 10 | 11 | 12

TAKE A BREAK!

ISAK says ...

Keeping your head stationary, rotate your eyes to form a circle, both eyes focusing together, five times clockwise and then five times counterclockwise.

D. SPECIAL HAND DRILLS

Alternate-Hand Words

24 fight neuritis Blanche lay world amend eighth bicycle Japan
25 or apt Vic box Rod fish land flaps if Bud fix coal fir dock
26 problem Janey name girl Sydney pay downtown pep handy Diane
27 bus Guthrie half city turn hang risk spent sock Dubuque Rob

Double-Letter Words

28 bass Nelly noon mamma hall broom cook Barry deep ditto bill
29 Anna Lynn mill Gabby queen free booth feet Anne Greek Ellen
30 Jenny feed fee feel shook teeth apple deer food Betty annex
31 Bobby spell sees hook Allan off tattoo Ella creek inn class

Lower-Row Words

32 beacon coccyx comedic dynamic mansion melanin manic manikin
33 pizzazz denizen cocoon cabin sunburn acerbic vermin vitamin
34 raccoon unclean Bombay embalm benign convex bandbox minicam
35 chicken bourbon bunion minicab blacken nonfarm cancan canon

E. PACED PRACTICE

Follow the software directions for this exercise to improve keystroking speed and accuracy.

F. 5-MINUTE TIMED WRITING

Take two 5-minute timed writings.

Goal: Push moderately for speed while keeping your accuracy under control.

36 The key to success in a small business is to generate	11
37 sales, and often that means sending out sales letters. Can	23
38 you say that your product is the best on the market? Yes,	34
39 you may legally express an opinion about your product if	46
40 that is your honest judgment. You cannot, however, make a	57
41 claim that can be proven false.	64
42 You cannot include a sample of your product with your	75
43 letter and require the reader to remit payment or return	86
44 the produce at your expense. Instead, the recipient may	97
45 legally treat the product as a gift from you.	107
46 You may legally accept orders from minors. However,	117
47 until they reach the age of adulthood, they may cancel a	129
48 contract and return the merchandise to you.	137
49 If you advertise a product in a magazine and run out,	148
50 you must either take orders for later delivery, give rain	160
51 checks, or sell a similar product at the same price.	171
52 Finally, if your assistant writes a letter advertising	182
53 a product at a price without your knowledge, you have to	193
54 honor the prices that were quoted.	200

1 | 2 | 3 | 4 | 5 | 6 | 7 | 8 | 9 | 10 | 11 | 12

ISAK says ...

TECHNIQUE TIP

Ensure that only your fingertips touch the keyboard. Let your fingers do the moving; the rest of your hand should be as still as possible.

Speed

Goals

- Build speed on:
  - ✓ 15-Second Speed Sprints and 30-Second Progressive Practice drills.
  - ✓ Common letter combinations and special hand drills.
- Assess speed and accuracy on a 5-minute timed writing.

A. WARMUP

Accuracy	1	The magical wizards jinxed folks by their quivering pranks.	12
Technique: SPACE BAR	2	I can. Al came and went. Why? Now you can do it. We do. So?	24
Speed	3	We all love when you tell us what you do with your own day.	36

          1 | 2 | 3 | 4 | 5 | 6 | 7 | 8 | 9 | 10 | 11 | 12

B. PRETEST-PRACTICE-POSTTEST: COMMON LETTER COMBINATIONS

PRETEST

Take a 1-minute timed writing, pushing moderately for speed.

4	It was now evident that the eminent dentist had both	11
5	the education and the mental capacity to prevent any more	22
6	emotional pain in his current patient. He had spent much	34
7	time with her and, in my mind, he did an exemplary job.	45

          1 | 2 | 3 | 4 | 5 | 6 | 7 | 8 | 9 | 10 | 11 | 12

PRACTICE
Common Letter Combinations

in 8 inuring opining insuring printing staining jinxing defining
9 wing swinging incliner pint wind inching lint blinding akin
10 in instinct cringing whining pinpoint singing gin hind mind
11 divining pin kindling sinking clinking ink fine inn quinine

ent 12 segment dentist sapient genteel aplenty entered lent cogent
13 portent dissent salient mental trident memento cements dent
14 stent invent eminent fervent evident prevent exigent rental
15 talent rent spent gent gently centric resent regent current

tion 16 motioning gradation assertion defection emotional agitation
17 lotion portioned rotation desertion reduction action potion
18 dictation injection rationing secretion deviation induction
19 erection education oration adoption ovation diction edition

POSTTEST

Repeat the Pretest. *Goal:* Improve speed and accuracy.

C. 15-SECOND SPEED SPRINTS

Goal: Increase your speed on each retyping of the same sentence.

20 She does love to cook; too bad she does not do it too well.
21 If you hold tight to an ice pack, it will help you so much.
22 Put that pen to a pad if you want to tell her how you feel.
23 Just face the fact that you did miss a very nice boat trip.

22

Accuracy

Goals

- Build accuracy on:
  - ✓ Corresponding-finger and confusable keys.
  - ✓ Spelling.
  - ✓ Alphabetic, horizontal, and number reaches.

A. WARMUP

Accuracy	1 The girls wove six dozen plaid jackets before my wife quit.	12
Technique: Concentration	2 incommensurableness noninterventionists reprehensiblenesses	24
Speed	3 If you hold tight to an ice pack, it will help you so much.	36

1 | 2 | 3 | 4 | 5 | 6 | 7 | 8 | 9 | 10 | 11 | 12

B. PRETEST-PRACTICE-POSTTEST: CORRESPONDING-FINGER KEYS

PRETEST Take a 1-minute timed writing, pushing moderately for speed.

4	Don't lose sight of the fact that the excess taxes	10
5	may slow our growth or even lead to a loss. It looks like	22
6	the lessons we learned during the last recession are slowly	34
7	being forgotten. The sums of money involved are large.	45

1 | 2 | 3 | 4 | 5 | 6 | 7 | 8 | 9 | 10 | 11 | 12

PRACTICE
Corresponding Fingers

S Finger

8 sis skews lows buss sews sash sups spas cows waits Wes sews
9 axes shows mass Cass toss sums sexes sobs wise excess wades
10 sirs swans wares wigs wow execs wasps wars wakes loss stows
11 taxes stew waxes suds wanes axles slow sows swash pass slaw

L Finger

12 toil blot atoll Mon. billow bola lbs. poodle loge roil glow
13 slowly looks. pole noodle clot locale lose Molly oval bloom
14 viol lope lolled boll old saloon lowly color soil plop floe
15 lonely clod long Oct. loot pillow Flo floor folk alto colon

S and L Fingers

16 shows yowls fowls slopes bosses pools swoons igloos lassoes
17 sloshes Swiss scowls stools loll folios spills looms bowwow
18 scoops colors swoops loon. jowls lessons fellows woos sills
19 bowels slops salvos powwow solo sorrows knolls lobos blooms

POSTTEST Repeat the Pretest. *Goal:* Improve speed and accuracy.

C. BUSINESS SPELLING

These spelling words are from a list of the most used and most misspelled words in business writing. Study the words that cause you problems.

20 structural schedule dedicated cassette drainage propagation
21 auditorium together auditing reason terminal fiscal zoology
22 agricultural city's termination committed recipient routine
23 partial subsequently superintendent technical inconvenience

D. SYMBOL PRACTICE

Keep your eyes on the copy as you type these top-row symbols.

24 all-day (lag) Fuentes* qli@bsu.edu #5 egg $1.68 sngo@az.gov
25 (lair) $1 aho@cs.com 4# of ham uely@az.gov Noe & Ray be-all
26 729% Harrison* 3# of sand $0.34 uely@az.gov age-old Parker*
27 57.2% (lamb) Ngo & Ely (lack) West & Little Ely & Foy $1.04

E. PRETEST-PRACTICE-POSTTEST: CONCENTRATION
Take a 1-minute timed writing, pushing moderately for speed.

PRETEST

Concentrate on keeping your eyes on the copy as you type these vocabulary words. How many of these terms do you know?

28   Our trade representatives may have overemphasized the   11
29 misunderstandings of their confidant, but they are able to   23
30 specifically rebut all of the charges so far and are able   34
31 to clearly explicate our fealty to international law.   45

    1 | 2 | 3 | 4 | 5 | 6 | 7 | 8 | 9 | 10 | 11 | 12

PRACTICE   Short Words
Vocabulary Words

32 vivify vendor pathos grotto bier fealty
33 pious taut specie laud awry egress aura
34 influx vortex arrant twinge deign prate
35 rondo revert apiary penury rebut levity

Medium-Length Words

36 penurious querulous defalcate explicate confidant
37 volition autarchy languor dastard fatuous abridge
38 vacuous foppery eiderdown rampart proffer retinue
39 progeny alluvion quixotic requite acetate clarion

Long Words

40 incomprehensibility overemphasized constituency equilibrium
41 superficially acquaintance misunderstandings unquestionable
42 representatives luminescence misinformation congratulations
43 magnification republication quasigovernmental theoretically

POSTTEST

Repeat the Pretest. *Goal*: Improve speed and accuracy.

F. PUNCTUATION PRACTICE

Eyes on copy!

44 Jr. 1/9 flea's Drink? How? link: Ms. aid, Stop! star; pond;
45 Always? Walk? "peg" net; Asia: 2/10 pine; Inc. Danger! Tue.
46 cars, neat; each, mart; Mon. big, Break? Hear? c.o.d. Lynn;
47 pave; seat; equally/as 3/4 card, Duck! act, Candy? pp. Thu.

48 most; Quit! Morning? band, noon; learn/teach bats, Nothing?
49 Jan. Assn. Aug. lace, barn, loom; Sun. some; cog, tab; Fri.
50 let; Bart: Where? "peel" Dale's Run! knew, bars, Wed. camp,
51 pack; sky; Enough? pin; intl. Stan; know, pain; axed, Sign?

TECHNIQUE TIP

ISAK says...

Center your body on the alphabetic portion of the keyboard.

D. MAP+: ALPHABET

Follow the software instructions for this exercise to improve accuracy.

E. PRETEST-PRACTICE-POSTTEST: CONFUSABLE KEYS

PRETEST

Take a 1-minute timed writing, pushing moderately for speed.

Pay special attention to these consecutive-finger reaches that often get confused.

24	The expert may be trying to avert the jury's attention	11
25	away from the obvious weakness in his conclusions, which, I	23
26	believe, are truly unmerited. He went overboard in looking	35
27	at only part of the evidence that was available to him.	46

1 | 2 | 3 | 4 | 5 | 6 | 7 | 8 | 9 | 10 | 11 | 12

PRACTICE

Consecutive Fingers

rt-tr

28 try expert deport avert desert trip assert part apart trill
29 triad curt cavort treble tread trauma tropic tract trio ort
30 blurt thwart abort trunk troll unhurt trig fort Troy trudge
31 resort triage treaty skirt truly start trying trough effort

mn-nm

32 unmarred firmness calmness mnemonic enmity rainmaker unmade
33 unmasked condemn omnivore unmoving nonmilitary nonmalignant
34 alumnus Denmark circumnavigate omnipotence unmoved unmapped
35 nonmajor gymnastics condemns enlightenment unmerited inmost

vb-bv

36 breakeven vibes observe bivouac cabdriver unlivable brevity
37 beverage curveball believe adverb advisable bravo overboard
38 vagabond oblivious unlovable abusive bedeviled obvious vibe
39 movable bravado above obsessive bedevil available invisible

POSTTEST

Repeat the Pretest. *Goal:* Improve speed and accuracy.

F. REACH DRILLS: HORIZONTAL REACHES

we and ip

40 cower jawed lip strip bowed welt swell hip slip dweeb weave
41 weigh awe weary tweed unwed flip ship wedge jewel lower tip
42 bower yip weak ripen chip wet gripe swipe swear pawed cowed
43 pipe tower bowel wed dippy rip wend dip wean sweat skip nip

Horizontal reaches move to a different key on the same row.

ga and pi

44 pile gaff pique gang gaily gaze piece gave gam pig pi spite
45 gauze gaffe pity gay pipe pike spill topic pied omega spike
46 sugar gate pie gash aspic pita aping toga gab pin again gap
47 regal gable gas spice gale sepia pint gaudy epic gamma game

G. MAP+: NUMBERS

Follow the software instructions for this exercise to improve accuracy.

TAKE A BREAK!

ISAK says ...

With your left arm stretched out in front of you, with your right hand pull the left hand backward and hold for 10 seconds; then pull the left hand downward and hold for 10 seconds. Repeat with the right hand.

Technique

Goals

- Improve technique on nonprinting, number, symbol, and punctuation keys.
- Improve concentration.

A. WARM-UP

Accuracy	1	Why did those wrong jobs quickly faze their moving experts?	12
Technique: Transpositions	2	item tile|alto lamp|isle silo|Eton test|Enid near|oral roar	24
Speed	3	Go tell that old man that I like his good golf game so far.	36

1 | 2 | 3 | 4 | 5 | 6 | 7 | 8 | 9 | 10 | 11 | 12

B. PRETEST-PRACTICE-POSTTEST: NONPRINTING KEYS

PRETEST

Take a 1-minute timed writing, pushing moderately for speed. Type each sentence; then press TAB to move from column to column.

4	Drop it now.	Go home now.	I saw a man.	Take my bag.	11
5	I am a lady.	File it now.	I dare them.	Who is here?	21
6	We are late.	Oh, not him.	Be a friend.	Key quickly.	31
7	Add me also.	Let me stay.	I was tired.	I can do it.	41

PRACTICE
Nonprinting Keys

ENTER Key

Press ENTER after each word to format each word on a new line.

8 Now. Fast! Underline. Hide. Leave. Gosh. Erase. Whoa! Alas!
9 Rush. Whisper! Lift. Certainly. Man! Up! Sit. Silly! Great.
10 Next. So? Pay. Hello. Hit. Remember? Evidently. Hey! Start.
11 Who? Later. When? Stir. Amen. Congratulations. Play. Reach.

TAB Key

Type each word; then press TAB to move from column to column.

12	query	await	abysmal	quint
13	abash	amass	quince	acreage
14	zealot	qualify	quality	appear
15	algebra	amoral	zombie	queasy

SPACE BAR

16 Let me have it. How dare you? We are up. Jo saw Al at home.
17 I am up. Go up to the man. See me at ten. Ed was up at one.

Bounce the thumb quickly off the SPACE BAR.

18 Me? I can. We do. How are you? Do it for me. I do not know.
19 When? I may just do it. What gives? Don't do it now. I may.

POSTTEST

Repeat the Pretest. *Goal*: Improve speed and accuracy.

C. NUMBER PRACTICE

Press TAB to move from column to column in each row.

Eyes on copy!

20	880	897	277	754	408	428	392	620	325	152
21	851	399	147	608	951	987	265	543	398	114
22	740	127	346	944	291	308	356	922	491	558
23	468	890	457	432	197	326	937	171	923	688

Technique

Goals

- Improve technique on nonprinting, number, symbol, and punctuation keys.
- Improve concentration.

A. WARMUP

Accuracy	1 He quickly trained a dozen brown foxes to jump over a gate.	12
Technique: Double Letters	2 good well Glenn Harry deep Nelly look I'll teeth Otto occur	24
Speed	3 If he puts that gift in the mail now, it will ship in time.	36

1 | 2 | 3 | 4 | 5 | 6 | 7 | 8 | 9 | 10 | 11 | 12

B. PRETEST-PRACTICE-POSTTEST: NONPRINTING KEYS

PRETEST

Take a 1-minute timed writing, pushing moderately for speed. Type each sentence; then press TAB to move from column to column.

4 Run quickly.	Type it now.	Drive there.	Come to her.	11
5 Key quickly.	Listen here!	Believe him.	File it now.	21
6 You're okay.	I was tired.	Read my map.	Let's do it.	31
7 Are we late?	Why not now?	Be a friend.	Tell me why.	41

PRACTICE
Nonprinting Keys   ENTER Key

Press ENTER after each word to format each word on a new line.

8 Aim. Pause. Play. Sip. Hurry. Continue. Steady. Watch. Yea!
9 Hello. Congratulations. Write. Encore. Proceed. Good. Heel.
10 Granted. So? Spell. Ouch! Eat. Hit. Freeze! Taste. Me? Not!
11 Danger! Catch. Yes! Sit. Naturally. Dig? Erase. Print. How?

TAB Key

Type each word; then press TAB to move from column to column.

12 abstain	abysmal	appear	airfare
13 attain	acreage	quiver	alfalfa
14 appall	qualm	await	quaint
15 airmail	quell	altar	attack

SPACE BAR

16 See Mr. Dye. Is it too big? I am up. The ox may die. I see.
17 I think so. Why? Buy a map for me. I go. Be here. Jo is up.

Bounce the thumb quickly off the SPACE BAR.

18 Don't do it now. Now is the time. He is. Why me? Do it now.
19 I do. When? I do not know. You may go on up. She may do it.

POSTTEST

Repeat the Pretest. *Goal:* Improve speed and accuracy.

C. NUMBER PRACTICE

Press TAB to move from column to column in each row.

Eyes on copy!

20 320	591	472	584	159	342	469	149	184	800
21 773	109	535	361	554	404	520	398	655	478
22 388	530	224	189	177	846	182	381	172	445
23 920	147	150	778	493	709	363	116	229	402

D. MAP+: ALPHABET

Follow the software instructions for this exercise to improve accuracy.

E. PRETEST-PRACTICE-POSTTEST: CONFUSABLE KEYS

PRETEST

Pay special attention to these consecutive-finger reaches that are often get confused.

Take a 1-minute timed writing, pushing moderately for speed.

```
24        Our attorneys are trying to keep track of the court        11
25  hearings and have a favorable opinion of the way in which        22
26  the case is moving. They believe that the court will assert      34
27  its power and move to indemnify our company for any losses.      46
        1 | 2 | 3 | 4 | 5 | 6 | 7 | 8 | 9 | 10 | 11 | 12
```

PRACTICE
Consecutive Fingers

rt-tr

```
28  trance triad tram art tragic court deport troll true assort
29  curt heart tart trying inert thwart trough overt trap track
30  tray trunk trio truism trill trash tread tract import trail
31  hurt wart revert desert trike tried tort chart assert sport
```

mn-nm

```
32  unmade nonmedical remnants inmate insomnia firmness gymnast
33  nonmoving rainmaker alumni hymnal omnivore grimness omnibus
34  inmost amnesiac columnar amniotic indemnify nonmajor damned
35  enlightenment autumn unmined hymn remnant unmarred unmailed
```

vb-bv

```
36  favorable bravery unmovable bravado beehive abusive voluble
37  overboard bovine obviate combative believe adverb overbaked
38  viable cabdriver above adverbial avoidable verbalize verbal
39  abusive bedcovers oblivious behaved obvert bivalve bi-level
```

POSTTEST

Repeat the Pretest. *Goal*: Improve speed and accuracy.

F. REACH DRILLS: HORIZONTAL REACHES

we and ip

Horizontal reaches move to a different key on the same row.

```
40  trip mowed sweep weary sowed swear wet cawed ripe dweeb lip
41  dower wiper vowel snipe snip we Swede bowed weave were well
42  welt nippy weld newel wean dip jawed nip rawer pip ship rip
43  wowed newer quip swipe bowel towel ripen skip wept wee flip
```

ga and pi

```
44  Pima sugar sepia spike gale epic pi cigar gad gasp pick gag
45  gam spite spine ping pagan gamut gait gaily gavel pike gape
46  rapid gab Garth spice pita gang pill pigmy pupil gaff opium
47  agave pivot gas piety tepid pinch pitch gay pie gaffe spill
```

G. MAP+: NUMBERS

Follow the software instructions for this exercise to improve accuracy.

TAKE A BREAK!

ISAK says...

Standing at attention, breathe in while you bend backward and then breathe out as you return to the normal position. Then repeat, bending forward.

D. SYMBOL PRACTICE

Keep your eyes on the copy as you type these top-row symbols.

24 (lad) qli@bsu.edu West & Little boo-boo Ngo & Ely bad-badly
25 Han & Hsu $1.14 697% $1 cli@bsu.edu 157.2% (lady) Noe & Ray
26 932% (laid) 958% sngo@az.gov 233% (lace) Owens & Young 102%
27 729% 6% Shan* Mills & Ham $1.68 also-ran aorr@cs.com Berry*

E. PRETEST-PRACTICE-POSTTEST: CONCENTRATION
Take a 1-minute timed writing, pushing moderately for speed.

PRETEST

Concentrate on keeping your eyes on the copy as you type these vocabulary words. How many of these terms do you know?

28   It will have little effect if we vigorously inveigh   11
29 against all of the inane countermeasures the competition   22
30 has instituted. We cannot stop their investigations without   34
31 jeopardizing our own fine reputation in the marketplace.   45

   1 | 2 | 3 | 4 | 5 | 6 | 7 | 8 | 9 | 10 | 11 | 12

PRACTICE   Short Words
Vocabulary Words

32 effect bide taut licit acrid mite inane
33 retch posit enigma beck dyne cant arbor
34 jocose allay fresco vertex wry teem lea
35 yaw evert egoist gamut feint dun rancor

Medium-Length Words

36 amalgam polyglot inveigh polemics conduce culvert
37 desultory litigious indigence tenebrous explicate
38 distrain acetate solecism comport ignoble epicure
39 turpitude reprobate effluvium cacophony fugacious

Long Words

40 survivorship plenipotentiary regionalization investigations
41 cornucopia hallucinogenic jeopardizing counterrevolutionary
42 ragamuffin vigorously reconnoiter meretricious pertinacious
43 countermeasure unsuccessfully preconstruction grandiloquent

POSTTEST

Repeat the Pretest. *Goal:* Improve speed and accuracy.

F. PUNCTUATION PRACTICE

Eyes on copy!

44 tag; stay; Esq. fwd. 1/7 Bus? cont'd lab, Lucy; Here? acre:
45 knew, boa, line; Escape? Eat! Leon; Knox, Wed. next; "peak"
46 chg. luck; skin; 1/9 rain; pain; tact; You! pin; John, Dec.
47 jack, qtr. New? Sun. Break? M.D. it, dept. onto; elf, know,

48 Yea! don't safe; Dance? Feb. Drive! pink; Dave, axis, calm,
49 axle, 4/10 loud; Gas? ppd. Morning? bank, "peek" Cut! flax,
50 one; son; mdse. omit; Better? acct. flea's cave, Lou; Bart:
51 let; amt. fed, 2/10 bars, a.k.a. band, room; Nov. recd. Go!

ISAK says ...

TECHNIQUE TIP
Type with a light touch and steady rhythm.

Accuracy

Goals

- Build accuracy on:
  - ✓ Corresponding-finger and confusable keys.
  - ✓ Spelling.
  - ✓ Alphabetic, horizontal, and number reaches.

A. WARMUP

Accuracy | 1 Jeff moved those six dozen quail last night by power truck. | 12
Technique: Lower Row | 2 convex novice moving mix neb conch mob can, ebb. evince ban | 24
Speed | 3 If you go look on my desk now, you will find what you seek. | 36

1 | 2 | 3 | 4 | 5 | 6 | 7 | 8 | 9 | 10 | 11 | 12

B. PRETEST-PRACTICE-POSTTEST: CORRESPONDING-FINGER KEYS

PRETEST Take a 1-minute timed writing, pushing moderately for speed.

4   The oil from West Texas has lost much of its value, | 11
5 having dropped more than a dollar last week. We will need | 22
6 to boost prices in the global market in order to make up | 34
7 the shortfall. We may also need other fixes next month. | 45

1 | 2 | 3 | 4 | 5 | 6 | 7 | 8 | 9 | 10 | 11 | 12

PRACTICE   S Finger
Corresponding Fingers

8 assays fixes Texas sops shows sexy waxers awes wanes Sphinx
9 sets uses sans Swiss wasp assist news sips snows expos boss
10 sway bows jaws sags whew waxy wakes sixths slaws sows swish
11 twos miss so-so sups owls west swat Ross owes bus sis wards

L Finger

12 oil droll foil loch flop Lou collar lobo poll toll lion low
13 dollar colony coal volley loaf willow Ont. mold global loom
14 plot mellow foul lock loam hello Sun. color also loyal goal
15 lost flow folk slot wool allow loan hole Laos tallow boldly

S and L Fingers

16 boost slobs wills sloops wolves hollows osmosis walls plows
17 slops slopes cellos lessons stroll yowls losers solos slots
18 floors lowbrow fossils loll woos looks extols lasso shallow
19 solo Apollo silos folios snoops bolls sows wool slow salvos

POSTTEST Repeat the Pretest. *Goal*: Improve speed and accuracy.

C. BUSINESS SPELLING

These spelling words are from a list of the most used and most misspelled words in business writing. Study the words that cause you problems.

20 efficiency consistent enrollment sense established monitors
21 vendor establishment quarterly bargaining consultants yield
22 function unique secretaries advisory maximum identification
23 negative attended maturity bearing recommendation dividends

Speed

Goals

- Build speed on:
  - ✓ 15-Second Speed Sprints and 30-Second Progressive Practice drills.
  - ✓ Common letter combinations and special hand drills.
- Assess speed and accuracy on a 5-minute timed writing.

A. WARMUP

Accuracy	1	Do quiz just two more of eight executives on back pay only.	12
Technique: Upper Row	2	pot retype Tory tee Euterpe tort put wire Peter eerie petty	24
Speed	3	Go grab the pink pot on the sill to fill it up to the edge.	36

1 | 2 | 3 | 4 | 5 | 6 | 7 | 8 | 9 | 10 | 11 | 12

B. PRETEST-PRACTICE-POSTTEST: COMMON LETTER COMBINATIONS

PRETEST

Take a 1-minute timed writing, pushing moderately for speed.

4 The main reason I'm inclined to comment on the new 10
5 retention plan is that it is urgent that, to the extent 22
6 possible, we maintain control of the whole promotion of the 34
7 concept. Let's look into the notion of refining the plan. 45

1 | 2 | 3 | 4 | 5 | 6 | 7 | 8 | 9 | 10 | 11 | 12

PRACTICE
Common Letter Combinations

in 8 inclined mink clinging fainting joining main hind mini ruin
9 wink paining ginning loin clinking sinning whining inlaying
10 shin maintain refining into stinting evincing lint jingling
11 lining wind inking bind ins zing oink repining winning thin

ent 12 entitle extent comment sapient reenter scent vented evident
13 repent polenta torrent lucent figment mentor urgent genteel
14 absent cogent entrap salient raiment venture rental dentist
15 invent ardent segment entered central assent resent exigent

tion 16 potion affection ovation vibration tuition lotion adulation
17 pulsation formation retention deduction gestation elocution
18 rotation ration hydration optioning notion execution nation
19 attrition promotion exudation cognition inception erudition

POSTTEST

Repeat the Pretest. *Goal:* Improve speed and accuracy.

C. 15-SECOND SPEED SPRINTS

Goal: Increase your speed on each retyping of the same sentence.

20 I will not get far if my bike will not move when I push it.
21 If you type this word and then five more, you will be done.
22 She did warn me to go easy when I comb her hair; I can try.
23 Sit up here next to me and we will see the red sun go down.

D. SPECIAL HAND DRILLS

Alternate-Hand Words

24 work both snap girls keys Rob air the visual tidy hair rush

25 risks Guam ant lay form die born Pamela he city fir do make

26 also by maid go fix land big audit Glen formal bushel spend

27 sit laugh foe fish pay towns amendment chairman Panama pays

Double-Letter Words

28 spell Eddie sorry hall free call greet loom weed mill Peggy

29 Hyatt seek noon ill look cliff foot tells add zoo Anne tail

30 tool apple comma fussy will nanny see occur annoy miss roof

31 blood cell Ella Emma asset been Bobby door petty Bess small

Lower-Row Words

32 icebox canteen monsoon calcium bantam bumpkin minicab mimic

33 baboon nomadic vitamin cubic bandbox manikin chicken cocoon

34 mailbox benign bonbon denizen nonfarm entomb hobnob albumen

35 Cayman masonic coccyx oceanic abuzz dynamic complex mansion

E. PACED PRACTICE

Follow the software directions for this exercise to improve keystroking speed and accuracy.

F. 5-MINUTE TIMED WRITING

Take two 5-minute timed writings.

Goal: Push moderately for speed while keeping your accuracy under control.

36 If you are a college student, maybe hold down a full-	11
37 or part-time job, and maybe have family responsibilities,	22
38 you do not have to be reminded of the need for competent	34
39 time-management skills.	39
40 First, you should plan out your fixed blocks of time,	50
41 such as classes, jobs, eating, sleeping, and other tasks.	61
42 Other duties must be planned around these. Set realistic	73
43 goals for your other duties. If you know that it usually	84
44 requires you two hours to do your weekly grocery shopping,	96
45 don't plan to cut it down to one hour. You are just setting	108
46 yourself up for failure.	113
47 Set aside a reasonable amount of time for studying,	123
48 typically two hours for each hour of credit. Remember that	135
49 several shorter study periods are more effective than one	147
50 long marathon session just before your assignment is due.	158
51 Be flexible in your schedule and recognize that some	169
52 unexpected events will occur, so build some unplanned time	181
53 in your schedule to allow for these. In other words, do not	193
54 plan out every minute of every day.	200

1 | 2 | 3 | 4 | 5 | 6 | 7 | 8 | 9 | 10 | 11 | 12

TECHNIQUE TIP

ISAK says ...

Keep your wrists in a neutral position, with your forearms, wrists, and hands in a straight line.

D. SPECIAL HAND DRILLS

Left-Hand Words

Maintain the nontyping hand in home-row position.

24 trees readers grew saves grades bag rate sat regret reserve
25 degree attract car addressers fare few target feared faster
26 defer based deserve weave greet waste Caracas waters server
27 treated dad bear rage rave tag refers tact bears Dave Bates

Right-Hand Words

28 uplink hum Polly mum lop unholy kimono you hook ohm kin Kim
29 oilily lymph kiln poi pylon oil nylon lion inky homily hunk
30 plunk ion unhook nymph pink jumpy jump oink loop Philip ink
31 ump opinion join inn I'll yolk look monopoly noun hilly pun

Left- and Right-Hand Words

32 state July minimum oink waves rage exceed dated defer hilly
33 west Caesar case saved nymph cards water Exeter served noon
34 him debts rag areas revere arts bag mom saw bet hymn arrest
35 affect treat hominy access cave ever ilk Stewart Abe excess

E. 30-SECOND PROGRESSIVE PRACTICE

Follow the software directions for this exercise to improve keystroking speed and accuracy.

F. 5-MINUTE TIMED WRITING

Take two 5-minute timed writings.

Goal: Push moderately for speed while keeping your accuracy under control.

36   Plagiarism can be a potential problem for anyone who   11
37 writes. For example, a well-known minister was criticized   22
38 for lifting numerous sections from someone else's book to   34
39 include in his own book. Dishonest work has become such a   46
40 major problem, in fact, that the federal government has   57
41 issued new rules designed to police scientific work.   67
42   You can, of course, go too far in the other direction   78
43 and provide too much documentation. Such a practice not   90
44 only distracts the reader but also leaves the impression   101
45 that the writer is not an original thinker. One published   113
46 study contained almost four-thousand citations.   122
47   You must give due credit to your sources and ensure   133
48 the quality and accuracy of all data you use. Never accept   145
49 any data, whether words, photographs, or charts, as true   156
50 unless you can verify them. Your company's reputation, not   168
51 to mention your own, demand no less.   175
52   While in school, make sure that all of the work you   186
53 submit in class is your own. Be proud of all the work that   198
54 you submit.   200

    1 | 2 | 3 | 4 | 5 | 6 | 7 | 8 | 9 | 10 | 11 | 12

ISAK says ...

TAKE A BREAK!

Shut your eyes tightly for 3 seconds; then open them wide and blink rapidly.

Goals

- Build speed on:
  - ✓ 15-Second Speed Sprints and Paced Practice drills.
  - ✓ Common letter combinations and special hand drills.
- Assess speed and accuracy on a 5-minute timed writing.

A. WARMUP

Accuracy 1 When did that quick brown fox jump over the very lazy dogs? 12
Technique: Home Row 2 sales fled dad's sheds self sags add heals jags ladle salad 24
Speed 3 Put your hand up if you know how to deal with the rude man. 36
  1 | 2 | 3 | 4 | 5 | 6 | 7 | 8 | 9 | 10 | 11 | 12

B. PRETEST-PRACTICE-POSTTEST: COMMON LETTER COMBINATIONS
PRETEST Take a 1-minute timed writing, pushing moderately for speed.

4   We need advance assurance that we have the votes to 11
5 pass the sales tax measure when it moves to the floor of 22
6 the House. We should continue to confer on the concept and 34
7 perhaps to conduct a straw poll for further guidance. 44
  1 | 2 | 3 | 4 | 5 | 6 | 7 | 8 | 9 | 10 | 11 | 12

**PRACTICE
Common Letter
Combinations**

es 8 dues does boxes these Bess tapes bores bless hoes ukes ires
9 pies pest mesa zesty guest mess ages times quest comes cues
10 votes nest hies peso dyes clues moves races byes ales taxes
11 takes mixes sales bakes gazes cures oozes rests notes trees

con 12 conceit contrite continue icon beacon falcon connive confer
13 confide concur console conceal concept content confess cone
14 confused conquest conserve scone conduct sconce concise con
15 conduit conch contain contend condor consult convoy contort

ance 16 fragrance nuisance attendance imbalance financed imbalanced
17 severance sustenance assurance advanced instance assistance
18 appearance allowance guidance vigilance poignance dominance
19 glance chance balance vengeance ambulance refinance advance

POSTTEST Repeat the Pretest. *Goal:* Improve speed and accuracy.

C. 15-SECOND SPEED SPRINTS

Goal: Increase your speed on each retyping of the same sentence.

20 When the day is very hot, we like to swim in the cold pool.
21 If you hold tight to an ice pack, it will help you so much.
22 The sea was cold, but she was too keen to surf to stay out.
23 When we meet, I will ask you to read the mail they sent us.

Accuracy

Goals

• Build accuracy on:
 ✓ Corresponding-finger and confusable keys.
 ✓ Spelling.
 ✓ Alphabetic, vertical, and symbol reaches.

A. WARMUP

Accuracy	1 High zinc expense very quickly bankrupted a famous jeweler.	12
Technique: SHIFT Keys	2 Gladys Hall tried. Ivan Jacobs might. Kristen Lawson could.	24
Speed	3 I do like dogs and cats, but a nice pet for me is the best.	36

  1 | 2 | 3 | 4 | 5 | 6 | 7 | 8 | 9 | 10 | 11 | 12

B. PRETEST-PRACTICE-POSTTEST: CORRESPONDING-FINGER KEYS
PRETEST Take a 1-minute timed writing, pushing moderately for speed.

4	For meeting her sales quota, Ava received an award of	11
5	a trip to Qatar. Will she go in January or in May? It will	23
6	amaze me if she doesn't opt to add a side trip to Haifa to	35
7	visit her friends Ralph and Eliza and/or to visit Howard.	46

  1 | 2 | 3 | 4 | 5 | 6 | 7 | 8 | 9 | 10 | 11 | 12

PRACTICE
Corresponding Fingers

A Finger
8 agape aorta amaze sauna tzar Jan Qatar papa array razor cab
9 quad basal pasta Samoa dad zeta Aqaba mafia baa Howard java
10 Tampa azure Macie Ava abash adze raze parka May Mabel quack
11 naval Bad razz lazy Matt aha quit act add qualm quart salad

; Finger
12 popping; per par pie spa Pam? opt may/can pay Pat? gap pop;
13 asp tip lip per/a gyp pry; pap pet; Rupert paw pep Poe? ply
14 Daphne rap Phil? nip cup psi pet ups pix zap Ralph pol spa;
15 pry; imp sap pry sop phi lend/loan set/sit pot; pit on/onto

A and ; Fingers
16 madam Poe per/a await nip ply; laze sap spa; pro award maze
17 quota ajar quake per; papa gala mania Poe? fizzy Tip? quack
18 pod Pam Pete? Aye pin; Eliza pap Haifa apt aha lip phi; gap
19 llama quad tip Qatar amass aqua radar paw Pele? imp Dad pat

POSTTEST Repeat the Pretest. *Goal*: Improve speed and accuracy.

C. BUSINESS SPELLING

These spelling words are from a list of the most used and most misspelled words in business writing. Study the words that cause you problems.

20 courses brochure whether inquiries equitable simultaneously
21 negotiations complement adequately definite its accumulated
22 excessive laboratory further anniversary essential canceled
23 dependents environmental commensurate carrying installation

D. SYMBOL PRACTICE

Return your fingers immediately to home-row position after typing each of these top-row symbols.

24 Sokolov* Han & Hsu sngo@az.gov Parker* 212% Noe & Ray #1-20
25 #8 nut $1 boo-boo Harrison* add-on (lair) aho@cs.com (lace)
26 6% A.D.-B.C. Owens & Young $2 baby-sit (lamb) West & Little
27 (lady) $1.09 rho@cs.com $1.04 Riley & Dow (laid) 268% (lad)

E. PRETEST-PRACTICE-POSTTEST: CONCENTRATION
Take a 1-minute timed writing, pushing moderately for speed.

PRETEST

Type the Pretest exactly as shown, but type the sentences below from right to left.

28   It may be difficult to avoid run-on sentences if you   11
29 type a sentence like this: ".secnetnes no-nur diovA." And   22
30 although we know what an adjective is, it is confusing to   34
31 think of it as ".nuonorp ro nuon a seifidom evitcejda nA."   46

     1 | 2 | 3 | 4 | 5 | 6 | 7 | 8 | 9 | 10 | 11 | 12

PRACTICE   **Reverse Typing**   Short Sentences

32 .secnetnes no-nur diovA
33 .serugif ni slamiced etirW
34 .gnitirw nehw stifeneb redaer ssertS
35 .nuonorp ro nuon a seifidom evitcejda nA

Medium-Length Sentences

36 .ecnetnes a snigeb taht rebmun a tuo llepS
37 .gnieb fo etats a ro noitca sesserpxe brev A
38 .nuonorp ro nuon rehtona semaner evitisoppa nA
39 .skram noitautcnup desu netfo tsom eht era sammoC

Long Sentences

40 .nuonorp ro nuon eht erofeb emoc syawla snoitisoperP
41 .redaer eht ediug ot pam daor a sa sevres noitautcnuP
42 .nosrep a fo sdrow tcaxe eht dnuora skram noitatouq esU
43 .etairporppa eb yam noitisoperp a htiw ecnetnes a gnidnE

POSTTEST

Repeat the Pretest. *Goal:* Improve speed and accuracy.

F. PUNCTUATION PRACTICE

Eyes on copy!

44 ash: Danger! Dec. bawl, am, Dave, stow; 1/9 kid, aid, Leon;
45 Now? Break? Drive! Hear? neat; lacy, Oct. pink; Walk? must;
46 Taxi? shall/will Here? rare; sack; he, pond; room; No! qty.
47 Drink? pie; div. "peal" dep't Call? dad's Lucy; lack, only;

48 film, bats, axed, 4/10 att. Where? lab, Angry? whsle. gave,
49 lost; mfg. asst. 13/24 Safe! act, pain; acre, soon; Escape?
50 lazy, "peck" Well? egg, cont'd camp, ring; Assn. line; New?
51 post; In! stem; "peek" First? skin; baby, don't none; save;

TAKE A BREAK!

ISAK says …

Hold your arms out to the sides and make small circles, first clockwise, then counterclockwise. Relax. Now repeat, making large circles.

D. MAP+: ALPHABET

Follow the software instructions for this exercise to improve accuracy.

E. PRETEST-PRACTICE-POSTTEST: CONFUSABLE KEYS

PRETEST

Pay special attention to these consecutive-finger reaches that often get confused.

Take a 1-minute timed writing, pushing moderately for speed.

24	The new manager will look to solve a lot of issues by	12
25	proposing fresh and powerful innovations. Please feel free	24
26	to look deeply within your own departments for cuts, since	35
27	you must get used to a whole new management structure.	46

1 | 2 | 3 | 4 | 5 | 6 | 7 | 8 | 9 | 10 | 11 | 12

PRACTICE
Consecutive Fingers

de-ed

28 creed deter lied deft decoy bleed deaf cede abide edge hide
29 yodel axed blade used redo derby bide lode defer deity sped
30 boxed mode fed biped breed decaf zoned edger glade died ode
31 deed video desk chide debug cadet bred deep den death alder

ol-lo

32 carol wool idol cold lo sold lock loot lord extol lone look
33 bolt fool lot pole lox troll lop solve volt load Colin loom
34 whole fold tool loam bolo polyp dolt Dolly loath loss polar
35 old local stole lout lost louse lotto jolt loupe logic polo

fr-rf

36 frond perform Frank fearful saffron frail French free frown
37 carfare freedom fracas fringe colorful freak frenzy frantic
38 affront frolic fry underfed serf dwarf frugal frost freckle
39 perfume powerful alfredo airfield earful fresh frozen froze

POSTTEST

Repeat the Pretest. *Goal*: Improve speed and accuracy.

F. REACH DRILLS: VERTICAL REACHES

st and *ly*

40 stout belly stow stem lynx crust dryly just coyly nest idly
41 must last rest jest steep pest pasta dully rely rusty stone
42 style least bully stalk stand steer gusty stair truly musty
43 exist ugly sly stern newly stag stuff stall twist taste lye

Vertical reaches move from one row to the adjacent row.

ar and *ul*

44 darn weary dart mulch party heard molar foul army argue bar
45 fare wharf larva arbor art bulb drear cull ardor bark Maria
46 barn diary earn Marge pearl hare tardy dull scar marsh warm
47 dear shear ovary bulk liar march could stare lull ark armed

G. MAP+: SYMBOLS

Follow the software instructions for this exercise to improve accuracy.

TECHNIQUE TIP

ISAK says ...

Sit so that all body angles are slightly more than 90 degrees: (a) shoulders, hips, and knees; (b) shoulder, elbow, and wrist; and (c) hips, knees, and feet.

Technique

Goals

- Improve technique on nonprinting, number, symbol, and punctuation keys.
- Improve concentration.

A. WARMUP

Accuracy	1	Janet moved their psychology quiz to next week for Roberta.	12
Technique: Substitutions	2	d-s ads studs sad side disks suds dash sided sends sod dish	24
Speed	3	Walk as fast as you can go and look out for that last step.	36

1 | 2 | 3 | 4 | 5 | 6 | 7 | 8 | 9 | 10 | 11 | 12

B. PRETEST-PRACTICE-POSTTEST: NONPRINTING KEYS

PRETEST

Take a 1-minute timed writing, pushing moderately for speed.

Backspace to correct all errors as you type.

4	Rosa Wood and Mack Mead drove Rosa's Ford Focus to	10
5	the mall, where Rosa purchased a pair of Thom McAn shoes	22
6	and Mack purchased two Izod shirts that he plans to wear	33
7	when he flies to Oahu in June or July on United Airlines.	45

1 | 2 | 3 | 4 | 5 | 6 | 7 | 8 | 9 | 10 | 11 | 12

PRACTICE
Nonprinting Keys

LEFT SHIFT Key

8 Newt Hamm Hess Mead Ubon Mack Lent Oahu Lena Ursa Ives Jesu
9 Leon Iggy Herb Jeff Marc Izzy Hals Kali Kane Kent Iran Iris
10 Otto Yank Pena Isis Hadj Mary Oslo Haru Urdu Nero Kral Levi
11 Nast Marx Hugh Palu Jean Utes Oran Lear Izod Laos Parr Pele

RIGHT SHIFT Key

12 Ames Glen Zulu Dona Anne Roma Chad Wolf Burr Rita Colt Cohn
13 Goya Elam Gish Fido Wise Emil Cola Tony Goth Guam Rowe Alps
14 Rosa Wood Buck Chen Ford Sikh Ritz Finn Amex Enid Shui Elks
15 Cuba Dunn Wilt Rose Anna Thom Dior Emma Toby Rice Fisk Fiji

BACKSPACE Key

When you reach the Backspace sign (←), backspace 1 time and then type the letter that follows.

16 are←k mad←n hot←p nag←p gym←p leg←i flu←y aid←l has←m dab←y
17 dab←m mob←m kid←n met←n zig←p art←m inn←k job←y rid←p she←y
18 car←p rig←m gee←l rag←m mow←p sob←n fro←y gas←p max←y wig←n
19 bag←m wow←n woe←k wag←y ski←y pub←n ill←k hoe←g dew←n hot←p

POSTTEST

Repeat the Pretest. *Goal*: Improve speed and accuracy.

C. NUMBER PRACTICE

Press TAB to move from column to column in each row.

Eyes on copy!

20	741	177	859	880	726	592	346	902	772	113
21	350	425	414	712	431	830	889	505	806	970
22	683	228	433	522	174	966	718	852	405	960
23	415	126	722	326	679	240	840	615	101	832

Technique

Goals

- Improve technique on the nonprinting, number, symbol, and punctuation keys.
- Improve concentration.

A. WARMUP

Accuracy | 1 | I just sent back oxygen equipment of the size we delivered. | 12
Technique: Substitutions | 2 | e-r reed rye rare eerie rely err rear care emery core rarer | 24
Speed | 3 | She does like to knit; she will make you a gift if you ask. | 36

1 | 2 | 3 | 4 | 5 | 6 | 7 | 8 | 9 | 10 | 11 | 12

B. PRETEST-PRACTICE-POSTTEST: NONPRINTING KEYS

PRETEST

Take a 1-minute timed writing, pushing moderately for speed.

Backspace to correct all errors as you type.

4   Lena Byrd wore a new Dior gown at the opening of the | 12
5 new Goya exhibit in Bonn. Her son, Mark Ford, is a senior | 23
6 next year at Penn State. He wants to drive his Ford sedan | 35
7 to the Florida Keys in June. Maybe Lena would prefer July. | 46

1 | 2 | 3 | 4 | 5 | 6 | 7 | 8 | 9 | 10 | 11 | 12

PRACTICE
Nonprinting Keys

LEFT SHIFT Key

8 Java Pate Iran Hale Yael Odin Kahn Yank Oran Jesu Lacy Hadj
9 Mark Matt Utah Marc Lego Ovid Penn Nami Haru Manx Page Nate
10 Keys Palu Mari Ubay Leif Ivan Hals Uris Iggy Oahu Lena Kara
11 Kazu Iraq Otos Jane Pena Maya Ural Mack Pele Nast Kent Owen

RIGHT SHIFT Key

12 Ruby Sikh Riga Elia Dior Guru Ella Finn Bull Ford Fiji Bonn
13 Soto Rose Tina Byrd Bose Goth Boer Ruiz Boyd Quan Alex Giza
14 Wolf Ross Aida Dodd Bill Suva Roma Elam Toby Guam Shaw Goya
15 Tony Fish Rico Dona Rowe Togo Zion Dima Fido Fitz Rolf Elks

BACKSPACE Key

When you reach the Backspace sign (←), backspace 1 time and then type the letter that follows.

16 pub←n cot←p bud←m tag←m par←n was←y hug←m job←y gig←n has←y
17 his←p sag←p hid←m dad←m are←k par←n box←n gee←m bag←m ill←k
18 ire←k nut←n gas←p nag←p bog←o dew←n sue←m put←p vat←n mad←n
19 nix←p her←n has←m mob←m and←y ice←y get←m pod←i toe←n wag←y

POSTTEST

Repeat the Pretest. *Goal:* Improve speed and accuracy.

C. NUMBER PRACTICE

Press TAB to move from column to column in each row.

20	302	100	203	949	298	394	401	472	547	461
21	820	405	935	813	829	897	706	663	588	505
22	228	346	713	578	821	102	507	433	749	351
23	867	189	612	200	355	621	944	227	162	653

D. MAP+: ALPHABET
Follow the software instructions for this exercise to improve accuracy.

E. PRETEST-PRACTICE-POSTTEST: CONFUSABLE KEYS

PRETEST

Pay special attention to these keys that are often substituted for each other.

Take a 1-minute timed writing, pushing moderately for speed.

24	Terry found four typos in one story in our literature	11
25	book today. He spoke to our instructor, who said she keeps	23
26	track of these errors and will report them to the proper	34
27	party. It looks like that is now being taken care of.	45

1 | 2 | 3 | 4 | 5 | 6 | 7 | 8 | 9 | 10 | 11 | 12

PRACTICE
Substitutions

s-k
28 leaks whisk swank risks ducks knobs shank skews tanks sleek
29 spoke takes perks keeps dunks masks wakes beaks smoke pecks
30 lurks kilts stuck looks skill kites sakes cocks backs shake
31 spunk knits books slick banks tasks skimp frisk decks flask

y-t
32 thy yeast nifty itchy story patty tidy sty ratty amity tray
33 lofty tangy witty today style tardy dirty Betty bitsy putty
34 Terry booty party fifty kitty rusty artsy pithy gusty Tyler
35 fatty toy ditzy stay try deity tying aptly dusty typos tyke

r-u
36 drub four rouse lurch upper auger ruse crude purr grub rule
37 lurid fruit usher cruet argue cur truss our Ruth trump purl
38 sugar ulcer urn murky truck fury hour truly quart rue virus
39 grout incur drunk curry runt brunt brush ecru rut rub lunar

POSTTEST

Repeat the Pretest. *Goal*: Improve speed and accuracy.

F. REACH DRILLS: JUMP REACHES

ct and mi
40 octane middle timid admit mite midway misled mix exact mine
41 actual insect expect effect deduct mind active taming erect
42 remiss doctor act mishap atomic mild mitt sector swami tact
43 milk simile comic fact evict edict remind might aspect mice

Jump reaches move from the upper row to the lower row or vice versa.

ze and mp
44 eczema tamp cramps compel glaze daze hemp umpire temp cramp
45 laze tamper seize limp chump imply slump doze dampen seized
46 mumps comp gaze empty tempt frozen champ ampere trump dozen
47 impugn sample haze zeal nymph bumpy thump ramp temper amaze

G. MAP+: SYMBOLS
Follow the software instructions for this exercise to improve accuracy.

TECHNIQUE TIP

ISAK says …

Sit so that all body angles are slightly more than 90 degrees: (a) shoulders, hips, and knees; (b) shoulder, elbow, and wrist; and (c) hips, knees, and feet.

D. SYMBOL PRACTICE

Keep your eyes on the copy as you type these top-row symbols.

24 #9 jib 697% sngo@az.gov (lag) aho@cs.com add-on 233% (lair)
25 Eng & Morris 3# of sand (lady) Owens & Young bad-badly 212%
26 Batista* aorr@cs.com rorr@ua.edu Berry* Noe & Ray 3# of wax
27 4# of ham baby-sit 970% 6% $2 $1 268% A.D.-B.C. cli@bsu.edu

E. PRETEST-PRACTICE-POSTTEST: CONCENTRATION
Take a 1-minute timed writing, pushing moderately for speed.

PRETEST

Pay attention to what you're typing.

28   If you are hungry in the Netherlands, you might say,   12
29 "Ik heb honger." In the Philippines, you would say, "Ako   23
30 ay gutom," and in Portugal, "Estou com fome." Closest to   34
31 the English phrase is the German "Ich bin hungrig."   45

    1 | 2 | 3 | 4 | 5 | 6 | 7 | 8 | 9 | 10 | 11 | 12

PRACTICE   *Short Phrases*
Foreign Phrases

32 Italian: Ho fame.
33 Basque: Gose am I.
34 Latin: Ego esuriit.
35 Dutch: Ik heb honger.

Medium-Length Phrases

36 English: I am hungry.
37 Danish: Jeg er sulten.
38 Spanish: Tengo hambre.
39 Filipino: Ako ay gutom.

Long Phrases

40 Indonesian: Saya lapar.
41 Afrikaans: Ek is honger.
42 German: Ich bin hungrig.
43 Portuguese: Estou com fome.

POSTTEST

Repeat the Pretest. *Goal:* Improve speed and accuracy.

F. PUNCTUATION PRACTICE

Eyes on copy!

44 pile: When? room; Apr. Who? led, dig, Corp. sat; load; Gas?
45 card, tab; ear, Now! pie; pin; Dance? How? Ohio; knew, aid,
46 pump; bays, past; Feb. that/which pain; Escape? Busy? Stay!
47 Ltd. intl. hog, Ed.D. cans, pink; main: Tue. att. Ms. sing;

48 path; Exciting? Always! calm, caps, egg, "peep" New? Drink!
49 R.N. did, acct. Inc. pp. pad: www.cnn.com/ do, Candy? noun;
50 P.O. Phil; Full? pack; stub; let; Sun. Lynn; Walk? Against?
51 acts, cave, Rome; son; cont. ppd. lube: enc. c.o.d. Danger!

ISAK says ...

TAKE A BREAK!

Hold your arms out to the sides and make small circles, first clockwise, then counterclockwise. Relax. Now repeat, making the largest circles possible.

Accuracy

Goals

- Build accuracy on:
  - ✓ Corresponding-finger and confusable keys.
  - ✓ Spelling.
  - ✓ Alphabetic, jump, and symbol reaches.

A. WARMUP

Accuracy	1	Vic found Jack was right: Pam was being quite lazy and lax.	12
Technique: SHIFT Keys	2	Sonia Torres saw. Uday Vila is. Wu Xie may. Yvonne Zoe can.	24
Speed	3	When we hear the bell ring, we must then put down our pens.	36

1 | 2 | 3 | 4 | 5 | 6 | 7 | 8 | 9 | 10 | 11 | 12

B. PRETEST-PRACTICE-POSTTEST: CORRESPONDING-FINGER KEYS

PRETEST

Take a 1-minute timed writing, pushing moderately for speed.

4	Once Jackie returns from Waikiki and Kauai, she will	11
5	be done with her travels and was kind enough to offer her	22
6	free help during the brisk selling season if Alec or Rick	34
7	should become sick. Her offer may come in handy then.	45

1 | 2 | 3 | 4 | 5 | 6 | 7 | 8 | 9 | 10 | 11 | 12

PRACTICE
Corresponding Fingers

D Finger

8 odd done cad deny dime Ted code Ned Alec wade doe lace lead
9 Clem acme deal Eric cote etch curd acre desk duet coke dude
10 ewe cent tend ache cone bead cute cape wed dud Eve fee held
11 cede cane free dodo once fend come Chet ecru cord duel dele

K Finger

12 ark flick eke, strike dike sickle sky, Nike pike sky Mikado
13 Minsk Jackie milk Rick spike kill kimono brisk dickie brink
14 troika frisk skid kind skill blink wok kite kit haiku eking
15 kith kin Kauai whisk uke, wick whisky ark, ink knit Waikiki

D and K Fingers

16 birdie icier hick trick binding Mickey wick fiction keeping
17 lick abiding tiepin sicken midi hijack disdain iodide flick
18 kiddie tickle tick icily sick Dick knack deficit pick idiot
19 nickel codicil bricked incise aiding biscuit bidding wicket

POSTTEST

Repeat the Pretest. *Goal*: Improve speed and accuracy.

C. BUSINESS SPELLING

These spelling words are from a list of the most used and most misspelled words in business writing. Study the words that cause you problems.

20 suite reimburse facilities associated derived alleged entry
21 herein ledger accidents criteria jewelers solely supplement
22 closing achievement asbestos principal breaker universities
23 variance priority capacity discussing existence hereinafter

Speed

Goals

• Build speed on:
  ✓ 15-Second Speed Sprints and Paced Practice drills.
  ✓ Common letter combinations and special hand drills.
• Assess speed and accuracy on a 5-minute timed writing.

A. WARMUP

Accuracy 1 Five wobbly jockeys fixed the four gleaming bronze plaques. 12
Technique: Home Row 2 sad; leas gash; jells "dad" flak shall fall addles ash keg; 24
Speed 3 The cell does not ring well, so you may miss a call or two. 36

  1 | 2 | 3 | 4 | 5 | 6 | 7 | 8 | 9 | 10 | 11 | 12

B. PRETEST-PRACTICE-POSTTEST: COMMON LETTER COMBINATIONS

PRETEST Take a 1-minute timed writing, pushing moderately for speed.

4   In order to comment on the new ruling about our new 11
5 merger agreement, we are going to have to be very careful 22
6 to mention it the moment they enter the discussions and 33
7 bring in our best negotiators to implement our strategies. 45

  1 | 2 | 3 | 4 | 5 | 6 | 7 | 8 | 9 | 10 | 11 | 12

PRACTICE
Common Letter Combinations

er 8 order eerier beer paper Mercer merger lever veer very lower
9 terrier ever water enter buyer eager inner dozer goer toner
10 pier verger doer peril pert derby caterer biker deter mover
11 opera owner herd herder ruler tiger tern ferry perkier hers

ing 12 ruling boxing dying dazing hating zinging king sizing bring
13 diving going sling ring eating citing flying zing lingering
14 aiming seeing acting drying ruing hiring eying owing making
15 bringing fringe stinging binge asking crying slinging vying

ment 16 agreement battlement fragment implement annulment alignment
17 determent pimento deferment rudiment mental garment segment
18 mentor mention ointment allotment armament cement amusement
19 condiment moment lament comment detriment tenement liniment

POSTTEST Repeat the Pretest. *Goal:* Improve speed and accuracy.

C. 15-SECOND SPEED SPRINTS

Goal: Increase your speed on each retyping of the same sentence.

20 If we go too far past our turn, just toss out the old maps.
21 Push and pull with all you have got if you plan to make it.
22 She must find the one file by nine, or we will lose it all.
23 When the bulb goes too dim, it can be hard to read my book.

D. SPECIAL HAND DRILLS

Left-Hand Words

Maintain the nontyping hand in home-row position.

24 debts gates ears wears tab fear aware fees free Edward care
25 tea feet eraser wasted rarest gave greeted average bet gage
26 faster reserves degree Caesar stated Bart reader wages text
27 revere raw cartage breezes dressed grader grew tree careers

Right-Hand Words

28 lip Honolulu ill Yukon Jill hymn oil join hum hill monopoly
29 mom Ohio pink John lump pin oink Jim you hypo polo yolk hop
30 onion plunk look Lou phylum inn Jimmy honk ply I'm puny phi
31 minimum pony mum hominy inky ink mil mink pop milk ploy ump

Left- and Right-Hand Words

32 waters Joplin Bess tract fear face sets Stewart swear dress
33 pony arts pull adverbs phi inn Kohl Fred degree loop states
34 onion star serves added read deed dated arrears rear beasts
35 sew Seward age saves tea Phil red sea access linkup created

E. 30-SECOND PROGRESSIVE PRACTICE

Follow the software directions for this exercise to improve keystroking speed and accuracy.

F. 5-MINUTE TIMED WRITING

Take two 5-minute timed writings.

Goal: Push moderately for speed while keeping your accuracy under control.

36   You should not wait until you have graduated from   10
37 college to begin saving money. Even if you have student   21
38 loans to repay, you should begin an organized system of   33
39 regular savings today. Your economic survival depends upon   44
40 it. First, you need to save enough money to ensure that you   56
41 have funds equal to three to six months of living expenses   68
42 in case you lose your job. You should make doing this your   80
43 very first savings goal because it is the most important.   92
44   Then, you can put money aside for short-term goals,   102
45 such as buying a new suit, mid-term goals, such as buying   114
46 a used car next year, and long-term goals, such as putting   126
47 a down payment on a house or condominium. Finally, remember   138
48 that you will not likely be working for the rest of your   149
49 life, so you will require a nest egg to retire on.   159
50   See a bank representative or investment advisor for   170
51 the best advice about investing. You want to avoid getting   182
52 investment advice from someone who has anything specific to   194
53 sell you, such as a stockbroker.   200

1 | 2 | 3 | 4 | 5 | 6 | 7 | 8 | 9 | 10 | 11 | 12

TAKE A BREAK!

ISAK says ...

Hold your shoulders with your palms and rotate your elbows ten times clockwise, then ten times counterclockwise.

D. SPECIAL HAND DRILLS

Alternate-Hand Words
24 spend Helen forms Lakeland apt cork Claudia lay fix map toe
25 Dixie goals flaps fuel big clay such laugh bow Kay Jay firm
26 sod tie dial paid spent rock if Ivory cut of Burma hang man
27 is downtown the goal Rufus England us oak visit height city

Double-Letter Words
28 hook broom apple deer Barry gross heed spree inn spell week
29 Ross funny Jimmy press Anna creek root happy ball kill buzz
30 swell error cliff too occur Billy bull Emma allow bass Dunn
31 Lloyd proof Tommy look feet noon took Jeff motto merry hall

Home-Row Words
32 salad gal's jells slake gas leaks fake seas sage age: sleds
33 shag feds gaffs gal ads deal ladled adages "jag" dash lake:
34 flasks kales fakes "has" shags shaded head shake falls asks
35 ask leaf's deals slags slash glad; Hades shells shall Degas

E. PACED PRACTICE
Follow the software directions for this exercise to improve keystroking speed and accuracy.

F. 5-MINUTE TIMED WRITING

Take two 5-minute timed writings.

Goal: Push moderately for speed while keeping your accuracy under control.

36   When you are required to give a presentation in class,   11
37 do you, for example, feel faint, get shaking hands or a   22
38 rapid heartbeat, or tend to speak quickly and in a high-   34
39 pitched voice?   37
40   If so, you are suffering from stage fright. Research   47
41 has shown that having to make a presentation is the number   59
42 one fear of most people, even more than a fear of death for   71
43 many people. Fortunately, this phobia is not difficult to   83
44 overcome.   85
45   In this case, the best defense is a good offense, that   96
46 is, you should overprepare. There is no such thing as too   108
47 much practice. The more familiar you are with the content   119
48 of your presentation and the more time you spend practicing   131
49 it, the better you will be able to focus on the delivery   143
50 when you make your presentation.   149
51   Being just a little nervous, however, is a good thing,   160
52 because it gets the adrenaline flowing. If you find that   172
53 you have to make a lot of presentations, you might want to   184
54 join an organization like Toastmasters that will give you   195
55 help in giving speeches.   200

   1 | 2 | 3 | 4 | 5 | 6 | 7 | 8 | 9 | 10 | 11 | 12

ISAK says ...

TECHNIQUE TIP
Keep your forearms, wrists, and hands in a straight line as you type.

Speed

Goals

- Build speed on:
  - ✓ 15-Second Speed Sprints and 30-Second Progressive Practice drills.
  - ✓ Common letter combinations and special hand drills.
- Assess speed and accuracy on a 5-minute timed writing.

A. WARMUP

Accuracy	1	Two jobbers quickly analyzed the pecks of mixed vegetables.	12
Technique: Upper Row	2	petite trip typewriter rote wept quitter root opt wiper two	24
Speed	3	Call her at noon to talk over the plan we made at the cafe.	36

1 | 2 | 3 | 4 | 5 | 6 | 7 | 8 | 9 | 10 | 11 | 12

B. PRETEST-PRACTICE-POSTTEST: COMMON LETTER COMBINATIONS

PRETEST Take a 1-minute timed writing, pushing moderately for speed.

4	Closing on the old Macon estate may be complex and	10
5	complicated, and we'll need a competent realtor to compose	22
6	the language of the contract and to mediate any disputes	34
7	once the deal is done. I predict a long, drawn-out debate.	45

1 | 2 | 3 | 4 | 5 | 6 | 7 | 8 | 9 | 10 | 11 | 12

PRACTICE
Common Letter
Combinations

on 8 money on Don font ton solon futon wonk melon crony cone Ono
9 bony prong one bacon scion pond month rayon only once colon
10 prone gong sonar honor long moon condone pontoon neon ionic
11 irony pony bonbon phony iron donation nylon Macon pong done

ate 12 elevate notate operate goatee actuate sedate fixate citrate
13 mediate palate state isolate satiate radiate debate prorate
14 cognate opiate imitate treated inflate irate mutate greater
15 animate sate estate eaten hydrate gate seated cater narrate

comp 16 compact complicated accomplice compose computation comprise
17 subcompact complex competent compartment compute compensate
18 compliment compound complaint compare comprehend complexity
19 compel comparison compliance encompass composure compendium

POSTTEST Repeat the Pretest. *Goal*: Improve speed and accuracy.

C. 15-SECOND SPEED SPRINTS

Goal: Increase your speed on each retyping of the same sentence.

20 His name is kind of lame, but he will just keep it for now.
21 If you go look on my desk now, you will find what you seek.
22 Put your hand up if you know how to deal with the rude man.
23 The chair is very nice; I wish I had two of them to sit on.

Accuracy

Goals

- Build accuracy on:
  ✓ Corresponding-finger and confusable keys.
  ✓ Spelling.
  ✓ Alphabetic, jump, and number reaches.

A. WARMUP

Accuracy	1 In a den below, six crafty judges provoke the amazed queen.	12
Technique: Lower Row	2 zinc comma Nancy? beacon Bob, convoy ammine conch bemoaning	24
Speed	3 Do not drop that item; if you do, it will not work for you.	36

1 | 2 | 3 | 4 | 5 | 6 | 7 | 8 | 9 | 10 | 11 | 12

B. PRETEST-PRACTICE-POSTTEST: CORRESPONDING FINGERS

PRETEST

Take a 1-minute timed writing, pushing moderately for speed.

4 For more than twenty years, Timothy taught tourism to	11
5 many students who wanted to get out of their college debt	23
6 by starting their own businesses. He taught them how to	34
7 apply to a venture fund to get started in hospitality.	45

1 | 2 | 3 | 4 | 5 | 6 | 7 | 8 | 9 | 10 | 11 | 12

PRACTICE
Corresponding Fingers

F Finger

8 bar gate rib tot thug gulf far rare beef get gear rift Beth
9 agog robe Rita rag rat goof rub roar Viv off tiff stag Cobb
10 veer debt rove err bang tar bulb tact roof fry rot rave for
11 vat beg ebb gut aft toga Bob art vet vast frog buff gag tug

J Finger

12 mum mom bum chin fund jury urn name bush buy Maui many dumb
13 Juan hump Judy Jim horn harm inn memo mug any nut ugly nine
14 Amy rum jug hen mind fun Nan hut Jane Hugh Jan noun hub gym
15 mud jump ham hem yam yen jut jay joy jam gnu Utah undo main

F and J Fingers

16 grungy venting finery gurney tinting beneath binary fluting
17 tankful fudging bypath burning reentry bonbon thrash gnarly
18 tugging tourism Timothy rhythm thirdly taught twenty gluten
19 tantrum fishery venture vinery rupture ringing ranging guru

POSTTEST

Repeat the Pretest. *Goal*: Improve speed and accuracy.

C. BUSINESS SPELLING

These spelling words are from a list of the most used and most misspelled words in business writing. Study the words that cause you problems.

20 edition distribution restaurant component maintenance acres
21 designate receiving audit perusing co-op analyses municipal
22 calendar encourage sufficient material indicating aggregate
23 negotiated occurred mining electricians issuance compliance

D. SYMBOL PRACTICE

Keep your eyes on the copy as you type these top-row symbols.

24 also-ran $1.14 baby-sit Ely & Foy 6% qli@bsu.edu 3# of sand
25 729% A-frame (lack) Berry* $1.09 (lair) 3# of wax Harrison*
26 Li & Ng, Inc. 212% all-day 57.2% (lain) 970% Sokolov* (lad)
27 7# of stew 932% $1.04 $0.34 #2 cap Mills & Ham 697% Santos*

E. PRETEST-PRACTICE-POSTTEST: CONCENTRATION
Take a 1-minute timed writing, pushing moderately for speed.

PRETEST

Concentrate on keeping your eyes on the copy as you type these foreign phrases.

28   Most of us are pleased to meet new people. In Mexico   11
29 City, we might say, "Me alegra encontrarme con usted" to a   23
30 new acquaintance, whereas in Heidelberg, we would tell a   34
31 new acquaintance, "Ich freue mich, Sie kennen zu lernen."   46
    1 | 2 | 3 | 4 | 5 | 6 | 7 | 8 | 9 | 10 | 11 | 12

PRACTICE   Short Phrases
Foreign Phrases

32 Basque: zu bete pozik nago.
33 Filipino: Ako makilala kayo.
34 Latin: Placet in occursum tui.
35 Dutch: Ik ben blij u te ontmoeten.

Medium-Length Phrases

36 English: I am pleased to meet you.
37 Estonian: Mul on hea meel kohtuda.
38 Swahili: Nafurahi kukutana na wewe.
39 Indonesian: Saya senang bertemu Anda

Long Phrases

40 Spanish: Me alegra encontrarme con usted.
41 French: Je suis heureux de vous rencontrer.
42 Italian: Sono lieto di incontrarmi con voi.
43 German: Ich freue mich, Sie kennen zu lernen.

POSTTEST

Repeat the Pretest. *Goal:* Improve speed and accuracy.

F. PUNCTUATION PRACTICE

Eyes on copy!

44 in, In? Duck! none; Ms. Out! came, 8/10 stop; Bus? Morning?
45 rust; one; Wed. net; dig, can, "peck" All! gov't ring; sat;
46 Inc. fed, i.e. mgt. avg. pat; "peg" nine; jog, former/first
47 acre, avid, bats, "peep" When? labs, ear, pack; elk, "peat"

48 Corp. sing; fwd. noon; have, Finish? cog, sack; Break? Yea!
49 big, flax, How? P.O. lab, bid, axed, axis, led, bath, palm;
50 Give? elf, Hot? let; am, incl. asst. some; equally/as Soon?
51 acid, load; Mack; knee, pad; near; Nothing? Well! beg, Mrs.

TECHNIQUE TIP

ISAK says ...

Type with a light touch and a steady rhythm.

D. MAP+: ALPHABET
Follow the software instructions for this exercise to improve accuracy.

E. PRETEST-PRACTICE-POSTTEST: CONFUSABLE KEYS

PRETEST

Pay special attention to these adjacent-finger reaches that often get confused.

Take a 1-minute timed writing, pushing moderately for speed.

24   What are the odds of our passing a motion that gives   11
25 each senior the option to ask for cash instead of consumer   23
26 goods? The point of the motion would be that then seniors   34
27 could save their cash for their choice of basic necessities. 46

    1 | 2 | 3 | 4 | 5 | 6 | 7 | 8 | 9 | 10 | 11 | 12

PRACTICE

Adjacent Fingers

oi-io

28 radio adjoin memoir broil point anoint iodide axiom koi bio
29 devoid lotion motion poi coif viola scion ionic notion riot
30 coin coil choice pious folio soil boil senior savior wooing
31 joist idiot oink dioxin biopsy odious ion olio option ratio

as-sa

32 vast safe abash pasta rash slash bass spas yeas salon paste
33 sable save sagas grasp gash blast dash astir boast sake gas
34 sodas basic asp spasm Judas cash basis tunas has sash leash
35 askew alas comas sat ask ascot salvo oasis sauté east colas

sd-ds

36 heads odds feeds suds rods goods bards wads binds eavesdrop
37 misdoing herds acids fads quads ads grads prods maids feuds
38 coeds bands duds toads tads nods girds raids lids aids kids
39 lauds bids lends misdeed winds rinds tends roads moods pads

POSTTEST

Repeat the Pretest. *Goal*: Improve speed and accuracy.

F. REACH DRILLS: JUMP REACHES

ct and mi

Jump reaches move from the upper row to the lower row or vice versa.

40 remind factor misery vomit abject mice misuse Mickey vermin
41 hectic domino select mien strict roomie simile doctor exact
42 tactic Arctic remiss insect direct victor amino family tact
43 affect mix effect induct timid midair octad mine act aspect

ze and mp

44 size dampen prize craze tramp booze tweeze dump breeze ooze
45 glaze bumper hazel tamp import gaze blaze lump seize frozen
46 nymph faze chump prompt lumpy primp Tampa damp impugn swamp
47 oomph maze zesty seized plump impel adze simply pump shrimp

G. MAP+: NUMBERS
Follow the software instructions for this exercise to improve accuracy.

TAKE A BREAK!

ISAK says ...

Standing at attention, breathe in while you bend backward and then breathe out as you return to the normal position. Then repeat, bending forward.

Technique

Goals

- Improve technique on the nonprinting, number, symbol, and punctuation keys.
- Improve concentration.

A. WARMUP

Accuracy	1 Those ten zebras quickly jumped high over the twelve foxes.	12
Technique: Double Letters	2 pool Bess fee Cobb apply lobby Scott miss Greek Jenny Peggy	24
Speed	3 I sent the memo to my boss, but I hope he does not read it.	36

1 | 2 | 3 | 4 | 5 | 6 | 7 | 8 | 9 | 10 | 11 | 12

B. PRETEST-PRACTICE-POSTTEST: NONPRINTING KEYS

PRETEST

Take a 1-minute timed writing, pushing moderately for speed. Type each sentence; then press TAB to move from column to column.

4 Let me stay.	Let's do it.	I like them.	Who is here?	10
5 I dare them.	Believe him.	Do not stay.	I was tired.	21
6 So be quiet.	Why not eat?	Take my bag.	Come to her.	31
7 He is tired.	Drop it now.	Here you go.	Why not her?	41

PRACTICE ENTER Key

Nonprinting Keys

Press ENTER after each word to format each word on a new line.

8 Rest. Guess. Outside. Drag. Super. Maybe. Lift. So? Beware.

9 Think. Play. Crazy. Vote. What? Answer. Sleep. Later. Down.

10 Jump. Explain. Proceed. Sorry. Yea! Cool. Leave. Ugh! Okay.

11 Granted. Whew! Nope. Continue. Beautiful. Sure. Good. Clap.

TAB Key

Type each word; then press TAB to move from column to column.

12 zombie	quint	zippy	already
13 affair	applaud	abase	ahead
14 abash	quotient	appeal	zooms
15 agenda	alfalfa	animal	quantify

SPACE BAR

16 Oh. What gives? I see. I know. Ed was up at one. Who knows?

17 When? Who does? I say I can. Who? Give it to me. Do it now.

Bounce the thumb quickly off the SPACE BAR.

18 She may do it. Help me. Don't do it now. Jo saw Al at home.

19 Here you go. I dare you. I am up. Why? Go. How? Step on it.

POSTTEST

Repeat the Pretest. *Goal:* Improve speed and accuracy.

C. NUMBER PRACTICE

Press TAB to move from column to column in each row.

20 813	549	560	151	944	555	342	590	802	397
21 947	933	224	906	192	697	197	211	300	612
22 622	748	146	620	756	402	835	243	231	584
23 112	744	226	202	388	446	438	961	248	815

Technique

29

Goals

- Improve technique on the nonprinting, number, symbol, and punctuation keys.
- Improve concentration.

A. WARMUP

Accuracy	1	Jack quietly exited the seven jazz groups by way of my map.	12
Technique: Transpositions	2	Ann nag|edge deed|ash say|on no|all lap|Etna tell|itch tide	24
Speed	3	I love to read in bed; I wish I knew of a good book to get.	36

1 | 2 | 3 | 4 | 5 | 6 | 7 | 8 | 9 | 10 | 11 | 12

B. PRETEST-PRACTICE-POSTTEST: NONPRINTING KEYS

PRETEST

Take a 1-minute timed writing, pushing moderately for speed. Type each sentence; then press TAB to move from column to column.

4	I dare them.	Let's do it.	Drop it now.	Key quickly.	10
5	Take my bag.	I saw a man.	When was it?	Is it alive?	21
6	He is tardy.	What was it?	We think so.	I was tired.	31
7	Come to her.	Why not her?	She is sick.	We are late.	41

PRACTICE
Nonprinting Keys

ENTER Key

Press ENTER after each word to format each word on a new line.

8 Slow. Bye. Translate. Shoot. Rush. Drive. Sip. Save. Smile.
9 Confirm. Talk. Danger! Beware. Proceed. Alas! Hit. Retreat.
10 Speak. Remember? Erase. Hi. Here. Sorry. No! Hike. Replace.
11 Promise? Swim. Bad. Ready? Inhale. Always! Attention. Heck.

TAB Key

Type each word; then press TAB to move from column to column.

12	quiver	areas	quantify	zapper
13	quarrel	zodiac	annual	zanier
14	attach	quibble	quota	quantity
15	adage	abash	airbag	queasy

SPACE BAR

Bounce the thumb quickly off the SPACE BAR.

16 We are up. What? I dare you. No one is to go. How dare you?
17 I see. One at a time. I can. I think so. Do not do it. Who?
18 Why? How much? Do it now. Mark it in red. How? I see an ax.
19 What gives? Give it to me. You may go on up. I know. We do.

POSTTEST

Repeat the Pretest. *Goal:* Improve speed and accuracy.

C. NUMBER PRACTICE

Press TAB to move from column to column in each row.

20	320	591	472	584	159	342	469	149	184	800
21	773	109	535	361	554	404	520	398	655	478
22	388	530	224	189	177	846	182	381	172	445
23	920	147	150	778	493	709	363	116	229	402

D. MAP+: ALPHABET
Follow the software instructions for this exercise to improve accuracy.

E. PRETEST-PRACTICE-POSTTEST: CONFUSABLE KEYS
Take a 1-minute timed writing, pushing moderately for speed.

PRETEST

Pay special attention to these keys that are often substituted for each other.

24	It might be rough for our team to maintain our growth	11
25	this year due to the weak economy. It would be ideal if we	22
26	were given a larger area in which to market our products,	34
27	but other regions have also sought larger territories.	45

1 | 2 | 3 | 4 | 5 | 6 | 7 | 8 | 9 | 10 | 11 | 12

PRACTICE
Substitutions

e-i 28 rinse merit spine tithe spire aegis miser dries image befit
29 given bride shine sepia inner vie ire tilde ideal emir ride
30 wire field vise swine tide Zaire bicep chide nice wine lied
31 brine quiet tiger feign yield slice being binge prime arise

g-h 32 chug night tight plight hog grouch height laugh huge hating
33 dinghy alight wright homage change hedge might rough ghetto
34 bought thug cough gopher hungry glitch hiking hunger trough
35 gush haggle sought gash hug fright eight hung eighth growth

a-e 36 eave haze Dale tame aerosol mate acne kale larvae area seam
37 year mane cage ape beam bare Caesar flea rake gaze lea case
38 beau peat weak Earl hare wane sane fake ahem heat earn gear
39 aloe heal era awe ear jade tape ale team Vera bead age dead

POSTTEST

Repeat the Pretest. *Goal*: Improve speed and accuracy.

F. REACH DRILLS: VERTICAL REACHES

st and ly 40 study gaily start daily frost stool slyly waist roost testy
41 stomp feast badly stilt early stock first sting jolly midst
42 doily fully stitch lowly aptly folly roast angst west jelly
43 post stub Billy stuff stem least oily best fist guest ghost

Vertical reaches move from one row to the adjacent row.

ar and ul 44 gull mulch mare care heart tulip bulb parka Marge pare arch
45 scull farm bark rule gear smear hull hoard start scar alarm
46 mark quart polar share wart soar dare annul weary czar near
47 are park par hare bard ultra lark truly ardor oar card bear

G. MAP+: NUMBERS
Follow the software instructions for this exercise to improve accuracy.

TAKE A BREAK!

ISAK says ...

With your left arm stretched out in front of you, with your right hand pull the left hand backward and hold for 10 seconds; then pull the left hand downward and hold for 10 seconds. Repeat with the right hand.

D. SYMBOL PRACTICE

Keep your eyes on the copy as you type these top-row symbols and return your fingers immediately to home-row position.

24 imply-infer aorr@cs.com Batista* 233% be-all958% Ngo & Ely
25 Ely & Foy age-old $1.68 A.D.-B.C. $1.04 (lake) 970% Santos*
26 also-ran (lair) qli@bsu.edu Shan* $1 boo-boo $2 rorr@ua.edu
27 add-on $1.68 Parker* Li & Ng, Inc. sngo@az.gov (laid) $1.09

E. PRETEST-PRACTICE-POSTTEST: CONCENTRATION
Take a 1-minute timed writing, pushing moderately for speed.

PRETEST

Type the Pretest exactly as shown, but type the Practice sentences below from right to left.

28   Longer words are more difficult to type in reverse   10
29 than are shorter words. For example, the word "confidently"   22
30 becomes "yltnedifnoc," "explanatory" becomes "yrotanalpxe,"   34
31 and "unnecessary" becomes "yrassecennu." How confusing!   45

    1 | 2 | 3 | 4 | 5 | 6 | 7 | 8 | 9 | 10 | 11 | 12

PRACTICE
Reverse Typing
Short Sentences

32 .yltnedifnoc etirW
33 .eciov evitca eht referP
34 .serugif ni segatnecrep etirW
35 .flesti yb esnes ekam tsum ecnetnes A

Medium-Length Sentences

36 .tcejbus larulp a htiw brev larulp a esU
37 .thguoht ni kaerb neddus a setacidni hsad A
38 .gnitirw ssenisub tsom ni snoitcejretni diovA
39 .lairetam yrotanalpxe esolcne ot sesehtnerap esU

Long Sentences

40 .ammoc a naht noitarapes regnorts a si nolocimes A
41 .elcitra na fo eltit eht dnuora skram noitatouq esU
42 .yranoitcid a ot refer ot sdeen yllanoisacco enoyrevE
43 .aedi na fo noititeper yrassecennu eht si ycnadnuder A

POSTTEST

Repeat the Pretest. *Goal:* Improve speed and accuracy.

F. PUNCTUATION PRACTICE

Eyes on copy!

44 Walk! Give? Where? most; Escape? lazy, Aug. Apr. rare; qtr.
45 7/10 babe, bed, pack; boa, First? Sara; are: Wed. bog, one;
46 tag; ea. load; Beg! Morning? bawl, raise/rise Finish? stow;
47 so/so that Stu; cane, Oct. Ely, Ltd. film, that/which loom;

48 calm, stub; our; acid, big, cog, Better? c.o.d. bats, once;
49 bays, Jr. camp, i.e. stay; shall/will axis, 2/10 barn, R.N.
50 Fire! Why? go, Dave, all's lube; he, Sell! Sat. Ph.D. Lucy;
51 Gas? Call? Yes! gave, Clean? "peer" pump; lost; Sign? Bart:

ISAK says ...

TECHNIQUE TIP

Center your body vertically on the alphabetic portion of the keyboard, which is the J key on most keyboards.

Accuracy

Goals

- Build accuracy on:
  - ✓ Corresponding-finger and confusable keys.
  - ✓ Spelling.
  - ✓ Alphabetic, vertical, and number reaches.

A. WARMUP

Accuracy	1	Was Joe puzzled by the czar's quip about five oxygen masks?	12
Technique: Concentration	2	antirevolutionaries deinstitutionalized conventionalization	24
Speed	3	If we go too far past our turn, just toss out the old maps.	36

    1 | 2 | 3 | 4 | 5 | 6 | 7 | 8 | 9 | 10 | 11 | 12

B. PRETEST-PRACTICE-POSTTEST: CORRESPONDING-FINGER KEYS

PRETEST

Take a 1-minute timed writing, pushing moderately for speed.

4	Juan is the fourth man to give the five families in	11
5	Yuma a free trip, but the fact is that the vast majority of	23
6	the families also got further help for their other expenses	35
7	in the form of either cash or other helpful donations.	45

    1 | 2 | 3 | 4 | 5 | 6 | 7 | 8 | 9 | 10 | 11 | 12

PRACTICE
Corresponding Fingers

F Finger

8 bulb tear Greg robe rot trip goof fit bib vast urge rig vat
9 Rita gang fat agog free golf got fib ebb gust vote but rang
10 bag gear tube tot stub frog form tab brag vet rest Bob rate
11 rave grab tub Beth far gate five Gobi rag for gob give fact

J Finger

12 Juan dumb Ann hub ugly gym Josh snub Yuma maim Lynn hen mug
13 man noun high inn Fuji jut hash gnu hour hum Jane none much
14 jamb mud June army Utah yawn huge navy emu jam guy holy shy
15 hem yarn Judy main Hyde fun yam memo Nan horn hue name Mary

F and J Fingers

16 rueful fourth thrifty bygone furnish rubbing tenting binary
17 bunting grubby rough rhythm gauging gingham buffoon butcher
18 gouging further faulty fungus bypath bureau bathtub royalty
19 bighorn bulrush golfing fury theorem tuneful gluten thereby

POSTTEST

Repeat the Pretest. *Goal*: Improve speed and accuracy.

C. BUSINESS SPELLING

These spelling words are from a list of the most used and most misspelled words in business writing. Study the words that cause you problems.

20 miscellaneous implementation clarification therapy decision
21 residents waiver congratulations analysis lien particularly
22 confirmed affects considerable referral separately statutes
23 approximately position discrepancies percentage immediately

Speed

Goals

- Build speed on:
  - ✓ 15-Second Speed Sprints and 30-Second Progressive Practice drills.
  - ✓ Common letter combinations and special hand drills.
- Assess speed and accuracy on a 5-minute timed writing.

A. WARMUP

Accuracy	1	Vance squeezed orange juice before they made waxed pickles.	12
Technique: Space Bar	2	Why not? I am. Pay Jon his fee now. I see an ax. I am fine.	24
Speed	3	The chair is very nice; I wish I had two of them to sit on.	36

          1 | 2 | 3 | 4 | 5 | 6 | 7 | 8 | 9 | 10 | 11 | 12

B. PRETEST-PRACTICE-POSTTEST: COMMON LETTER COMBINATIONS

PRETEST

Take a 1-minute timed writing, pushing moderately for speed.

4	They are debating the ratio of the real taxable income	11
5	that will be payable under the new system. I know they are	24
6	required to provide verbatim instructions when updating the	35
7	system, so we should be patient for the rest of the session.	47

          1 | 2 | 3 | 4 | 5 | 6 | 7 | 8 | 9 | 10 | 11 | 12

PRACTICE
Common Letter Combinations

re

8 wire bare pare pore fret fore rehire prefired treasure bred
9 surefire real revere reek pure referee redrew trek are acre
10 hire ogre core ream reared carefree hare required dare reed
11 rest Rex repaired grew wren red restored care mere rein ore

ati

12 meatiest creation notating sedative ratio taxation berating
13 clematis cheating heating equating verbatim patient meatier
14 donation native debating aromatic curative aquatic laxative
15 grating station patio Latina satire stratify batik updating

able

16 lovable gable cable towable fable payable provable valuable
17 loanable flyable mailable taxable affable bearable sociable
18 viable sealable bribable burnable syllable eatable culpable
19 shakable huggable leasable passable huggable tablet salable

POSTTEST

Repeat the Pretest. *Goal*: Improve speed and accuracy.

C. 15-SECOND SPEED SPRINTS

Goal: Increase your speed on each retyping of the same sentence.

20 Call her at noon to talk over the plan we made at the cafe.
21 I sent the memo to my boss, but I hope he does not read it.
22 Walk as fast as you can go and look out for that last step.
23 When we hear the bell ring, we must then put down our pens.

D. SPECIAL HAND DRILLS

Alternate-Hand Words

24 fight sick giant sir Uruguay mend and Jay Claudia bible woe
25 idle or foe chap dug social rich proficiency firm name both
26 Durham own it wit eye works entitle toe such busy authentic
27 handle Yale for thrown Lakeland visitor Kay he chairman bus

Double-Letter Words

28 buzz soon speed loss Anna seed motto pass Mann tattoo guess
29 patty bell wheel three jell cross press happy seek mass ill
30 weed inn class Anne Peggy tool well cliff alley fleet stood
31 good pool small dwell less been food beef Jeff access spoon

Upper-Row Words

32 potty petty tort power tore yeti outer your outwore pie woe
33 peyote pout Euterpe rut out rot top putty queer otter trout
34 rye epee port wept quit wore twit ewe erupt two repute writ
35 petit ort piety rep equity wee typewrote eye wire typo were

E. PACED PRACTICE
Follow the software directions for this exercise to improve keystroking speed and accuracy.

F. 5-MINUTE TIMED WRITING

Take two 5-minute timed writings.

Goal: Push moderately for speed while keeping your accuracy under control.

36 You will undoubtedly be assigned many group projects	11
37 while in school. One reason is that a team's output often	22
38 exceeds the sum of each person's own efforts. The down side	34
39 of this, of course, is that conflict sometimes arises.	45
40 Conflict is a greatly misunderstood part of teamwork.	56
41 Some people try to avoid all conflict, thinking that it	68
42 detracts from the group's goals. In fact, quite the reverse	80
43 happens if conflict is handled properly. While you will	91
44 want to minimize personal conflicts, conflicts of ideas are	103
45 the very heart of teamwork.	109
46 The purpose of teamwork is to generate as many ideas	119
47 as possible and to test these ideas before you implement	131
48 them. Thus, the diverse views of team members should be	142
49 heard and even encouraged. Only then will the team be able	154
50 to generate the most appropriate solution to a problem.	165
51 When you work in a team, always try to solicit the	175
52 views of all team members so that you can then determine	187
53 what will and what will not work. That way, everyone will	198
54 succeed.	200

1 | 2 | 3 | 4 | 5 | 6 | 7 | 8 | 9 | 10 | 11 | 12

TECHNIQUE TIP

ISAK says ...

Ensure that only your fingertips touch the keyboard. Let your fingers do the moving; the rest of your hand should be as still as possible.

D. SPECIAL HAND DRILLS

Left-Hand Words

24 beverages red eat reserved raw sewer gates rewarded careers

Maintain the nontyping hand in home-row position.

25 wasted affected Bert tract stewardess Ted race arrears fare

26 started egg dated bad ads gas swears gate fast water Edward

27 cave text acted deed era taxed addressed defect rave street

Right-Hand Words

28 lumpy unhook you'll junky Phil pull puny million oink phony

29 mill Lynn ink pony pink phylum Polly lop unpin polo pumpkin

30 milk uplink mum hunk ion yip minion onion hump upon ill hop

31 holy only nook honk ilk kiln link loin mil July linkup oily

Left- and Right-Hand Words

32 bag fares defects extra exceeded dressed deferred hill fast

33 ears unholy tact degree ward reserved yon mom state reserve

34 awards served bear beast bad Kohl greeted readers dad jumpy

35 ilk treat junk deeds beverages aware rewards taste rag bees

E. 30-SECOND PROGRESSIVE PRACTICE

Follow the software directions for this exercise to improve keystroking speed and accuracy.

F. 5-MINUTE TIMED WRITING

Take two 5-minute timed writings.

Goal: Push moderately for speed while keeping your accuracy under control.

36   Being effective on the job means that you must have   11

37 effective listening skills. No matter if you are giving a   22

38 formal speech to a large group or simply talking with a   33

39 colleague, your efforts will be in vain if your audience   45

40 tunes you out.   48

41   Listening involves more than hearing because hearing   59

42 is a passive act that simply involves perceiving sound.   70

43 Listening is an active act that requires you to interpret   81

44 the meaning of these sounds.   87

45   Listening is the communication skill that we use the   98

46 most. Yet, the average person remembers only half of the   109

47 facts heard during a ten-minute talk.   117

48   To listen better, tune out distractions and maintain   128

49 eye contact with the speaker. Focus on the content of what   140

50 is being said, and do not be too concerned about how the   151

51 talk is delivered. What is said is always more important   162

52 than how it is said. Also, remember that boring does not   174

53 mean not important. Even boring and complex data may be   185

54 critical to your job success, so you should maximize every   197

55 chance to learn.   200

    1 | 2 | 3 | 4 | 5 | 6 | 7 | 8 | 9 | 10 | 11 | 12

ISAK says ...

TAKE A BREAK!

Keeping your head stationary, rotate your eyes to form a large circle.

Speed

Goals

- Build speed on:
  - ✓ 15-Second Speed Sprints and Paced Practice drills.
  - ✓ Common letter combinations and special hand drills.
- Assess speed and accuracy on a 5-minute timed writing.

A. WARMUP

Accuracy   1   The amazed boy mixed equal parts of juice and weak vinegar.   12

Technique: Concentration   2   parapsychologically electroluminescence unselfconsciousness   24

Speed   3   She must find the one file by nine, or we will lose it all.   36

     1 | 2 | 3 | 4 | 5 | 6 | 7 | 8 | 9 | 10 | 11 | 12

B. PRETEST-PRACTICE-POSTTEST: COMMON LETTER COMBINATIONS

PRETEST

Take a 1-minute timed writing, pushing moderately for speed.

4   I will make a motion to provide our native artists   10

5   with proper display studios to entice them to stay on our   22

6   property and maybe earn a tidy profit and improve their   33

7   welfare. Another option is to improve their present space.   45

     1 | 2 | 3 | 4 | 5 | 6 | 7 | 8 | 9 | 10 | 11 | 12

PRACTICE
Common Letter
Combinations

ti   8   motion stilt tin stick entity tilting tinting option static

9   motive feting erotic Arctic entice softie tipsy tiepin tile

10   tick mating native nation artists septic tilt sating Scotia

11   tidy cretin tidbit antics tint toting artistic tinsel tinge

pro   12   prostate provide protect promote protest proof prompt prose

13   improve protrude apron project product proper probe propjet

14   uproar pronto profane profit promo property prodigal uproot

15   proxy proviso provost provoke prof prowl repro prod proverb

ther   16   neither therewith either southern therapy thereupon panther

17   smoother dither there other weather thermal loather blather

18   lather slither another hither therein leather wither rather

19   tether thereon feather therapist therefore breather heather

POSTTEST

Repeat the Pretest. *Goal:* Improve speed and accuracy.

C. 15-SECOND SPEED SPRINTS

Goal: Increase your speed on each retyping of the same sentence.

20   Do not drop that item; if you do, it will not work for you.

21   I love to read in bed; I wish I knew of a good book to get.

22   She does like to knit; she will make you a gift if you ask.

23   The cell does not ring well, so you may miss a call or two.

Accuracy

Goals

• Build accuracy on:
  ✓ Corresponding-finger and confusable keys.
  ✓ Spelling.
  ✓ Alphabetic, horizontal, and symbol reaches.

A. WARMUP

Accuracy	1 The prancing wizards quickly jumped over fifty green boxes.	12
Technique: Punctuation	2 (lit) x-ray (opt) no-no pep; (lily) run-on You! deal; jell;	24
Speed	3 His name is kind of lame, but he will just keep it for now.	36

       1 | 2 | 3 | 4 | 5 | 6 | 7 | 8 | 9 | 10 | 11 | 12

B. PRETEST-PRACTICE-POSTTEST: CORRESPONDING-FINGER KEYS

PRETEST

Take a 1-minute timed writing, pushing moderately for speed.

4 Does Mickey think the deal approved last week leaves	11
5 us with a weak exit strategy? If so, we can ask that an	23
6 additional fee be paid at the end of the contract, like we	35
7 did for the Viking contract last month. Please ask him.	46

       1 | 2 | 3 | 4 | 5 | 6 | 7 | 8 | 9 | 10 | 11 | 12

PRACTICE
Corresponding Fingers

D Finger

8 bee tree dame puce due cad did cage heck deal cent red dove
9 cape died cute fee dew Clem cue chew daze bed etch ewe doze
10 doe rice gee date Dave rude ode den epic aide Lee edge dive
11 pace Cody idle wed Celt cock tide ice Eden end nude nee fed

K Finger

12 kiss hiking bike kit ark think whisky oak skin Katie Viking
13 kill link ask chink sheik keying brink sky slink kid tickle
14 pike skiing stick like kind dinky nickel bicker slick brisk
15 Sikh chick tinkle irk, Mickey taking Sitka risk fickle rink

D and K Fingers

16 woke bake tie dire sack sickle ice cider lack keg veil wine
17 week knew tickle bike die mite vice mice eke wind diet buck
18 decode paid lire tied leak dank rich dark rock Id kind cite
19 beak mire smirk bicker nick lied dais weak exit Kodiak dunk

POSTTEST

Repeat the Pretest. *Goal*: Improve speed and accuracy.

C. BUSINESS SPELLING

These spelling words are from a list of the most used and most misspelled words in business writing. Study the words that cause you problems.

20 paragraph pagers whereas proposals deductible button hazard
21 alloy professional coordination institutions owing apparent
22 certification tariff receipt maintaining sector explanation
23 stations trustees compressor corporations indication notify

D. SYMBOL PRACTICE

Keep your eyes on the copy as you type these top-row symbols.

24 qli@bsu.edu 970% 268% Fuentes* (lady) boo-boo (laid) laser*
25 Berry* Li & Ng, Inc. cli@bsu.edu Ngo & Ely 697% uely@az.gov
26 $1.09 (lamb) West & Little 932% $1 rorr@ua.edu 233% Parker*
27 729% be-all Han & Hsu (lack) Portillo* (lair) Owens & Young

E. PRETEST-PRACTICE-POSTTEST: CONCENTRATION
Take a 1-minute timed writing, pushing moderately for speed.

PRETEST

Concentrate on keeping your eyes on the copy as you type these vocabulary words. How many of these terms do you know?

28   It might be an overgeneralization on my part, but I   11
29 think that the influx of such torrid weather this summer   22
30 has had an egregious effect on intercontinental behavior,   34
31 causing either apathy or raucous behavior among people.   45

     1 | 2 | 3 | 4 | 5 | 6 | 7 | 8 | 9 | 10 | 11 | 12

PRACTICE
Vocabulary Words

Short Words

32 torrid lyric endue ponder batten effuse
33 vendor natal penury beset influx virile
34 gibe assay waif bier awry evince apathy
35 vapid deflect maxim enmity wizen prolix

Medium-Length Words

36 labyrinth sagacious fugacious virulence derisible
37 scintilla contusion rigmarole reliquary ebullient
38 cabalism raucous comport epiphany obviate forfend
39 egregious unanimous insidious leviathan erudition

Long Words

40 disjunctive opalescence hyperparathyroidism philosophically
41 horticultural intercontinental parliamentarian ecologically
42 examinations anemometers interdivisional overgeneralization
43 discrimination surprisingly professionalization pandemonium

POSTTEST

Repeat the Pretest. *Goal:* Improve speed and accuracy.

F. PUNCTUATION PRACTICE

Eyes on copy!

44 have, Funny! Break? flea's part; aid, 13/24 Yea! But? only;
45 bail, net; caps, "peat" don't axle, incl. Fast? bawl, know,
46 Today? "peek" sat; avg. Ed.D. gal's sing; New? Candy? pack;
47 ea. jack, 1/5 some; Mon. bog, shall/will Fire! sink; whsle.

48 film, that/which roar; Dale's dad's cars, P.O. noon; Drive!
49 1/9 Lucy; back, acre, past; lacy, palm; "peg" ax, Jr. Ph.D.
50 balk: safe; Better? "peep" size: Roy; Tue. mdse. pin; Whew!
51 hid, Help! fig, Soon? onto; No? slab; face, camp, am, pine;

TAKE A BREAK!

ISAK says ...

Massage each finger slowly and gently, starting with the space between the finger and moving toward the nail.

D. MAP+: ALPHABET
Follow the software instructions for this exercise to improve accuracy.

E. PRETEST-PRACTICE-POSTTEST: CONFUSABLE KEYS

PRETEST

Take a 1-minute timed writing, pushing moderately for speed.

Pay special attention to these adjacent-finger reaches that often get confused.

24	Eric will need to recruit fewer faculty in the ensuing	11
25	years because so many of his former recruits were given	22
26	tenure here at the college last year. In the future, Eric	34
27	can simply ignore the task of issuing job announcements.	45

1 | 2 | 3 | 4 | 5 | 6 | 7 | 8 | 9 | 10 | 11 | 12

PRACTICE
Adjacent Fingers

re-er 28 future ogre ampere fare spire encore Erica pore adore chore
29 ignore mere here attire tore errand acre rehire manure mire
30 ashore tenure erne cadre rare admire sphere fore sore shore
31 bore snore injure nature wore sure lore ore era were desire

iu-ui 32 Jesuit emporium guild Louis penguin annuity gluing geranium
33 quiz quibble ruin triumph ensuing opium quiet ruining Bruin
34 biscuit helium quinine squint squirt magnesium calcium quid
35 barium ruing recruit quiche aquarium issuing radius pursuit

we-ew 36 ewe rewrap vowed rower yew nephew grew reward Newton trowel
37 wept fewest Weber sweep blew tweak flew swept flowed sewage
38 chew lower twenty threw anew newest west showed brew weasel
39 drew webcam wear eschew newer rawest weep fewer reword crew

POSTTEST

Repeat the Pretest. *Goal*: Improve speed and accuracy.

F. REACH DRILLS: HORIZONTAL REACHES

xc and kl 40 inkling excesses except exceed coxcomb meekly sickly tackle
41 excellence briskly excitement excuse buckle excrete chuckle
42 weakly excess twinkle freckle fickle excise knuckle exclaim
43 booklet shackle excerpt exceeding excursion backlit wrinkly

Horizontal reaches move to a different key on the same row.

ds and iu 44 odium deeds uranium needs radius aids reads grads bends ads
45 magnesium kinds cranium rids opium coeds words hands sodium
46 tedium potassium geranium aquarium podium acids odds atrium
47 barium calcium leads cards feeds multiuser genius kids ends

G. MAP+: SYMBOLS
Follow the software instructions for this exercise to improve accuracy.

TECHNIQUE TIP

To avoid excessive twisting of the neck, position the monitor directly in front of you—about an arm's length away—with the top of the monitor tilted slightly away from you.

ISAK says ...

Technique

Goals

- Improve technique on the nonprinting, number, symbol, and punctuation keys.
- Improve concentration.

A. WARMUP

Accuracy	1	Six jolly men are quickly operating a few heavy bulldozers.	12
Technique: Alternate-Hand	2	clan Laurie corps Vivian proficiency Keith bicycle Shanghai	24
Speed	3	When the bulb goes too dim, it can be hard to read my book.	36

                1 | 2 | 3 | 4 | 5 | 6 | 7 | 8 | 9 | 10 | 11 | 12

B. PRETEST-PRACTICE-POSTTEST: NONPRINTING KEYS

PRETEST

Take a 1-minute timed writing, pushing moderately for speed.

Backspace to correct all errors as you type.

4	Jeff Hayes and Ross Wood may join the Elks Lodge in	11
5	Orem, Utah, in July. Meanwhile, Rita Todd and Tina Rice	22
6	flew to Mesa, Arizona, to visit their friends Jane Wouk	33
7	and Toby Kahn. They stayed at the Ritz Carlton Hotel.	44

                1 | 2 | 3 | 4 | 5 | 6 | 7 | 8 | 9 | 10 | 11 | 12

PRACTICE
Nonprinting Keys

LEFT SHIFT Key

8 Kane Java Meir Ural Jena Utes Levi Mann Penn Oran Levi Mesa
9 Hays Iggy Nell Macy Marx Hale Manx Mace Hadj Jeff Utah Hank
10 Kent Lena Yale Ochs Parr Oahu Iraq Kral Magi Yael Kahn Hedy
11 Mach Pena Hamm Urdu Mark Nast Odin Jane Kern Pate Palu Keys

RIGHT SHIFT Key

12 Wood Ford Rolf Rita Dunn Cody Alex Ahab Dior Todd Burr Rice
13 Cuba Ruby Roma Wouk Coke Elam Toby Amex Cohn Chad Gigi Tiki
14 Tina Ritz Elks Cole Guam Eyre Enid Aida Finn Buck Tojo Ross
15 Apia Fitz Quos Tory Suez Elia Ella Ruiz Boer Tito Anna Quon

BACKSPACE Key

When you reach the Backspace sign (←), backspace 1 time and then type the letter that follows.

16 she←y art←m put←p the←y dew←n vie←m flu←y sot←y big←n dug←n
17 max←y bud←m ire←k per←p box←y age←o job←y ash←k toe←n zig←p
18 rig←m leg←i yea←n was←y hex←y yaw←m hid←m zag←p dab←m cow←y
19 hoe←g are←k pod←i pug←n sob←n kid←n mar←p sag←p hot←p mad←n

POSTTEST

Repeat the Pretest. *Goal:* Improve speed and accuracy.

C. NUMBER PRACTICE

Press TAB to move from column to column in each row.

20	177	470	887	439	860	816	472	921	529	584
21	428	206	651	784	286	862	550	587	723	957
22	947	759	551	170	572	825	847	391	327	851
23	565	117	675	521	817	376	330	291	948	581

Technique

Goals

- Improve technique on the nonprinting, number, symbol, and punctuation keys.
- Improve concentration.

A. WARMUP

Accuracy	1	Jane's big deluxe quiz form was very easy to check in pink.	12
Technique: One-Hand	2	kimono estate pink fact mill sweater poplin greater upon as	24
Speed	3	The rain is wet on my feet, but the sun will soon dry them.	36

    1 | 2 | 3 | 4 | 5 | 6 | 7 | 8 | 9 | 10 | 11 | 12

B. PRETEST-PRACTICE-POSTTEST: NONPRINTING KEYS

PRETEST

Take a 1-minute timed writing, pushing moderately for speed.

Backspace to correct all errors as you type.

4	Kate Hans from Yale University and Gina Boer from Shaw	11
5	University just flew to Fiji but had a layover at the Orly	23
6	Airport in Paris. They stayed at the Ritz Hotel and were	34
7	able to have dinner at the Park Lake Restaurant on Friday.	46

    1 | 2 | 3 | 4 | 5 | 6 | 7 | 8 | 9 | 10 | 11 | 12

PRACTICE
Nonprinting Keys

LEFT SHIFT Key

8 Kate Hans Haru Lacy Nast Yale Ural Herb Pete Pate Ochs Iris
9 Nami Iggy Mace Kahn Jack Mead Ovid Macy Mars Yves Odin Yael
10 Park Lent Otos Iran Owen Orly Jess Nero Hart Yank Yang Hall
11 Pena Hedy Mays Pele Iraq Lear Ivan Hugh Uris Palu Lake Kent

RIGHT SHIFT Key

12 Sikh Glen Gila Burt Fuji Gobi Goya Amex Dodd Bill Emma Boer
13 Dior Coke Fitz Boyd Wouk Bond Ritz Tito Zion Suez Fiji Emil
14 Todd Ames Roma Tiki Ella Diaz Finn Rock Shui Shaw Guam Quan
15 Anna Rolf Sims Burr Bose Zola Anne Andy Gina Rosa Elia Elam

BACKSPACE Key

When you reach the Backspace sign (←), backspace 1 time and then type the letter that follows.

16 woe←k had←m nut←n own←l his←p car←p ire←k add←o nag←p cow←p
17 hid←m oaf←k yaw←m gym←p mud←m log←o leg←i hex←y tot←p cot←p
18 cue←p jar←y yea←n dim←p hot←p rut←n cab←n elf←k are←k nix←p
19 wag←y tag←m vie←m zig←p rig←m flu←y tar←p bag←m keg←y ash←k

POSTTEST

Repeat the Pretest. *Goal:* Improve speed and accuracy.

C. NUMBER PRACTICE

Press TAB to move from column to column in each row.

20	302	100	203	949	298	394	401	472	547	461
21	820	405	935	813	829	897	706	663	588	505
22	228	346	713	578	821	102	507	433	749	351
23	867	189	612	200	355	621	944	227	162	653

D. MAP+: ALPHABET

Follow the software instructions for this exercise to improve accuracy.

E. PRETEST-PRACTICE-POSTTEST: CONFUSABLE KEYS

Take a 1-minute timed writing, pushing moderately for speed.

PRETEST

Pay special attention to these consecutive-finger reaches that often get confused.

24	Given a new breakeven point, it wouldn't be advisable	11
25	for us to depart from our usual effort and begin to export	23
26	the device. Apart from our unmet sales goal, we may need to	35
27	triple our domestic sales in an effort to increase revenue.	47

1 | 2 | 3 | 4 | 5 | 6 | 7 | 8 | 9 | 10 | 11 | 12

PRACTICE
Consecutive Fingers

rt-tr

28 tart tragic trough tread mart fort apart trip trudge export
29 trend dirt travel tremor tray trawl ort trophy yogurt tress
30 expert effort trace trust tryout trail cohort retort depart
31 triple insert hurt trivia trauma desert tried trying escort

mn-nm

32 unmask hymnal unmarred glumness nonmetal unmasked indemnify
33 unmet column amniotic chimney circumnavigate unmade remnant
34 unmade enmity alumni remnants unmoving amnesiac abandonment
35 damned grimness alignment enlightenment detainment unmapped

vb-bv

36 breakeven bivouac vibrant voluble bravado curveball Bolivar
37 coverable behoove Bolivia verbal absolvent beaver favorable
38 venerable vestibule subversive cabdriver advisable obviated
39 bi-level dividable obviate subvert abrasive beloved vibrate

POSTTEST

Repeat the Pretest. *Goal*: Improve speed and accuracy.

F. REACH DRILLS: HORIZONTAL REACHES

fa and *up*

40 upturn facile puppet fasten up cup superb backup setup coup
41 coupe fat recoup faster defame fact lay-up pup fault update

Horizontal reaches move to a different key on the same row.

42 blowup pupil facial fatal fax upkeep upward far infant faze
43 pickup holdup uproar slipup abrupt fan fad tossup fake fail

ad and *oi*

44 stead foible grad head add choice evade jaded oink adage ad
45 squad read bread boil lady badge foil sad salad radar adobe
46 loin admit recoil madam noise mad avoid ado coin glad radio
47 toilet broad nomad soil made spade anoint adept going glade

G. MAP+: SYMBOLS

Follow the software instructions for this exercise to improve accuracy.

TECHNIQUE TIP

ISAK says ...

Sit about a hand width away from the keyboard. If your keyboard has pop-up legs in the back, do not engage them. Instead, the keyboard should either be horizontal or have a slightly negative tilt.

D. SYMBOL PRACTICE

Keep your eyes on the copy as you type these top-row symbols.

24 Harrison* uely@az.gov Portillo* (lain) aho@cs.com Noe & Ray
25 233% #10 station #9 jib 7# of stew (lag) Eng & Morris 57.2%
26 Shan* $2 sngo@az.gov also-ran 6% 729% (lamb) Parker* Naser*
27 (lace) 958% be-all add-on $1.09 $1 Batista* Ely & Foy $1.68

E. PRETEST-PRACTICE-POSTTEST: CONCENTRATION
Take a 1-minute timed writing, pushing moderately for speed.

PRETEST

Concentrate on keeping your eyes on the copy as you type these vocabulary words. How many of these terms do you know?

28   We will be remiss if we do not castigate the demagogue   11
29 for his desultory remarks about our company's intentions.   23
30 He was prone to speak without rectitude and exhibited an   34
31 astonishing level of moral turpitude for a public servant.   46
   1 | 2 | 3 | 4 | 5 | 6 | 7 | 8 | 9 | 10 | 11 | 12

PRACTICE   Short Words
Vocabulary Words

32 remiss horde dispel fathom impel accost
33 idiom solder fez bask palsy cull mishap
34 educe caucus mettle indict guile volant
35 ode pique covey theism wane miser canon

Medium-Length Words
36 castigate desultory execrable sophistry turpitude
37 winsome probity nihilist denizen solecism vestige
38 extenuate cacophony elucidate sentience rectitude
39 demagogue sumptuous indigence imbroglio immutable

Long Words
40 ventricular deinstitutionalizing forbearance rejuvenescence
41 entertainingly inconvenienced transportation occupationally
42 disenfranchisements incandescent dissuasion acknowledgement
43 counterdemonstration octogenarian consonance distinguishing

POSTTEST

Repeat the Pretest. *Goal:* Improve speed and accuracy.

F. PUNCTUATION PRACTICE

Eyes on copy!

44 be, it, In? only; onto; tab; elk, lace, 3/4 cave, Mark; So?
45 acre, dad's Nothing? Here? 2/10 cane, lace, Sit! shall/will
46 Type! beg, do, egg, www.cnn.com/ cans, ask: sat; Ltd. pick;
47 Stan; learn/teach Drink? Start! son; stem; tag; soon; long;

48 tact; fact, Sell! Roy; past; Asia: Lou; Burglar? sing; let;
49 neat; Quit! See? maybe/maybe Duck! Enough? Luis; Dave, pig;
50 Safe? Fire! link: More? once; lube; skin; park; Ohio; Sign?
51 First? can, know, flea's mfg. axis, fwd. near; "peep" luck;

ISAK says ...

TAKE A BREAK!

Relax and place one hand on your abdomen and the other hand on your chest; inhale slowly through the nose and hold for 4 seconds; then exhale slowly through the mouth. Repeat 3 times.

Accuracy

Goals

- Build accuracy on:
  - ✓ Corresponding-finger and confusable keys.
  - ✓ Spelling.
  - ✓ Alphabetic, horizontal, and symbol reaches.

A. WARMUP

Accuracy	1 She'd seen five or six big jet planes zoom quickly by town.	12
Technique: Transpositions	2 era red|ink kin|arm raw|anew name|ore row|Ali lag|Erma rear	24
Speed	3 Push and pull with all you have got if you plan to make it.	36

1 | 2 | 3 | 4 | 5 | 6 | 7 | 8 | 9 | 10 | 11 | 12

B. PRETEST-PRACTICE-POSTTEST: CORRESPONDING FINGERS

PRETEST

Take a 1-minute timed writing, pushing moderately for speed.

4 Maybe Laura will opt to quit smoking again in April,	12
5 when she reviews the data about the dangers that lie ahead.	24
6 As Liza knows only too well, it could be a fatal mistake	35
7 if Laura does not pay attention to the medical facts.	45

1 | 2 | 3 | 4 | 5 | 6 | 7 | 8 | 9 | 10 | 11 | 12

PRACTICE
Corresponding Fingers

A Finger

8 Laura alas Liza data alpha papa Sara aorta java Mamie ahead
9 tzar aha quota arena asea cab rajah Paula fatal larva Eliza
10 await raze quark Kate amass Iraq parka gaze Zach Gaza pasta
11 quit Hope drama Ozark banal madam Alamo llama again Ava aye

; Finger

12 set/sit pro; cop pan pew; lay/lie yip pop; Poe; yap pet pie
13 Pat? pin; sop pap ape its/it's Poe par per ply pin pal pig;
14 of/have pay fop tap pat pry tip; ply; opt pot; ups top Peg?
15 pet; yep Pip? pus pop Kip? Pia type/key April pew pep Ralph

A and ; Fingers

16 mezzo per nip amass Japan abase nasal aloha quaff Bah Paula
17 hazy spa quart sop put quad daze laze Sara pit; pro aye pet
18 pup yap maze anal Eliza mop pen; Alva award Alma agaze Dana
19 adage hazel Aztec dizzy rap afar pix imp ply rajah alas pad

POSTTEST

Repeat the Pretest. *Goal*: Improve speed and accuracy.

C. BUSINESS SPELLING

These spelling words are from a list of the most used and most misspelled words in business writing. Study the words that cause you problems.

20 commitment physician warehouse claimant absence utilization
21 academic substantial executives procedure lesson procedural
22 international suspension initiated guarantee specifications
23 voluntary economy similar capabilities violation disclosure

Goals

- Build speed on:
  - ✓ 15-Second Speed Sprints and Paced Practice drills.
  - ✓ Common letter combinations and special hand drills.
- Assess speed and accuracy on a 5-minute timed writing.

A. WARMUP

Accuracy 1 Those two jobs require our packing five dozen axes monthly. 12

Technique: Substitutions 2 m-n norm monk mine moon mend mane mink amen Nome moan unman 24

Speed 3 As you knew it was to be, you must not make a fuss over it. 36

1 | 2 | 3 | 4 | 5 | 6 | 7 | 8 | 9 | 10 | 11 | 12

B. PRETEST-PRACTICE-POSTTEST: COMMON LETTER COMBINATIONS

PRETEST
Take a 1-minute timed writing, pushing moderately for speed.

4   Our firm will not prosper until we produce some other 11

5 rating system for our sales representatives, rather than 22

6 still relying on our present approach. Therefore, I will 34

7 provide a profit motive to help us improve our tactics. 45

1 | 2 | 3 | 4 | 5 | 6 | 7 | 8 | 9 | 10 | 11 | 12

PRACTICE
Common Letter Combinations

ti 8 dating poetic tibia tiring haptic tick entities tier retire

9 biotic active still autism stilt tactic duties ratio erotic

10 aortic tic motive tilt sting siting softie patio doting tip

11 feting until ties critic stir cities rating tinge tidal tie

pro 12 proclaim prosy prof propane progeny prosper proviso produce

13 uproar profit prohibit proton approach profess prop provide

14 protrude profane prompt improve probable profuse probe prom

15 pro proper prove proud provost pronto propel promo province

ther 16 there lather rather hither northern thermal slither thermos

17 other zither southern leather father bather slather panther

18 therewith therefore thereby weather thereto whether thereof

19 tether smoother thereon therapist soother thereupon farther

POSTTEST
Repeat the Pretest. *Goal:* Improve speed and accuracy.

C. 15-SECOND SPEED SPRINTS

Goal: Increase your speed on each retyping of the same sentence.

20 If you go too deep and are not able to swim, call for help.

21 She has a torn seam on the right cuff of her new suit coat.

22 The boys and girls all sat in a ring to hear the wild tale.

23 When the day is very hot, we like to swim in the cold pool.

D. SPECIAL HAND DRILLS

Left-Hand Words

Maintain the nontyping hand in home-row position.

24 eat gage stages arts bars vast bat fear garage drafted edge
25 regarded crafts bases award crew Egbert reserve gear grades
26 verbs egg beaver assets bears act stewardesses Baxter tests
27 rates Bess dad tax feet ease serve decreased Everett extras

Right-Hand Words

28 ohm ion pumpkin milk inn nil junk hop oil punk pony homonym
29 unholy plunk holy Kohl only Jon mink honk ink oily kill Kim
30 phony monk mop Molly lop onion hypo puppy Lynn moon minimum
31 p.m. Jill pink oink loom Yukon link upon polo pinky joy hip

Left- and Right-Hand Words

32 tract baggage treated kin desert greatest poi free seat ads
33 erasers extras wears exceed Johnny Vera rewards face stages
34 acreage base wages Molly vast barber Bart cassette gas I'll
35 ion ohm dresser dared honk bee bread seed union imply nylon

E. 30-SECOND PROGRESSIVE PRACTICE
Follow the software directions for this exercise to improve keystroking speed and accuracy.

F. 5-MINUTE TIMED WRITING

Take two 5-minute timed writings.

Goal: Push moderately for speed while keeping your accuracy under control.

36 Creative thinking is a way of looking at problems or	12
37 situations with a fresh outlook that suggests unorthodox	23
38 answers. It can expand our awareness and open the door to	35
39 new points of view. Most of our thinking in school is to	46
40 acquire knowledge. Creative thinking, on the other hand,	57
41 helps us to create knowledge. The purpose of brainstorming	69
42 is to come up with as many new solutions as we can. Write	81
43 down everything, no matter how crazy it may sound at first.	93
44 Stress quantity rather than quality. You can go through	104
45 your list of ideas later and analyze them and then throw	115
46 out what doesn't work.	120
47 Creative thinking is an attitude, that is, it is a	131
48 willingness to play with ideas. It helps us to enjoy the	143
49 good while looking for ways to improve it. The creative	154
50 person knows that there is always room for improvement.	165
51 Most advances in the workplace come from those whose	177
52 job is outside the area of the innovation. A good mind with	189
53 a positive attitude will surely help in solving problems.	200

1 | 2 | 3 | 4 | 5 | 6 | 7 | 8 | 9 | 10 | 11 | 12

TAKE A BREAK!

ISAK says... Let your hands hang loosely at your side; rotate your right hand clockwise in a circle, then counterclockwise. Repeat with the left hand.

D. SPECIAL HAND DRILLS

Alternate-Hand Words

24 suspend Shenandoah cow Uruguay amendment world did giant by
25 Pamela pep Diana civic panel dock busy man handy cycle corn
26 bus sir Burke visual Bud vivid wit emblem authentic Guthrie
27 keys proficient Provo torn laid snap hair Chris signs Burma

Double-Letter Words

28 sees seen swell wheel food bloom good merry Nelly pass Anne
29 Quinn fill see cool feed tool seed wall loose I'll till odd
30 loom speed call Scott well poor deed flood Benny spell seek
31 happy Jeff ill assess egg feet tells been arrow steel Polly

Upper-Row Words

32 pout outwit typo ore tout quite ire tire quit tier poet yip
33 wee trite quo pewter pyrite pert pity equip Tory riot queer
34 pretty out weir retype wire potter tour petit ewe woo weepy
35 ewer rope ere your petri Troy trip wet port try weepier rut

E. PACED PRACTICE

Follow the software directions for this exercise to improve keystroking speed and accuracy.

F. 5-MINUTE TIMED WRITING

Take two 5-minute timed writings.

Goal: Push moderately for speed while keeping your accuracy under control.

36	Many of us grew up thinking vitamins were good for us,	11
37	but recent research published in medical journals shows	22
38	that taking a daily multivitamin is a waste of money for	34
39	most people. Extensive research shows that people who take	46
40	multivitamins are no healthier than those who do not.	56
41	Taking vitamins came into style a hundred years ago,	67
42	when it was difficult for most people to get a wide variety	79
43	of fresh fruits and vegetables year round. But these days,	91
44	you are unlikely to be deficient if you eat a typical diet,	103
45	because so many of the foods we buy are enriched with added	115
46	vitamins. Multivitamins have about two dozen compounds, but	127
47	food plants have hundreds of unique compounds to keep us	138
48	healthy and strong our whole life.	145
49	In short, vitamin pills do not prevent colds, do not	156
50	prevent heart disease, and do not defend against cancer.	168
51	One exception is that research does show that vitamin D	179
52	does protect against a long list of ills, and most people	190
53	do not make enough of this vitamin on their own.	200

1 | 2 | 3 | 4 | 5 | 6 | 7 | 8 | 9 | 10 | 11 | 12

ISAK says ...

TECHNIQUE TIP

Sit so that your lower back touches the back of the chair. Doing so enables the chair to help support your back.

Goals

- Build speed on:
  ✓ 15-Second Speed Sprints and 30-Second Progressive Practice drills.
  ✓ Common letter combinations and special hand drills.
- Assess speed and accuracy on a 5-minute timed writing.

A. WARMUP

Accuracy	1	Roxy saw him first and lazily jumped off the big quick van.	12
Technique: Substitutions	2	i-o trio toil oil iron polio viol obit folio kilo Ohio olio	24
Speed	3	I will not get far if my bike will not move when I push it.	36

1 | 2 | 3 | 4 | 5 | 6 | 7 | 8 | 9 | 10 | 11 | 12

B. PRETEST-PRACTICE-POSTTEST: COMMON LETTER COMBINATIONS

PRETEST

Take a 1-minute timed writing, pushing moderately for speed.

4	If Rex were able to prepare a different seating chart,	12
5	doing so would then restore a suitable arrangement for the	24
6	upcoming debates, leading to less negative interactions.	35
7	Have Matilda ask Rex to prepare the required charts today.	47

1 | 2 | 3 | 4 | 5 | 6 | 7 | 8 | 9 | 10 | 11 | 12

PRACTICE
Common Letter Combinations

re
8 required tree respire ogre red mere wire redirect rein trek
9 rent retreat rev reek Rex brethren rely mare bore Bren reed
10 revere sore redrew crew rehire reap purebred pare read redo
11 reel dare restore premiere fore rest prepare gore were bred

ati
12 seating lattice fixation creation citation elation climatic
13 satisfy aquatic emphatic curative relative relating coating
14 satire sciatic patio spatial eating ecstatic notating batik
15 volatile floating negative Matilda beating debating grating

able
16 readable bribable burnable sable culpable rentable closable
17 durable able gable sizable wearable playable salable doable
18 causable potable sellable provable parable tamable syllable
19 amicable suitable portable stable likeable loanable flyable

POSTTEST

Repeat the Pretest. *Goal*: Improve speed and accuracy.

C. 15-SECOND SPEED SPRINTS

Goal: Increase your speed on each retyping of the same sentence.

20 Go grab the pink pot on the sill to fill it up to the edge.
21 I do like dogs and cats, but a nice pet for me is the best.
22 If he puts that gift in the mail now, it will ship in time.
23 Run over to the shop by noon so you can buy a roll of tape.

Accuracy

Goals

- Build accuracy on:
  - ✓ Corresponding-finger and confusable keys.
  - ✓ Spelling.
  - ✓ Alphabetic, vertical, and number reaches.

A. WARMUP

Accuracy	1	Jay quickly traps five extra owls a month during blizzards.	12
Technique: Concentration	2	unconstitutionality undercapitalization counterreformations	24
Speed	3	The cute dogs ran fast to get a ball to give it back to me.	36

1 | 2 | 3 | 4 | 5 | 6 | 7 | 8 | 9 | 10 | 11 | 12

B. PRETEST-PRACTICE-POSTTEST: CORRESPONDING-FINGER KEYS

PRETEST

Take a 1-minute timed writing, pushing moderately for speed.

4	There are ways for Texas to pass laws that will slow	11
5	down the speed on their freeway exits and that will still	22
6	allow the multiple uses of both sets of signals. It will	34
7	take a bold move for them to achieve their freeway goals.	45

1 | 2 | 3 | 4 | 5 | 6 | 7 | 8 | 9 | 10 | 11 | 12

PRACTICE
Corresponding Fingers

S Finger

8 bows waist suns ways Sphinx pass waxes faxes cuss swim owns
9 woes sown sways assays sewn swims exits axes Wes swaps show
10 wards Texas sods slaw swish assess sass lass sacs sits swan
11 sons waits sets sax kiss fixes rows slow uses sirs saw webs

L Finger

12 salon poll folio gallon foil Lola lore goals cold plod slob
13 sole lox look orally alloy toll Nov. loss lop old plot mole
14 Lou stool cool sold clod allow dollop pool droll tallow Leo
15 slow gold plop allot loin bold spool color lion mellow Leno

S and L Fingers

16 woods glosses slobs exodus silos bellows pillow loll swords
17 gallows loons souls looks Apollo lobos soles wolves lessons
18 cools knolls woofs skills billow rolls bowels smells closes
19 dolls clowns spool swell mellow osmosis sorrows slogs gloss

POSTTEST

Repeat the Pretest. *Goal*: Improve speed and accuracy.

C. BUSINESS SPELLING

These spelling words are from a list of the most used and most misspelled words in business writing. Study the words that cause you problems.

20 entertainment annuity customer premises diesel confirmation
21 license appearance eligible envelopes unanimously defendant
22 preceding contractors equivalent intermediate role commence
23 frequency concur obvious recognition unfortunately appendix

D. SYMBOL PRACTICE

Keep your eyes on the copy as you type these top-row symbols and return your fingers immediately to home-row position.

24 qli@bsu.edu 3# of sand 268% cli@bsu.edu (lain) 57.2% #8 nut
25 Shan* $1 aorr@cs.com Portillo* Owens & Young sngo@az.gov $2
26 729% all-day Santos* #9 jib Noe & Ray sngo@az.gov 3# of wax
27 932% (lag) 970% Riley & Dow (lack) 697% Li & Ng, Inc. (lad)

E. PRETEST-PRACTICE-POSTTEST: CONCENTRATION

Take a 1-minute timed writing, pushing moderately for speed.

PRETEST

Type the Pretest exactly as shown, but type the sentences below from right to left.

Eyes on copy!

28   Typing ".sevitagen elbuod diovA" instead of "Avoid   10
29 double negatives" will force you to keep your eyes on the   22
30 copy instead of looking at your fingers as you type. While   34
31 doing this, be sure to ".enot erecnis dna suoetruoc a esU."   46

    1 | 2 | 3 | 4 | 5 | 6 | 7 | 8 | 9 | 10 | 11 | 12

PRACTICE
Reverse Typing

Short Sentences

32 .sevitagen elbuod diovA
33 .egaugnal evitisop referP
34 .enot erecnis dna suoetruoc a esU
35 .krow etelpmoc a fo eltit eht eziciiatI

Medium-Length Sentences

36 .deilpmi eb yam ecnetnes a fo tcejbus ehT
37 .etaciderp dna tcejbus a sniatnoc ecnetnes A
38 .noisserpxe yrotcudortni na retfa ammoc a esU
39 .doirep a naht noitarapes rekaew a si nolocimes A

Long Sentences

40 .detelpmoc neeb sah taht noitca ot srefer esnet tsaP
41 .etaciderp eno dna tcejbus eno niatnoc secnetnes tsoM
42 .nuon a erofeb emoc taht sevitcejda dnuopmoc etanehpyH
43 .yfidom yeht snuon eht tuoba snoitseuq rewsna sevitcejdA

POSTTEST

Repeat the Pretest. *Goal:* Improve speed and accuracy.

F. PUNCTUATION PRACTICE

Eyes on copy!

44 Dave, all's 1/7 park; roar; Jr. flag's lab, qty. Mr. Clean?
45 lace, calm, Who? band, How? pile; But? Yea! equally/as aid,
46 ea. face, Busy? Call? Apr. area: part; each, luck; in, Mrs.
47 Sit! cane, led, ask: lack, kid, Sell! son; John, Stan; ins.

48 acts, Finish? pie; Help! ppd. Faster! Nov. Sign? one; bawl,
49 Corp. none; Today? room; bldg. noun; Fire! Candy? are: You?
50 hog, lacy, axle, do, lube; safe; Ida, it, Rome; Mack; plus;
51 mart; P.O. Cut! ear, 8/10 dig, addl. ax, sky; bog, Nothing!

ISAK says ...

TECHNIQUE TIP

Keep your elbows relaxed and close to your body as you type. Do not move them outward when typing.

D. MAP+: ALPHABET
Follow the software instructions for this exercise to improve accuracy.

E. PRETEST-PRACTICE-POSTTEST: CONFUSABLE KEYS
Take a 1-minute timed writing, pushing moderately for speed.

PRETEST

Pay special attention to these keys that are often substituted for each other.

24   The growth in the yield of the five- and eight-year   11
25 bonds caught us by surprise since we had invested in quite   22
26 safe securities. This has taught us that we must weigh the   34
27 length and growth of all of our investments in the future.   46

    1 | 2 | 3 | 4 | 5 | 6 | 7 | 8 | 9 | 10 | 11 | 12

PRACTICE
Substitutions

e-i
28 lime yield vice hire tie sheik mice mine dime bicep pie lei
29 dice devil brine die pine title gibe five slime ethic binge
30 rein feign irate dine opine ice vein wise since fiber grief
31 dike viper wife kite Stein pier vibe quite infer waive give

g-h
32 gush trough Goth taught hang gopher gosh weight light eight
33 weigh Graham blight dinghy caught fought nigh hating grouch
34 tight cough hug hog neigh growth plight aweigh gnash though
35 chug charge change bright homing length sight homage alight

a-e
36 ace easy Caesar awe teak ache beat fake yeah safe acre peak
37 seam Etna babe sage heat lea case made aye alumnae ate beta
38 dare nape larvae take fare rate maestro alee wear same pane
39 name daze meal lean beak rake cane feta aloe able game cape

POSTTEST

Repeat the Pretest. *Goal*: Improve speed and accuracy.

F. REACH DRILLS: VERTICAL REACHES

es and li
40 lily flies lie lit best tries chess dries press valid mazes
41 mess zest fixes jest bless geese comes lid taxes pries lint
42 limp essay blind lied like list lion slim resin guess calix
43 blimp slid beset does deli estop lib reset align nixes mesa

Vertical reaches move from one row to the adjacent row.

ra and pl
44 plumb imply gray cram upset plea fray cramp plot extra play
45 crack grant rag Kraft cobra maple raid draft gram rapt rail
46 brat rad grab drape coral plume brawn plus rang plump gravy
47 split crab rake grape rack zebra brag trap rant brave fraud

G. MAP+: NUMBERS
Follow the software instructions for this exercise to improve accuracy.

TAKE A BREAK!
ISAK says ...

Place your elbows on the desk and lean forward. Cup your hands over your eyes, close your eyes, and inhale deeply through the nose. Hold for 4 seconds, and then exhale through the mouth. Repeat 3 times.

Technique

Goals

- Improve technique on the nonprinting, number, symbol, and punctuation keys.
- Improve concentration.

A. WARMUP

Accuracy	1 Quickly a strange silver fox jumped between the zoo fences.	12
Technique: One-Hand Words	2 defect pop water uphill begged lion target uplink aggravate	24
Speed	3 She did warn me to go easy when I comb her hair; I can try.	36

1 | 2 | 3 | 4 | 5 | 6 | 7 | 8 | 9 | 10 | 11 | 12

B. PRETEST-PRACTICE-POSTTEST: NONPRINTING KEYS

PRETEST

Take a 1-minute timed writing, pushing moderately for speed. Type each sentence; then press TAB to move from column to column.

4 We are late.	Can he help?	Turn around.	How goes it?	10
5 Listen here!	I see an ax.	Drop it now.	Who is here?	21
6 I can do it.	I am so hot.	We think so.	Take my bag.	31
7 Why not eat?	Come to her.	Talk slowly.	Drive there.	41

PRACTICE **ENTER Key**
Nonprinting Keys

Press ENTER after each word to format each word on a new line.

8 Not! Sure. No! Still? Push. Hurry. Stay. Farewell. Outside.
9 Really? Goodbye. Surrender. Move. Yikes. March. Wrong. Who?
10 Answer. Read. Next. Unfortunately. Yea! Edit. Listen. Wait.
11 Good. Remember? Oh. So? Ready? Proofread. Talk. Gross! Bye.

TAB Key

Type each word; then press TAB to move from column to column.

12 quiet	quaff	zanier	zinger
13 queasy	quench	zebra	zealous
14 quilt	queen	appall	awkward
15 zesty	award	quiver	quack

SPACE BAR

16 One at a time. What do you want? Buy a map for me. I am up.
17 What is it for? I do. Why me? Me? Do not do it. What gives?
18 Who knows? Hi. Here you go. I can. When? Now you can do it.
19 See me at ten. Now is the time. I dare you. Who is at work?

Bounce the thumb quickly off the SPACE BAR.

POSTTEST

Repeat the Pretest. *Goal*: Improve speed and accuracy.

C. NUMBER PRACTICE

Press TAB to move from column to column in each row.

20 613	293	558	943	982	808	328	306	526	872
21 797	498	424	161	637	876	457	312	842	692
22 237	880	243	270	140	225	348	938	305	469
23 968	733	470	622	856	841	937	576	848	923

Technique

Goals

- Improve technique on the nonprinting, number, symbol, and punctuation keys.
- Improve concentration.

A. WARMUP

Accuracy	1 Six or seven flashing new jet planes quickly zoomed by him.	12
Technique: Alternate-Hand	2 risk amend Claudia visitor spend vigor giant rush amend the	24
Speed	3 We can beat the heat of the day if we go swim at that pond.	36

1 | 2 | 3 | 4 | 5 | 6 | 7 | 8 | 9 | 10 | 11 | 12

B. PRETEST-PRACTICE-POSTTEST: NONPRINTING KEYS

PRETEST

Take a 1-minute timed writing, pushing moderately for speed. Type each sentence; then press TAB to move from column to column.

4 Be a friend.	When was it?	Who does it?	So be quiet.	10
5 Talk slowly.	How goes it?	I see a cat.	I saw a man.	21
6 Let's do it.	Key quickly.	I say I can.	File it now.	31
7 See Mr. Dye.	Can he help?	Who knew it?	Read my map.	41

PRACTICE   ENTER Key

Nonprinting Keys

Press ENTER after each word to format each word on a new line.

8 Now. Resume. Ahoy! Taxi! Back! Steady. Unfortunately. Wash.

9 Tweet. Aim. Pray. Swallow. Ugh! Inhale. When? Sleep. Fetch!

10 Congratulations. Continue. Walk. Perfect. Yea! Bravo! Oops!

11 Possibly. Cough. Nope. Drink. Watch. Surrender. Think. Eek!

TAB Key

Type each word; then press TAB to move from column to column.

12 zinger	quick	amoral	algebra
13 atlas	algae	quiet	applaud
14 quill	aviator	zigzag	ahead
15 apathy	quits	zombie	await

SPACE BAR

Bounce the thumb quickly off the SPACE BAR.

16 Do it now. Who is here? Jo is up. So? He is. I do not know.

17 No one is to go. Me? See me at ten. I can do the job. What?

18 Mark it in red. See Mr. Dye. Give it to me. What is it for?

19 Why? It is a fact. We are up. How? Who, me? The ox may die.

POSTTEST

Repeat the Pretest. *Goal:* Improve speed and accuracy.

C. NUMBER PRACTICE

Press TAB to move from column to column in each row.

20 320	591	472	584	159	342	469	149	184	800
21 773	109	535	361	554	404	520	398	655	478
22 388	530	224	189	177	846	182	381	172	445
23 920	147	150	778	493	709	363	116	229	402

D. MAP+: ALPHABET

Follow the software instructions for this exercise to improve accuracy.

E. PRETEST-PRACTICE-POSTTEST: CONFUSABLE KEYS

Take a 1-minute timed writing, pushing moderately for speed.

PRETEST

Pay special attention to these adjacent-finger reaches that often get confused.

24   Prior to last month, the safe choice would have been   11
25 to avoid the southern region and, in fact, all areas south   23
26 of Tucson on the basis of their border-control problems.   34
27 But that is going to waste a lot of prior sales efforts.   45

   1 | 2 | 3 | 4 | 5 | 6 | 7 | 8 | 9 | 10 | 11 | 12

PRACTICE
Adjacent Fingers

oi-io
28 prior boil join iota kiosk pious audio biopsy dioxin choice
29 biotic odious coil droid voice avoid ionic void choir going
30 curio mooing points koi polio heroic poi adjoin onion union
31 viol idiom soil senior ratio region period riot lesion loin

as-sa
32 tasty sail mask waste last aspic vase peas Sally sawn sagas
33 auras sang tubas flash mesas grasp as asp lasso chasm sable
34 alias seas areas Sal hash trash sack askew blast pleas safe
35 gash basis tease saga dash pasta sad aspen tunas nasal alas

sd-ds
36 moods studs rods kids cords rinds rends mends holds misdone
37 clods hands rids reds vends heeds fends misdeal kinds colds
38 roads doomsday wands woods scads brads ads adds skids girds
39 bauds plods weds misdial nods gods feeds yards beds disdain

POSTTEST

Repeat the Pretest. *Goal*: Improve speed and accuracy.

F. REACH DRILLS: JUMP REACHES

ce and on
40 lemon cedar capon peony conch crone tenon niece colon among
41 puce dice twice ice arson croon salon price drone since one

Jump reaches move from the upper row to the lower row or vice versa.

42 soon noon done juice force bonus don cent goon cede son con
43 won voice donor pylon onto long on felon trace pounce wrong

ex and ni
44 Niger duplex nick unite expose Ninja sexy sniff amnio panic
45 hexad vex catnip exult Danish expert cortex exalt knife hex
46 extend bonier text excel exert extent animal exile Unix nit
47 animus enigma extra snipe snit index nil denial exceed knit

G. MAP+: NUMBERS

Follow the software instructions for this exercise to improve accuracy.

TAKE A BREAK!

ISAK says ...

Sitting back, raise your right foot slightly and rotate it clockwise in a big circle, then counter-clockwise. Repeat with the left foot. Repeat the routine 3 times.

D. SYMBOL PRACTICE

Keep your eyes on the copy as you type these top-row symbols.

24 Santos* #9 jib sngo@az.gov 212% #10 station (lain) also-ran
25 be-all Berry* 697% Naser* Riley & Dow #2 cap A-frame #8 nut
26 970% $1.68 Harrison* all-day cli@bsu.edu West & Little 729%
27 $1 268% Sokolov* 932% imply-infer Han & Hsu 57.2% Ely & Foy

E. PRETEST-PRACTICE-POSTTEST: CONCENTRATION

PRETEST

Take a 1-minute timed writing, pushing moderately for speed.

Concentrate on keeping your eyes on the copy as you type these foreign phrases.

28   How do you compliment a beautiful site in a foreign   11
29 country? In Malaysia, you might say, "Yang sungguh cantik,"   23
30 and in the Philippines, you would say, "Ay kaya maganda."   34
31 In Mexico or Spain, it would be "Eso es tan hermoso."   45

    1 | 2 | 3 | 4 | 5 | 6 | 7 | 8 | 9 | 10 | 11 | 12

PRACTICE   Short Phrases
Foreign Phrases

32 Latin: Sic pulchra.
33 Dutch: Dat is zo mooi.
34 Swahili: Hiyo ni nzuri.
35 Basque: Hau da hain eder.

Medium-Length Phrases

36 Estonian: See on nii ilus.
37 Filipino: Ay kaya maganda.
38 Malay: Yang sungguh cantik.
39 Croatian: To je tako lijepa.

Long Phrases

40 Estonian: Se on niin kaunis.
41 Spanish: Eso es tan hermoso.
42 Indonesian: Itu sangat indah.
43 English: That is so beautiful.

POSTTEST

Repeat the Pretest. *Goal:* Improve speed and accuracy.

F. PUNCTUATION PRACTICE

Eyes on copy!

44 Inc. i.e. past; pump; intl. Esq. P.O. tag; Hear? qtr. list:
45 pile; 1/7 lace, pp. Ltd. M.D. Wed. back, neat; Quick! Give?
46 area: Ms. Sara; Asia: So? have, Walk? bring/take sat; sing;
47 bare: Clean? att. Again? "peg" pond; Full? recd. New? know,

48 fog, Sell! But? Follow? camp, incl. gal's bed, Danger! ppd.
49 1/9 navy; it, acct. Jr. Ely, approx. Ohio; Well? bawl, son;
50 Yea! pin; band, Assn. No? Exciting? "peer" made; dept. Dec.
51 7/10 Safe? Lou; aid, that/which R.N. Yes? bail, flea's Apr.

ISAK says ...

TECHNIQUE TIP

Adjust the height of your chair so that your feet rest flat on the floor and your thighs are parallel to the floor. Use a seat cushion or a footstool if necessary.

Accuracy

Goals

- Build accuracy on:
  - ✓ Corresponding-finger and confusable keys.
  - ✓ Spelling.
  - ✓ Alphabetic, jump, and number reaches.

A. WARMUP

Accuracy	1	Peg quickly explained that many jobs involve a few hazards.	12
Technique: Punctuation	2	Ike, salad: vol. irk, Mac? ilk, Pat? bin, Alas! (Lola) Hey!	24
Speed	3	Sit up here next to me and we will see the red sun go down.	36

1 | 2 | 3 | 4 | 5 | 6 | 7 | 8 | 9 | 10 | 11 | 12

B. PRETEST-PRACTICE-POSTTEST: CORRESPONDING FINGERS

PRETEST

Take a 1-minute timed writing, pushing moderately for speed.

4	For the sixth year in a row, we will need to hire Lott	11
5	and Sons, Inc., to assist us in preparing our annual taxes.	23
6	They possess the skills needed to do the job, especially	35
7	considering all of the new requirements on excess wages.	46

1 | 2 | 3 | 4 | 5 | 6 | 7 | 8 | 9 | 10 | 11 | 12

PRACTICE
Corresponding Fingers

S Finger
8 assist bows sons sassy Cass woos show swash sway swam sixth
9 stews sags mows swaps wards six assays snow sow excess cows
10 taxes sex mass bass subs shows whew sax west Texas laws wax
11 wages axes moss fixes swats sods swans sew faxes swims wads

L Finger
12 Nov. enroll bowl willow collar mole Olga wallop lovely flop
13 oleo tallow alto plot lonely holy ogle blood sole soul Lott
14 love flow oriole gallop colt lout soil poll ploy blot aloof
15 oral hello Oka. bloc voodoo igloo sloe Ont. Mon. Ore. polio

S and L Fingers
16 willow spoils lobos toolbox kowtow polls slops loots igloos
17 looms silos gloss exodus spells follows shells skills oleos
18 hollow mellow spoons possess allows sorrows booboos lawless
19 lassos stroll rolls loll lasso fowls gallows fossils bosses

POSTTEST

Repeat the Pretest. *Goal:* Improve speed and accuracy.

C. BUSINESS SPELLING

20 industrial curriculum discretion successful characteristics
21 appraisal quickly anticipate substantially previously waive
22 commission received agriculture petition relevant efficient
23 employees brought accounted deposits manufacturer liability

Speed

Goals

- Build speed on:
  - ✓ 15-Second Speed Sprints and 30-Second Progressive Practice drills.
  - ✓ Common letter combinations and special hand drills.
- Assess speed and accuracy on a 5-minute timed writing.

A. WARMUP

Accuracy   1 Jeb was very quick when he fixed those zip codes for Gmail.   12

Technique: Transpositions   2 am ma|espy send|arm raw|item tile|Eden dean|Al la|alit last   24

Speed   3 It is such a long way to go in an old car, but we must try.   36

     1 | 2 | 3 | 4 | 5 | 6 | 7 | 8 | 9 | 10 | 11 | 12

B. PRETEST-PRACTICE-POSTTEST: COMMON LETTER COMBINATIONS

PRETEST

Take a 1-minute timed writing, pushing moderately for speed.

4   It will do no good to complain now about the complex   11

5 debate going on over how the union is spending the bonus   22

6 money. We will only need to educate them on all compliance   34

7 matters that might complicate their internal discussions.   45

     1 | 2 | 3 | 4 | 5 | 6 | 7 | 8 | 9 | 10 | 11 | 12

PRACTICE
Common Letter Combinations

on   8 Donna lion lone cone only axion union nylon once font clonk

9 demon sonic bonus agony iron irony conk ion honor bone fond

10 nonunion Mason won arson scion money blond Honda monk capon

11 croon salon ozone Ono upon sonar bond tone bison colon gong

ate   12 ate beaten prate neater debate state floated equate obviate

13 innate slate notate plateau probate pleated narrate satiate

14 educate oxidate patent climate dictate rate migrate testate

15 radiate aviate mandate heater curate greater treated donate

comp   16 competitor compute comprise complicate complain computation

17 compose comply encompass completion compel complex compress

18 composure competence compile compadre compliance compulsion

19 complaint compass complicit composition comprised component

POSTTEST

Repeat the Pretest. *Goal*: Improve speed and accuracy.

C. 15-SECOND SPEED SPRINTS

Goal: Increase your speed on each retyping of the same sentence.

20 Her dad puts the new oil in the car to keep it in top form.

21 She uses gold and blue a lot in her art; it will sell well.

22 The math test will be hard, but I am sure she will pass it.

23 We will not win this game if only half of the team is here.

D. SPECIAL HAND DRILLS

Alternate-Hand Words
24 idle problems to ruby lame rock bush throw Bud six dock apt
25 blame bushel spend dig cut Diane focus auto Lakeland Vivian
26 Rob proficiency torn pane angle soap bus cod Enrico ant eye
27 she own corps bow giant hang Kay neuritis but may pair goal

Double-Letter Words
28 nanny we'll heed Duffy access food booth three too deed see
29 motto room tooth wool well annex Ann apply stood inn assess
30 add took Lloyd annum Kelly roll skill hill soon Allen apple
31 Lee cliff Bobby spell need gross worry hurry sweet odd knee

Home-Row Words
32 elks shade: shad: "gad" sled: slags saddle hall Dahl shakes
33 asks adages aged slakes kale flea ages alas feds half gal's
34 gales flags Dale shaded gaff fall; flask lakes lad gad shad
35 slaked sale hell leak deal lake sheaf legs salad dash shade

E. PACED PRACTICE
Follow the software directions for this exercise to improve keystroking speed and accuracy.

F. 5-MINUTE TIMED WRITING

Take two 5-minute timed writings.

Goal: Push moderately for speed while keeping your accuracy under control.

36 Sexual harassment is real. It happens in schools and	11
37 colleges and in the workplace, not just in this country	22
38 but around the world. Nearly all of these incidents are	33
39 illegal and against school policies. This means you do not	45
40 have to put up with it.	50
41 Although men can be the objects of sexual harassment,	61
42 women are more likely to experience this unique form of	72
43 discrimination. You should value yourself and recognize	83
44 your right to an education and not have the distraction of	95
45 unwanted behavior from others.	101
46 The victim as well as the harasser may be a man or a	112
47 woman, and the victim does not have to be of the opposite	124
48 sex. The harasser can be one's boss, coworker, or someone	135
49 who is visiting the workplace. The one rule is that the	146
50 person's conduct must be unwelcome.	154
51 The best solution is to tell the harasser that his or	165
52 her conduct is not welcomed and must stop. If it does stop,	177
53 then you have made your point successfully and the problem	188
54 is solved. If it does not stop, tell someone in authority.	200

1 | 2 | 3 | 4 | 5 | 6 | 7 | 8 | 9 | 10 | 11 | 12

TECHNIQUE TIP

ISAK says ...

Rest your hands in your lap when not keyboarding. Doing so helps blood circulation.

D. SPECIAL HAND DRILLS

24 raw stars Babbage acts based deceased vast bar fares desert
25 set sea swear were aggregate exceed arrears bases age cases
26 dress degrees Sara facets verbs Dave data cast sat tree ads
27 seat dresses wear decade test aware regard garage fat fewer

Maintain the nontyping hand in home-row position.

Right-Hand Words

28 honk Ohio him oily kimono jumpy pump Jill hook ion lop yolk
29 inn hominy mom loom Kim jump unpin opinion puny nylon junky
30 John upon pumpkin Lou Lynn minion Johnny puppy Philip jolly
31 Molly pinky hum milk pylon ply phony pin oink poi hilly ink

Left- and Right-Hand Words

32 after refers card assets regarded reds hilly tested sweeter
33 Dave Rex decreased drag Seward tests sat Carter cards trade
34 yon phi mink milk ate adverbs art fee gets pull desert ears
35 dresses set rag moon award sad rate brave treat cases waves

E. 30-SECOND PROGRESSIVE PRACTICE

Follow the software directions for this exercise to improve keystroking speed and accuracy.

F. 5-MINUTE TIMED WRITING

Take two 5-minute timed writings.

Goal: Push moderately for speed while keeping your accuracy under control.

36 Learning how to balance work and family is especially	11
37 tough for single parents. In the work setting, your absence	23
38 on the job for child-related issues might be scrutinized	34
39 closely. Keep appointments as brief as possible, and always	46
40 give your company plenty of notice beforehand. Return from	58
41 your appointments quickly, without taking extra time to run	70
42 personal errands.	74
43 Plan ahead for unexpected events to minimize their	84
44 effects at work, and ensure that your coworkers do not have	96
45 to take up your slack. Have an acquaintance you can rely on	108
46 for emergencies. You should not complain about child care	120
47 issues on the job. When your coworkers think of you, you	131
48 want them to think about your job skills and not about the	143
49 fact that you're a single parent who causes them more work.	155
50 The best way to ensure that management will tolerate	166
51 your family demands is to be a pleasant employee who always	178
52 does outstanding work. If you want the boss to go the extra	190
53 mile for you, you should do the same for him or her.	200

1 | 2 | 3 | 4 | 5 | 6 | 7 | 8 | 9 | 10 | 11 | 12

TAKE A BREAK!

ISAK says ...

Shut your eyes tightly for 3 seconds; then open them wide and blink rapidly. Repeat 3 times.

Unit 12 • Lesson 36   72

Speed

Goals

- Build speed on:
  - ✓ 15-Second Speed Sprints and Paced Practice drills.
  - ✓ Common letter combinations and special hand drills.
- Assess speed and accuracy on a 5-minute timed writing.

A. WARMUP

Accuracy	1	Peg quickly explained that many jobs involve a few hazards.	12
Technique: Punctuation	2	Ike, salad: vol. irk, Mac? ilk, Pat? bin, Alas! (Lola) Hey!	24
Speed	3	Sit up here next to me and we will see the red sun go down.	36

1 | 2 | 3 | 4 | 5 | 6 | 7 | 8 | 9 | 10 | 11 | 12

B. PRETEST-PRACTICE-POSTTEST: COMMON LETTER COMBINATIONS
Take a 1-minute timed writing, pushing moderately for speed.

PRETEST

4	The owner is being forced to use cheaper laser paper	11
5	during the summer months, but he is hoping to be using our	23
6	regular brand for the next shipment. He is asking all our	34
7	typing staff to conserve our present allotment until then.	46

1 | 2 | 3 | 4 | 5 | 6 | 7 | 8 | 9 | 10 | 11 | 12

PRACTICE
Common Letter Combinations

er 8 power hero caterer eerier fever owner opera otter edger era
9 overt outer Xerox eager skier terser loser ulcer query serf
10 err erode wager berserk sober server paper pert laser sever
11 pervert mower miser utter herder nerd erupt jerk adder seer

ing 12 loving bringing busing wing mingling wringing hiring cringe
13 ruling springing using dining winging during voting pinging
14 binge vying mingle ginger icing hoping asking aching jingle
15 typing towing axing being having oiling cling hiking noting

ment 16 figment movement deferment allotment momentum moment lament
17 garment easement cement atonement mental parchment fragment
18 adornment detriment battlement amazement shipment devilment
19 sediment regiment armament memento ailment torment ointment

POSTTEST

Repeat the Pretest. *Goal:* Improve speed and accuracy.

C. 15-SECOND SPEED SPRINTS

Goal: Increase your speed on each retyping of the same sentence.

20 Make your bed when you wake up so your mom will not be mad.
21 Once you mow the lawn, pull each weed you find by the path.
22 The map says to turn right when you come upon the oak tree.
23 When she sees the time, she will wish she had not slept in.

Accuracy

Goals

- Build accuracy on:
  - ✓ Corresponding-finger and confusable keys.
  - ✓ Spelling.
  - ✓ Alphabetic, jump, and symbol reaches.

A. WARMUP

Accuracy	1 Jo saw six big packs of cards and very quietly seized them.	12
Technique: Concentration	2 reinstitutionalized electromagnetically comprehensibilities	24
Speed	3 Just face the fact that you did miss a very nice boat trip.	36

     1 | 2 | 3 | 4 | 5 | 6 | 7 | 8 | 9 | 10 | 11 | 12

B. PRETEST-PRACTICE-POSTTEST: CORRESPONDING-FINGER KEYS
Take a 1-minute timed writing, pushing moderately for speed.

PRETEST

4	Maria and Harold should add the Omaha arena and plaza	11
5	to our list ahead of the deadline; just have them type/key	23
6	the addition and put it all together instead of keeping it	35
7	apart from the rest of the contract. That is my suggestion.	45

     1 | 2 | 3 | 4 | 5 | 6 | 7 | 8 | 9 | 10 | 11 | 12

PRACTICE
Corresponding Fingers

A Finger

8 abase alarm amass eat dizzy Jake Arab Omaha Aha Maria arena
9 altar Harold alpha Max zing aria Eliza jazz lanai gala Cara
10 anal Ozark kayak quaff haze awake agaze plaza Lara Ava adze
11 llama adz Liza ahead avail award add adage apart quiz hazel

; Finger

12 ups pet peg Daphne zap pit sop pub dip Pip? hop Pam imp bop
13 spy paw Pete? in/into pet; pay ply; pot; pin; type/key slip
14 Ralph peg; pea ply who/whom pic pep; Pele? pap dope set/sit
15 pen; pol Poe pad pry nip Eppie ump sip pub; Sophia Poe; lap

A and ; Fingers

16 pot pig pry; manna dop pap ply quart aha zebra tip Ajax zap
17 Japan Bah Ezra Pete? Ozark pro; Maria maze Aim pie type/key
18 lanai spa alpha Sara Quit spy mop hazy ajar panda Arp azure
19 Alamo per/a Ada adapt pub pal put area Aztec psi Adam quash

POSTTEST

Repeat the Pretest. *Goal:* Improve speed and accuracy.

C. BUSINESS SPELLING

These spelling words are from a list of the most used and most misspelled words in business writing. Study the words that cause you problems.

20 counseling ordering appropriate comptroller achieve regards
21 especially corridors tenant cafeteria competition necessary
22 permanent definitely administrative machinery proxy knowing
23 value deficit administration revenues techniques employee's

D. SYMBOL PRACTICE

Keep your eyes on the copy as you type these top-row symbols.

24 also-ran 697% all-day 4# of ham baby-sit #5 egg uely@az.gov
25 #8 nut boo-boo #9 jib 57.2% $1.09 (lair) imply-infer (lake)
26 #1-20 aho@cs.com $1.71 Parker* (lamb) Han & Hsu 932% (lady)
27 Li & Ng, Inc. 268% Portillo* Shan* Ngo & Ely A-frame be-all

E. PRETEST-PRACTICE-POSTTEST: CONCENTRATION

Take a 1-minute timed writing, pushing moderately for speed.

PRETEST

Pay attention to what you're typing.

28   It is simply polite to say "thank you very much" when   11
29 someone has done a kindness for you. You may be familiar   23
30 with the phrases "muchas gracias" in Spanish and "merci   34
31 beaucoup" in French, but how about "vielen dank" in German?   46

   1 | 2 | 3 | 4 | 5 | 6 | 7 | 8 | 9 | 10 | 11 | 12

PRACTICE Short Phrases
Foreign Phrases

32 Danish: Tak meget.
33 German: Vielen dank.
34 Swahili: Asante sana.
35 Basque: Eskerrik asko.

Medium-Length Phrases

36 Italian: Grazie mille.
37 French: Merci beaucoup.
38 Spanish: Muchas gracias.
39 Portuguese: Muito obrigado.

Long Phrases

40 English: Thank you very much.
41 Dutch: Heel hartelijk bedankt.
42 Filipino: Maraming salamat sa inyo.
43 Indonesian: Terima kasih sangat banyak.

POSTTEST

Repeat the Pretest. *Goal:* **Improve speed and accuracy.**

F. PUNCTUATION PRACTICE

Eyes on copy!

44 Today? cave, flea's knee, bang, agt. Dave, fed, Cold? know,
45 Here? mart; Eat! none; tab; Carl, Candy? bare: "peat" camp,
46 lace, Give? axed, pick; Dec. 2/10 Bart: sky; Type! Jr. 7/10
47 line; Sign? dig, Quick! Drink? go, hog, Nov. it, mgt. Fire!

48 Follow? Sara; dep't "pear" gal's lazy, each, are: 4/10 ask:
49 "peer" post; Danger! Jack, Call? omit; Ltd. Sun. film, i.e.
50 Enough? is, "peep" onto; by, Yea! New? bays, Feb. Mrs. pad;
51 fax, maybe/may be; e.g. Who? "peak" kid; wt. bid, chg. hid,

TAKE A BREAK!

ISAK says ...

Lock your hands behind your head, bring your elbows back as far as possible, inhale deeply, and hold for 20 seconds. Then exhale and relax. Repeat 3 times.

D. MAP+: ALPHABET
Follow the software instructions for this exercise to improve accuracy.

E. PRETEST-PRACTICE-POSTTEST: CONFUSABLE KEYS

PRETEST

Pay special attention to these keys that are often substituted for each other.

Take a 1-minute timed writing, pushing moderately for speed.

24	Betty likes to study the youth market in the city and	11
25	is proud of her campaign. It looks as if the teen buyer	22
26	knows about our efforts but will try to stay within their	34
27	budget. They will not fall for the empty claims of others.	45

1 | 2 | 3 | 4 | 5 | 6 | 7 | 8 | 9 | 10 | 11 | 12

PRACTICE
Substitutions

s-k
28 likes knees necks stork shack peeks skirt looks skins jocks
29 sunk skip dunks skew woks mask keys monks yanks skews kilts
30 stock locks fakes tasks slack beaks corks spike pocks knows
31 skits stack tusk sack skid kids shank lurks skin inks knobs

y-t
32 tardy yacht try tarry toy tiny youth myth stony pasty empty
33 Teddy stray study today hotly sty hefty stay yet patsy typo
34 yeast hasty Tommy witty antsy tummy booty kitty party misty
35 city arty tray Toby Betty petty cyst tyke zesty rusty aptly

r-u
36 brunt quirk euro syrup drub shrug upper crust rut rub occur
37 amour Ruth rugby argue incur burl truth quart cur lure pour
38 query truce trout crude serum scour buyer proud auger prude
39 blur runt spurn rump aura court sour cruel truer tour super

POSTTEST

Repeat the Pretest. *Goal*: Improve speed and accuracy.

F. REACH DRILLS: JUMP REACHES

ve and *in*
40 suave in Vera eave naïve event ever grave knave clove inert
41 inch live index hive agave veal vest save level peeve verve
42 rivet valve pave vet drive cover liver infer Eve over inept
43 vegan inane infer elves river navel five ink very hovel vex

Jump reaches move from the upper row to the lower row or vice versa.

cr and *on*
44 cruet onus cradle crush crept crack crane across cried crag
45 crypt creep scroll online creamy credo scruff onward accrue
46 acrid cravat scrape screen escrow onrush scrawl crown crick
47 micro Ono onset crust cry create onyx crania crocus crow on

G. MAP+: SYMBOLS
Follow the software instructions for this exercise to improve accuracy.

TECHNIQUE TIP

ISAK says ...

If you use a document holder, place it at the same height as the monitor and at the same distance from the eyes to prevent frequent eye shifts. It can be placed either to the left or the right of the monitor.

Technique

Goals

- Improve technique on the nonprinting, number, symbol, and punctuation keys.
- Improve concentration.

A. WARMUP

Accuracy	1	New jackets of my next book provide logarithms plus a quiz.	12
Technique: SPACE BAR	2	Jo saw Al at home. A big word can be odd. Go up to the man.	24
Speed	3	If you type this word and then five more, you will be done.	36

1 | 2 | 3 | 4 | 5 | 6 | 7 | 8 | 9 | 10 | 11 | 12

B. PRETEST-PRACTICE-POSTTEST: NONPRINTING KEYS

PRETEST

Take a 1-minute timed writing, pushing moderately for speed.

Backspace to correct all errors as you type.

4	Ryan Paul and Jeff Wood from Penn State visited Lima,	11
5	Peru, in June and July, while Jane Byrd spent the summer in	23
6	the Florida Keys working as a lifeguard at the Park Wood	34
7	Resort and Casino there. Oddly, Jane lives in Lima, Ohio.	46

1 | 2 | 3 | 4 | 5 | 6 | 7 | 8 | 9 | 10 | 11 | 12

PRACTICE
Nonprinting Keys

LEFT SHIFT Key

8 Ives Mays Mars Iraq Kane Pena Paul Lane Kara Herb Kean Lacy
9 Mack Nell Hank Jean Hess Utes Kate Kral Uday Penn Noll Pele
10 Peru Ubon Kern Mach Nast Leif Keys Park Maya Magi Levi Jane
11 Yang Hugh Parr Hamm Oslo Jeff Ural Hays Matt Page Leon Mara

RIGHT SHIFT Key

12 Elia Wouk Apia Byrd Quan Ryan Cuba Fido Gobi Roma Quon Tito
13 Alex Ahab Riga Bose Amur Soto Buck Wood Glen Dior Zion Coke
14 Burt Toby Alan Wise Duma Shaw Chad Bush Ames Andy Tony Diaz
15 Gina Ruby Amex Togo Aida Tiki Tory Gish Bonn Fish Zuni Burr

BACKSPACE Key

When you reach the Backspace sign (←), backspace 1 time and then type the letter that follows.

16 bog←o fro←y yaw←m big←n ill←k mob←m via←m was←y zig←p bud←m
17 own←l add←o zag←p air←m tag←m tow←y cot←p ice←y box←n per←p
18 has←y get←m put←p hex←y gee←l ash←k tea←n age←o bar←n log←t
19 inn←k cab←n fur←n dab←m lie←p the←y rat←p tee←n woe←k dig←m

POSTTEST

Repeat the Pretest. *Goal:* Improve speed and accuracy.

C. NUMBER PRACTICE

Press TAB to move from column to column in each row.

20	302	100	203	949	298	394	401	472	547	461
21	820	405	935	813	829	897	706	663	588	505
22	228	346	713	578	821	102	507	433	749	351
23	867	189	612	200	355	621	944	227	162	653

Technique

Goals

- Improve technique on nonprinting, number, symbol, and punctuation keys.
- Improve concentration.

A. WARMUP

Accuracy	1	Sixty wives quickly joined us from the big piazza in Italy.	12
Technique: Double Letters	2	egg keep speed Duffy broom steel ross apple class food boss	24
Speed	3	If she cuts it up in tiny bits for you, you can try a bite.	36

1 | 2 | 3 | 4 | 5 | 6 | 7 | 8 | 9 | 10 | 11 | 12

B. PRETEST-PRACTICE-POSTTEST: NONPRINTING KEYS

PRETEST

Take a 1-minute timed writing, pushing moderately for speed.

Backspace to correct all errors as you type.

4	Rose Mann and Ivan Bond went to Catholic Mass in Orem,	11
5	Utah, on Sunday. Meanwhile, Levi Meir and Otto Mann will	23
6	head to Overland Park, Kansas, in June to interview Alma	34
7	Byrd for the position of Director of Product Development.	45

1 | 2 | 3 | 4 | 5 | 6 | 7 | 8 | 9 | 10 | 11 | 12

PRACTICE LEFT SHIFT KEY
Nonprinting Keys

8	Ovid Ives Neal Pate Oaks Kern Java Orly Pete Jean Newt Jane
9	Iraq Mass Peke Hans Leon Jedi Kelt Lake Marx Lapp Utah Haru
10	Hals Iggy Mann Kazu Ivan Ursa Otto Meir Hess Lego Utes Hedy
11	Yang Oahu Lacy Nami Uris Hugh Kali Lena Levi Laos Ubon Park

RIGHT SHIFT KEY

12	Roma Siam Gila Bonn Rosa Duma Cuba Shaw Tory Fisk Chad Dodd
13	Elbe Shui Rome Dima Fitz Cola Goth Alma Byrd Quin Thom Todd
14	Fuji Bond Ruth Bose Zion Quan Zulu Wouk Burt Amex Toby Ahab
15	Elam Giza Fiji Finn Apia Burr Guam Bush Cole Coke Ryan Rose

BACKSPACE KEY

When you reach the Backspace sign (←), backspace 1 time and then type the letter that follows.

16	put←p rat←p ice←y cot←p has←y wow←n egg←o hid←m awe←l cog←n
17	vie←m zig←p ash←k lie←p aid←l hot←p age←o cue←p dug←n par←n
18	dew←n par←n gee←l tie←n wag←y was←y has←m jag←m big←n sin←p
19	leg←i ire←k tea←n pug←n woe←k ski←y gee←m gag←y own←l rug←m

POSTTEST

Repeat the Pretest. *Goal:* Improve speed and accuracy.

C. NUMBER PRACTICE

Press TAB to move from column to column in each row.

Eyes on copy!

20	613	293	558	943	982	808	328	306	526	872
21	797	498	424	161	637	876	457	312	842	692
22	237	880	243	270	140	225	348	938	305	469
23	968	733	470	622	856	841	937	576	848	923

D. MAP+: ALPHABET

Follow the software instructions for this exercise to improve accuracy.

E. PRETEST-PRACTICE-POSTTEST: CONFUSABLE KEYS

Take a 1-minute timed writing, pushing moderately for speed.

PRETEST

Pay special attention to these consecutive-finger reaches that often get confused.

```
24      Colin and Louis need to load the fragile shipment of        11
25  freight at the airfield today. Otherwise, the fresh fruit       22
26  may freeze in this frigid weather and cannot be sold. If        34
27  Frank is free, please ask him to help them with this job.       45
     1 | 2 | 3 | 4 | 5 | 6 | 7 | 8 | 9 | 10 | 11 | 12
```

PRACTICE
Consecutive Fingers

de-ed
```
28  deal creed feed adder abode toed dead deny coder fled decoy
29  hazed deep yodel deem guide abide deaf weed evade cued side
30  vied aged imbed decaf ledge bred tide code deity elude need
31  alder denim dew adept ode cede widen demo deed fade led bed
```

ol-lo
```
32  loam loud fool Colin loon lop solo sold look love lone role
33  fold polka lousy oleo holy long Holt loch golly stole lobby
34  lost loupe doll mold Louis loath olive droll lot logon lobe
35  bolt pole old lo loyal load whole cola idol lobo wool lotto
```

fr-rf
```
36  fray fresh refrain Frank froth freckle freight carful frown
37  fruit airfield forfeit defraud frenzy earful affront belfry
38  defrost barfly franc perfume saffron parfait freeze fragile
39  free froze French fearful frill warfare frazzle from frigid
```

POSTTEST

Repeat the Pretest. *Goal*: Improve speed and accuracy.

F. REACH DRILLS: VERTICAL REACHES

at and ho
```
40  pat peat vat bloat hoard rat spat feat flat horn swat great
41  stat hooky homage heat hotdog hop cravat hoop hoe seat goat
42  begat home squat holy house hot repeat hotel combat at hope
43  carat hog beat honey hocus hoist cheat hock splat scat hole
```

Vertical reaches move from one row to the adjacent row.

se and il
```
44  serf Seine fail oil seep till exile tense sewer lapse peril
45  case kitty dose hail rail silo asset rose phase pilaf prose
46  mild vile seat silt setup coil arise build false hilt whose
47  tease kill poise gild sever oases mill wild sedan pill bilk
```

G. MAP+: SYMBOLS

Follow the software instructions for this exercise to improve accuracy.

TECHNIQUE TIP

Curve your fingers naturally, with only the fingertips lightly touching the home-row keys.

ISAK says ...

D. SYMBOL PRACTICE

Return your fingers immediately to home-row position after typing each of these top-row symbols.

24 697% $1.14 729% cli@bsu.edu $1.71 boo-boo 233% 932% Parker*
25 970% Riley & Dow $1.04 add-on Santos* Noe & Ray sngo@az.gov
26 (lady) aho@cs.com A-frame 212% Berry* Ngo & Ely $1.68 $0.39
27 aorr@cs.com 268% $2 (lad) 3# of sand Naser* Sokolov* #8 nut

E. PRETEST-PRACTICE-POSTTEST: CONCENTRATION

Take a 1-minute timed writing, pushing moderately for speed.

PRETEST

Type the Pretest exactly as shown, but type the sentences below from right to left.

28   Which is easier to type: "An indefinite pronoun stands   11
29 for a nonspecific noun" or ".gnihtemos seman taht drow a   23
30 si nuon A"? Of course, that is a silly question, or, maybe,   35
31 ".noitseuq yllis a si taht ,esruoc fO." Concentrate!   45

    1 | 2 | 3 | 4 | 5 | 6 | 7 | 8 | 9 | 10 | 11 | 12

PRACTICE
Reverse Typing

Short Sentences

32 .setad rof serugif esU
33 .stnemgarf ecnetnes diovA
34 .egaugnal yrotanimircsidnon esU
35 .gnihtemos seman taht drow a si nuon A

Medium-Length Sentences

36 .noitome gnorts sesserpxe noitcejretni nA
37 .noitanidrobus dna sisahpme etairporppa esU
38 .ammoc a deen ton od secnetnes dnuopmoc trohS
39 .etaciderp a dna tcejbus a htob sniatnoc esualc A

Long Sentences

40 .nuon cificepsnon a rof sdnats nuonorp etinifedni nA
41 .noitca eht smrofrep tcejbus eht ,eciov evitca eht nI
42 .brevda na ro ,evitcejda na ,brev a seifidom brevda nA
43 .nosrep a fo sdrow tcaxe eht dnuora skram noitatouq esU

POSTTEST

Repeat the Pretest. *Goal:* Improve speed and accuracy.

F. PUNCTUATION PRACTICE

Eyes on copy!

44 past; Angry? Why? cave, pace; set; You? approx. cont. Sara;
45 fact, fig, incl. "peal" All? post; size: Whew! Drink? lost;
46 sack; acre, par; navy; is, 13/24 all's Type! agt. pat; i.e.
47 What? raise/rise Tue. in, road; jog, ppd. big, Funny! nest;

48 Start! knew, wt. bays, Ohio; rust; Escape? gov't led, jack,
49 Dance? sad; Drive! Break? list: Give? lace, Jr. acid, Hank,
50 link: Lucy; noon; sat; Quick! First? slab; back, elf, bawl,
51 Ph.D. he, pick; pine; Hot? Candy? chg. page: stow; egg, it,

TAKE A BREAK!

ISAK says ...

With your eyes closed, slowly move your eyes up to the ceiling, down to the floor, to the left, and then to the right. Repeat 3 times.

Goals

- Build accuracy on:
  - ✓ Corresponding-finger and confusable keys.
  - ✓ Spelling.
  - ✓ Alphabetic, vertical, and symbol reaches.

A. WARMUP

Accuracy 1 Mr. Block requested sixty jeeps for moving the prizes away. 12
Technique: Transpositions 2 eh he|Inez nine|ants navy|area rage|itch tide|on no|and nab 24
Speed 3 Let us sit down and eat the fine pile of food she has made. 36

  1 | 2 | 3 | 4 | 5 | 6 | 7 | 8 | 9 | 10 | 11 | 12

B. PRETEST-PRACTICE-POSTTEST: CORRESPONDING-FINGER KEYS

PRETEST Take a 1-minute timed writing, pushing moderately for speed.

4   Ted, the aide at the front desk, knocked and came into 11
5 the office, carrying a thick folder of parking tickets. I 23
6 had asked him to come at once so that we could redo all of 35
7 them without taking up too much of our time that afternoon. 46

  1 | 2 | 3 | 4 | 5 | 6 | 7 | 8 | 9 | 10 | 11 | 12

PRACTICE **Corresponding Fingers** D Finger

8 dear desk fade dive puce aide once deed Clem come held cane
9 cell dye dine Ted eke rode aced crew eye cute Edna end lice
10 redo ride drew eyed deer bend code dove scud cure pace rice
11 dope wed dude wee cole Lee cape dice Eve den coke dead cove

K Finger

12 Kiev fickle pipkin dickie kilo tick invoke ark, mink bicker
13 Kevin dirk knife bilk sickle Jackie Kuwait uke click kiting
14 Mickey disk picks kitty taking shrink wok, Waikiki kit Kim,
15 bike Sitka risk mike silk Okie kick kill nickel kiss ticket

D and K Fingers

16 chick iodide clicked abiding codicil wienie flicked bidding
17 midi idiom icing biscuit airsick kicked knocked wick licked
18 wicked suicide sickle kiddie nickel midsized cowlick tiepin
19 knack flick quick pickaxe thick quicken Mickey binding tick

POSTTEST Repeat the Pretest. *Goal*: Improve speed and accuracy.

C. BUSINESS SPELLING

These spelling words are from a list of the most used and most misspelled words in business writing. Study the words that cause you problems.

20 occupancy manufacture patient amendment architect specified
21 handicapped communication pregnancy admissions appreciation
22 endeavors career suction authorization studies consequently
23 delinquent utilize accommodate analytical decrease juvenile

Speed

Goals

- Build speed on:
  - ✓ 15-Second Speed Sprints and Paced Practice drills.
  - ✓ Common letter combinations and special hand drills.
- Assess speed and accuracy on a 5-minute timed writing.

A. WARMUP

Accuracy 1 John quietly picked six razors from the woven luggage bags.   12

Technique: Upper Row 2 rite rep outwit roe wiry repute poet write etui toupee riot   24

Speed 3 Both have a cold but will be all well once they have slept.   36

  1 | 2 | 3 | 4 | 5 | 6 | 7 | 8 | 9 | 10 | 11 | 12

B. PRETEST-PRACTICE-POSTTEST: COMMON LETTER COMBINATIONS

PRETEST

Take a 1-minute timed writing, pushing moderately for speed.

4   It will certainly be messy, but it will be best if   10
5 James can convince the Macon City Council of the importance   22
6 of its compliance with the rest of these enhanced consumer   34
7 protections, even if Council has to refinance its budget.   46

  1 | 2 | 3 | 4 | 5 | 6 | 7 | 8 | 9 | 10 | 11 | 12

PRACTICE
Common Letter Combinations

es 8 desk idles ores foes obese hies tires pages ties beset odes
9 ires nest goes messy gazes bides aides ewes rest less times
10 ales best notes bales wires mess jest James rues cases fest
11 these dyes west byes dress tries uses dues quest ukes fakes

con 12 consume icon contrive consign conned conquer condo confused
13 convince connect converge console conceit contrite continue
14 concert convert consent consist con convoy conserve confess
15 Macon sconce convict cone conform conquest consumer economy

ance 16 assurance dance ambiance enhanced guidance glance hesitance
17 compliance finances annoyance allegiance appearance finance
18 cognizance deviance radiance brilliance importance distance
19 ignorance enhance vigilance refinance accordance governance

POSTTEST

Repeat the Pretest. *Goal:* Improve speed and accuracy.

C. 15-SECOND SPEED SPRINTS

Goal: Increase your speed on each retyping of the same sentence.

20 It is a bold move to turn down any job at a time like this.
21 The fish tank has a leak; I knew we did not set it up well.
22 It is too hot in the sun, so I will sit near the tall tree.
23 It was not very wise to skip her last big exam of the year.

D. SPECIAL HAND DRILLS

Maintain the nontyping hand in home-row position.

Left-Hand Words

24 feet acreage tax reserve reads Bart bee exceeded debts ages
25 deed stages geared seeds Bates affect grades case deeds ear
26 deferred addressers estate Vera Eve star bags tags were act
27 weeds afterwards base few weave regrets effects added defer

Right-Hand Words

28 yolk unhook unholy kimono oink minimum kiln unlink pun pump
29 him oil joy loop lump ump ion hypo Kohl imp plunk only pony
30 link John puppy opinion union phylum mill imply Philip upon
31 I'll homonym monopoly Ohio uplink Johnny pill pinky pumpkin

Left- and Right-Hand Words

32 acre homily uplink baggage effect bad linkup bed regret wet
33 plunk ear badges face stress onion oilily saw dear pink add
34 arrest Polly lumpy case gage raw Baxter caves greater cards
35 Fred lop agreed deeds nil mom Caesar wave only secrets ease

E. 30-SECOND PROGRESSIVE PRACTICE

Follow the software directions for this exercise to improve keystroking speed and accuracy.

F. 5-MINUTE TIMED WRITING

Take two 5-minute timed writings.

Goal: Push moderately for speed while keeping your accuracy under control.

36   If you rise high enough in your organization, sooner   11
37 or later, you will be asked to take a visiting executive   22
38 out to lunch or dinner. The restaurant you select and how   34
39 you act will reflect on both you and your organization. It   46
40 is your responsibility to ensure that your visitor enjoys   57
41 the occasion.   60
42   If the headwaiter seats you, permit your guest to go   71
43 first. Give your guest the preferred seat, facing a window   83
44 with a pleasant view or facing the dining room if you are   94
45 seated next to a wall or have an unpleasant view.   104
46   The more important the guest, the nicer the restaurant   115
47 should be. Choose one where the food is of top quality and   127
48 the service is dependable. When making a food suggestion,   139
49 recognize that your guest will take your suggestion as a   150
50 guideline to suitable prices. Each guest should place his   162
51 or her own order; if the server asks you for your order,   173
52 simply indicate that your guest will order first. Doing   184
53 this will also let the server know that you should get the   196
54 check after eating.   200

   1 | 2 | 3 | 4 | 5 | 6 | 7 | 8 | 9 | 10 | 11 | 12

TAKE A BREAK!

ISAK says ...   Shut your eyes tightly for 3 seconds; then open them wide and blink rapidly. Repeat 3 times.

D. SPECIAL HAND DRILLS

Alternate-Hand Words
24 Pamela such profit Enrico spent amendment England lane turn
25 Bud height right visit chairman Bob pays Vic world lay Rico
26 handy bushel land man for cut Rob is wit Diana Jan mend dug
27 turns busy clan to tidy Peoria snap bus foe chap rocks Ruth

Double-Letter Words
28 cook Hyatt Bess keen annoy seen Danny will allow beef Allen
29 motto fee Bobby tattoo still yell zoo meet deed offer shell
30 grass root ditto Scott ill cool hurry feel quill swell moon
31 Aaron Jimmy small brass assess Barry Tommy cliff feed apple

Lower-Row Words
32 cocoon cyclic condemn cavern pizzazz mansion Batman almanac
33 ribbon corncob uneven dynamic abdomen acumen taxicab bemoan
34 cranium hobnob minicab vermin botanic maxim avionic denizen
35 beacon cobweb baboon bunion xenon embalm Macon abuzz emblem

E. PACED PRACTICE
Follow the software directions for this exercise to improve keystroking speed and accuracy.

F. 5-MINUTE TIMED WRITING

Take two 5-minute timed writings.

Goal: Push moderately for speed while keeping your accuracy under control.

36 Are you anxious about your credit rating? Although you   11
37 may owe nothing on your condominium and paid cash for your   23
38 automobile, you may have a poor credit score if you have   34
39 never used credit cards. A credit score is what financial   46
40 institutions use to determine if you qualify for credit and,   58
41 if you do, how much interest you will be charged. It is a   70
42 number that credit bureaus compute to estimate how likely   81
43 you are to pay bills promptly.   87
44 Credit bureaus factor in when you last paid an account   99
45 late, how frequently you pay late, and by how many days.   110
46 The longer you have had an account, the better. This means   122
47 that your score will increase if you maintain an old credit   134
48 card rather than apply for a new one. Cards from national   145
49 banks rate higher than department store cards.   155
50 Strangely, having a good job does not increase your   165
51 credit rating. The credit bureaus simply analyze how you   177
52 manage the resources you do have. There are three national   189
53 credit bureaus; you can review your credit rating online.   200

1 | 2 | 3 | 4 | 5 | 6 | 7 | 8 | 9 | 10 | 11 | 12

ISAK says ...

TECHNIQUE TIP
Tilt the top of the monitor back a little, with the top of the screen at eye level, at a comfortable distance for you to read the display.

Speed

Goals

- Build speed on:
  - ✓ 15-Second Speed Sprints and 30-Second Progressive Practice drills.
  - ✓ Common letter combinations and special hand drills.
- Assess speed and accuracy on a 5-minute timed writing.

A. WARMUP

Accuracy	1	Inez said Jack played a very quiet game of bridge with Rex.	12
Technique: Home Row	2	all's flask lags head false flag deaf gaffs flags alga lake	24
Speed	3	She does love to pull her big red cart at the farm at dawn.	36

1 | 2 | 3 | 4 | 5 | 6 | 7 | 8 | 9 | 10 | 11 | 12

B. PRETEST-PRACTICE-POSTTEST: COMMON LETTER COMBINATIONS

PRETEST

Take a 1-minute timed writing, pushing moderately for speed.

4	It was an emotional situation when students decided to	11
5	join us in developing the content of the new honor code.	23
6	They agreed that it did not infringe on their freedoms, and	35
7	they actually welcomed the creation of the new policies.	46

1 | 2 | 3 | 4 | 5 | 6 | 7 | 8 | 9 | 10 | 11 | 12

PRACTICE
Common Letter Combinations

in
8 rind mining infringe Einstein joining rink paining tininess
9 inhaling thinking find clinking sink pint binging kind thin
10 ninepin twin inking mingling tinting bringing drinking wind
11 spin fine tainting minx vain zing join inuring hinting inky

ent
12 entwine resent entered tenthly torrent unsent extent entrap
13 bent denture consent ambient segment advent gentler scented
14 exigent sapient gently detente pendent venture agent fluent
15 sent dissent aplenty ardent entomb content mordent students

tion
16 vibration emanation reduction situation probation oxidation
17 diction aviation action coalition rationing citation nation
18 election motioned rejection creation dilation lotion notion
19 fictional emotional indention urination infection detection

POSTTEST

Repeat the Pretest. *Goal*: Improve speed and accuracy.

C. 15-SECOND SPEED SPRINTS

Goal: Increase your speed on each retyping of the same sentence.

20 He must get some of this work done now, but it is not easy.
21 My home is now on the edge of town, just past the old mill.
22 She made her best pal feel sad, but what she said was true.
23 The old man has such a sad tale; she wept when he told her.

Accuracy

Goals

- Build accuracy on:
  - ✓ Corresponding-finger and confusable keys.
  - ✓ Spelling.
  - ✓ Alphabetic, horizontal, and number reaches.

A. WARMUP

Accuracy	1 The twelve jumping hares quickly fled by the rear zoo exit.	12
Technique: SHIFT Keys	2 Machiko Nakano spoke. Oscar Parks went. Quinton Rice wrote.	24
Speed	3 Take the bus away from camp to chop some wood with the axe.	36

1 | 2 | 3 | 4 | 5 | 6 | 7 | 8 | 9 | 10 | 11 | 12

B. PRETEST-PRACTICE-POSTTEST: CORRESPONDING-FINGER KEYS

PRETEST

Take a 1-minute timed writing, pushing moderately for speed.

4 What is our routine for tonight? Vera Cobb and Fred	11
5 Taft may join us if they are not too busy. I just want them	23
6 to have much fun with us since they have been huge fans of	34
7 the show since June or July. What games do you suggest?	45

1 | 2 | 3 | 4 | 5 | 6 | 7 | 8 | 9 | 10 | 11 | 12

PRACTICE
Corresponding Fingers

F Finger

8 robe bar tug Gobi rest gust err debt rub belt fat tiff tube
9 rate Cobb boor fave tear Rita glob roar stub gift veto iffy
10 tag raft Vera trap beg rob Fred fang art rang fig Taft vary
11 rest bet rave form rag gang bomb fog vat far buff frog vote

J Finger

12 July holy army envy hum Mary dun may mug June ugly busy jam
13 hub hem huge bush hug gum urn fun you harm nun mind hay emu
14 Yuma any rum hash none Lynn navy Nan hen jug name dumb hand
15 jamb bump much buy main mud bum Maui hue join them jut just

F and J Fingers

16 fungus rematch thermos budging thereby bough guilty bluntly
17 tough tyrant brambly trinity tonight bought thirsty buttery
18 venture fruity turmoil beanery thrush furry tenting routine
19 button granary vulture tangent gauging routing burley tangy

POSTTEST

Repeat the Pretest. *Goal:* Improve speed and accuracy.

C. BUSINESS SPELLING

These spelling words are from a list of the most used and most misspelled words in business writing. Study the words that cause you problems.

20 categories recognize depreciation accomplished participants
21 currently factor explained cooperative expenditures passage
22 legislative furnace enclose legislature constitute feasible
23 publicity instrument totally familiar cancellation adequate

D. SYMBOL PRACTICE

Keep your eyes on the copy as you type these top-row symbols.

24 Li & Ng, Inc. #8 nut Noe & Ray Naser* uely@az.gov bad-badly
25 imply-infer Harrison* baby-sit #5 egg Han & Hsu #10 station
26 $1.04 Portillo* $2 Ely & Foy add-on cli@bsu.edu 970% (lain)
27 Batista* 697% boo-boo (lamb) $1.68 (lake) rorr@ua.edu $0.39

E. PRETEST-PRACTICE-POSTTEST: CONCENTRATION
Take a 1-minute timed writing, pushing moderately for speed.

PRETEST

Concentrate on keeping your eyes on the copy as you type these vocabulary words. How many of these terms do you know?

28   Notwithstanding the fact that the demonstrations may   11
29 recur, I think it would be propitious for us to acquiesce   22
30 to their demands and base all of our relocation decisions   34
31 on the chronologically arranged date-of-hire list.   44

     1 | 2 | 3 | 4 | 5 | 6 | 7 | 8 | 9 | 10 | 11 | 12

PRACTICE   Short Words
Vocabulary Words

32 regale rebut wrest deify aura knead nil
33 done affix crag whet forte occult satyr
34 relent recant parley triad evolve wield
35 tilth ossify facile recur motley callow

Medium-Length Words

36 aerostat juncture specter noisome oblique languid
37 adumbrate zeitgeist acquiesce soporific mnemonics
38 sapience plenary bulwark copious augment parlance
39 polyglot assuage vignette halcyon inverse subvert

Long Words

40 chronologically propitious misanthropic counterinflationary
41 redundance notwithstanding sanguinary sequacious felicitate
42 decentralizing contemporaneous discursive industrialization
43 exceptionalities demonstrations fragmentation precipitating

POSTTEST

Repeat the Pretest. *Goal*: Improve speed and accuracy.

F. PUNCTUATION PRACTICE

Eyes on copy!

44 be, i.e. Wed. Oct. Duck! learn/teach Quick! 1/7 must; only;
45 Nov. Bart: fig, Cold? Ida, jack, pig; calm, More? Bus? egg,
46 axes, back, most; Follow? noon; qty. But! came, Ph.D. acre,
47 size: Alone? Aug. "peek" plus; next; Tue. caps, Hear? all's

48 Stan; tab; Gas? bats, Exciting! pine; band, Fri. ask: Sign?
49 dept. pump; led, Cut! bank, beg, ring; Ely, Mrs. 8/10 Type!
50 Morning? 7/10 bath, Stay! So? intl. pp. elk, neat; Ms. our;
51 pond; P.O. Dance? Sun. In? agt. once; Empty? enc. one; Now?

ISAK says ...

TECHNIQUE TIP

Position the mouse at the same height as the keyboard and on the side opposite the copy holder. Move the mouse with the forearm and not just with your wrist.

D. MAP+: ALPHABET
Follow the software instructions for this exercise to improve accuracy.

E. PRETEST-PRACTICE-POSTTEST: CONFUSABLE KEYS

PRETEST

Pay special attention to these consecutive-finger reaches that are often get confused.

Take a 1-minute timed writing, pushing moderately for speed.

24 That brave gymnast was hurt when she tried to do a	10
25 truly difficult maneuver. It was obvious that her failed	22
26 effort cost her points, and everybody made the effort to	33
27 congratulate her when they saw her depart the floor.	44

1 | 2 | 3 | 4 | 5 | 6 | 7 | 8 | 9 | 10 | 11 | 12

PRACTICE
Consecutive Fingers

rt-tr
28 insert overt trial trawl tribe inert tried trod track tryst
29 trip try wart ort hurt desert trunk sort quart tread unhurt
30 truth squirt trifle depart dirt trio truly tort trim deport
31 part trap flirt escort trivet alert fort exert apart effort

mn-nm
32 gymnast nonmoving condemn remnant nonmajor dimness unmapped
33 hymn alumnus enmity gymnastics nonmedical omnivore omnivore
34 abandonment alumni mnemonic columnar unmet condemned solemn
35 alumna rainmaker omnipotence unmanageable glumness nonmetal

vb-bv
36 verbal vibrant boulevard abusive curveball obvious variable
37 dividable brave beverage beaver vestibule overbaked abusive
38 bovine everybody subversive verbs obverse overbuilt visible
39 bravado verbalize behoove Bolivia overbid beehive observant

POSTTEST

Repeat the Pretest. *Goal:* Improve speed and accuracy.

F. REACH DRILLS: HORIZONTAL REACHES

er and io
40 violation radio region biopic terse fryer curio aioli nicer
41 over ever idiot brio hers tower perm olio idiom cuter poker
42 merry patio viola beret kiosk oiler verse hyper priory tern
43 lover berry stern serf ion zero fixer sober per there mercy

Horizontal reaches move to a different key on the same row.

te and pu
44 matte Peter puree enter tempo Terry noted pupil opted cater
45 teal pate text kite pun tee teeter haute tempted tear steak
46 utter item note punt teak step elate toted team route teeny
47 emote later iterate sated opus tempt pushy often saute teed

G. MAP+: NUMBERS
Follow the software instructions for this exercise to improve accuracy.

TAKE A BREAK!

ISAK says ...

Tilt your neck to one side (ear toward shoulder), hold for 10 seconds, relax; then tilt your neck to the other side and repeat. Using the same steps, tilt your neck forward and backward.

Goals

- Improve technique on nonprinting, number, symbol, and punctuation keys.
- Improve concentration.

A. WARMUP

Accuracy	1	Just lacquer the big boxes of amazing jewelry a vivid pink.	12
Technique: Substitutions	2	a-s pass bases spans sea areas visa stays sales saves eases	24
Speed	3	His high note was not so off; he jams just like a true pro.	36

1 | 2 | 3 | 4 | 5 | 6 | 7 | 8 | 9 | 10 | 11 | 12

B. PRETEST-PRACTICE-POSTTEST: NONPRINTING KEYS

PRETEST

Take a 1-minute timed writing, pushing moderately for speed. Type each sentence; then press TAB to move from column to column.

4	He is tardy.	We think so.	He is tired.	Take my bag.	11
5	See me soon.	I am up now.	Type it now.	How goes it?	21
6	Talk slowly.	See Mr. Dye.	Why not you?	Add me also.	31
7	Why not her?	Run quickly.	Is it alive?	Tell me why.	41

PRACTICE
Nonprinting Keys

ENTER Key

Press ENTER after each word to format each word on a new line.

8 Play. Probably. Certainly. Whew! See? Hey! Sit. Drive. Aim.
9 Go. Amazing. Pay. Crazy. Nope. No! Italicize. Heck. Enough!
10 Stretch. Closer. Catch. Sure. Explain. Maybe. Me? Drag. So?
11 Choose. Man! Sorry. Kneel. Neat. Absolutely. Fast! Awesome.

TAB Key

Type each word; then press TAB to move from column to column.

12	attain	afraid	quack	quell
13	quest	aflame	areas	academy
14	zillion	quantify	zanier	quotient
15	airfare	zombie	aerial	abstain

SPACE BAR

Bounce the thumb quickly off the SPACE BAR.

16 Is it true? Go up to the man. Help me. Who, me? I dare you.
17 How are you? When? I do not know. It is a fact. Step on it.
18 I am. Don't do it now. I may go to bed. Why? She may do it.
19 I say I can. How dare you? One at a time. Do it now. I can.

POSTTEST

Repeat the Pretest. *Goal*: Improve speed and accuracy.

C. NUMBER PRACTICE

Press TAB to move from column to column in each row.

Eyes on copy!

20	320	591	472	584	159	342	469	149	184	800
21	773	109	535	361	554	404	520	398	655	478
22	388	530	224	189	177	846	182	381	172	445
23	920	147	150	778	493	709	363	116	229	402